INDIANA BOY

Memoir of a Psychologist

Dr. Kenneth R. Starkey

Copyright © 2024 Dr. Kenneth R. Starkey
All rights reserved
First Edition

PAGE PUBLISHING
Conneaut Lake, PA

First originally published by Page Publishing 2024

ISBN 979-8-89315-874-8 (pbk)
ISBN 979-8-89315-932-5 (hc)
ISBN 979-8-89315-890-8 (digital)

Printed in the United States of America

To all those whose love and wisdom
Have helped me to answer questions,
To discover inner peace, and to realize a
Life of meaning: especially to my parents;
Siblings; friends; mentors; my wife Pam;
Our boys Patch and Tucker; and to all those
In my hometown of Columbus, Indiana.

CONTENTS

Introduction vii

1. Beginnings 1
2. Family, Friends, and the Gift of Music 30
3. Exploring the World 62
4. Out of Darkness 94
5. Studying Psychology 119
6. Substance-Use Counseling 141
7. Professional Training 170
8. Work and Love 198
9. Professional Psychology Services—Mobile 233
10. The Practice of Clinical Psychology 256
11. Modern Times 287
12. Endings 316

Acknowledgments 351
References 353

INTRODUCTION

Every life has its story: some long, some short; some happy, some sad; some magical, some tragic. None of us can know in advance what life will bring or how our story might unfold. And why some people seem more blessed or more given to suffer than others is something we may never understand. But for me, questioning such matters has long been important as it has allowed me to learn more about life and to better embrace the world of which I am a part. Asking questions has helped bring me peace and contributed to a life of meaning.

What follows is my story, as best I can tell it. I grew up in a small Midwestern American town during the 1950s and 1960s. The '50s was a simpler time, not necessarily better or worse, just simpler. And like many small children, my own life seemed uncomplicated, safe, and predictable. But all this changed following the divorce of my parents when I was eight years old. Their separation was bitterly contested. And for the first time, life became confusing, unsettled, and scary. My siblings and I would be introduced to poverty, hunger, shame, even despair. And though giving up would never be seen as a viable option, for me, the need to understand how all this had happened, why the world would play such a seemingly cruel joke on our family by causing so much pain and suffering, would forever impact my life.

Moving into my teenage years, the '60s would raise new questions. Suddenly, America had become a nation marked by social change, political unrest, and national upheaval. A president would be assassinated. A "women's liberation" movement would emerge that, along with the so-called sexual revolution, forever redefined the relationships of men and women throughout the country. Legalized abortion would become the law of the land, dividing the nation between "right to life" groups and those supporting a woman's "freedom to choose." Children were bussed from their homes across town in the name of desegregation, and civil rights protests strained the very fabric of our society. Race riots would ensue, resulting in a renowned civil rights leader being senselessly murdered. Finally, as America became increasingly involved with the Vietnam conflict, problems with drug abuse worsened, anti-war demonstrations erupted, and our nation would be caught up in what some called a generation gap.

In the end, many would declare the 1960s to have been instrumental in advancing social change, women's rights, racial equality, and the like. Still, others lamented that with the shift in our nation's values, the upheaval of cultural mores, and the resulting movement toward a more diverse and pluralistic society, our traditional way of life had been lost forever. As for me, for the first time in my life, I'd find myself struggling to understand what was real and what was not. How was I to know good from bad or right from wrong? What was truth, and what was not? Why did people experience sickness, death, and war? And what values should I adopt to help me realize the person I would one day become, to make my own life matter?

As an adult, as I pursued my formal education, went to work, got married, and sought my way in the world, the ques-

INTRODUCTION

tions would persist. They'd lead to my studying religion and psychology. And over time, I'd encounter others who had similar questions and who'd share with me their thoughts, insights, and wisdom. Ultimately, the journey would lead to my becoming a clinical psychologist that I might further learn to understand people and their reasons for behaving as they do. And this, I found, not only allowed me to help ease the struggles of others but to gain a better understanding of my own life as well.

Today, much like the 1960s, our nation again finds itself in a period of dramatic change. A pandemic emerged, disrupting economies around the globe and killing millions of people worldwide. Countries in Europe and the Middle East are waging war on one another. And all the while, American politicians have spent the best part of a decade refusing to work together so as to resolve concerns that could well threaten the very foundation of our nation. Republicans and Democrats alike have taken to treating one another with disrespect, even contempt, while hopelessly dividing our nation and leading it ever closer to what some fear might one day be another civil war. Elections, once representing the will of the people and serving as the crown jewel for American democracy, are all too often contested or settled by the courts. The judicial system itself seems to have become increasingly politicized, resulting in many questioning the legitimacy of its rulings. Progressive-minded people proclaim that "systemic racism" deprives minority groups of their dignity and from receiving their fair share of the nation's wealth. Conservative groups, on the other hand, protest that all the changes in recent decades have destroyed the nation's values and undermined the importance of those social institutions that once helped define our communities while preserving a sense of culture. Gun violence has become increasingly commonplace, and civil protests have again broken out in our larger cities. Indeed, for a society immensely blessed with material wealth, it is most troubling that, in the current day, so many people seem to have lost their way, that so many people seem to struggle with feeling confused about who they are as individuals or where they fit into this world, with feeling estranged from their neighbors and communities, and with feeling as though their lives hold little if any meaning or purpose. Again, I find myself questioning what it all means.

After a lifetime of searching, I must admit I've still not found the answers for many of my questions. There remain so many things I simply do not understand, things I cannot explain. And I'm certain I don't have solutions for all the problems we humans face in the present day and age. I look around at the world, and I continue wondering what's it all about. Are the current problems truly insurmountable, or are they just part of the ebb and flow of a greater evolutionary process? Are we destined to repeat the mistakes of our past, or could all the struggles we experience today simply be leading us to a "new day," an "Age of Aquarius"? I really don't know. But despite all my uncertainties, despite all the unanswered questions, in the darkest of moments, I continue to discover goodness, beauty, and light in this world. And I continue believing in the importance of caring about others, of compassion, and of love. At times, I *know* these things to have value. And believing in these things brings me peace, while incorporating them into my life gives it meaning. So I will go on questioning, and I will trust that all the struggles of our time are not beyond our understanding, that if we just ask the right questions, if we just listen a little more closely, care a little more deeply, and practice a little more love, a little more faith, eventually the answers to all our questions will make themselves known.

In the landscape of spring, there is neither better nor worse; the flowering branches grow naturally, some long, some short.
—Alan Watts

This quote is from *This Is It: and Other Essays on Zen and Spiritual Experience* (Alan Watts, New York, New York: Random House Inc., 1973).

BEGINNINGS

I WAS BORN ON MAY 16, 1951, to Carl and Martha Starkey of Columbus, Indiana. At the time I was born, Columbus was a small rural community of about thirty-three thousand residents nestled into the hills of south central Indiana, some forty miles due south of Indianapolis. It had long been the county seat for Bartholomew County, and to this day, Columbus remains a rather affluent small town due largely to its abundance of industry. It's the international headquarters for Cummins Engine Company Inc., a Fortune 500 company currently employing some eight thousand plus people in Columbus alone (and over sixty thousand people worldwide). At the time I was growing up, it was also the international headquarters for Arvin Industries, another Fortune 500 company, and served as the home for Reeves Pulley Inc., Cosco Industries, and several other manufacturing companies. Presently, Columbus is touted as being home to more than thirty international companies from countries as far away as Japan, China, India, Germany, Korea, and elsewhere. And all this industry, in addition to the many farming operations surrounding the town, has meant an abundance of jobs for anyone desiring to work.

With jobs being plentiful, unemployment would be historically low, hovering around 3 percent to 4 percent—even during times of economic hardship or national recession. And the high employment rate yielded a tax base providing benefits many other cities would never come to know. Public services were plentiful. And as a result of job opportunities being ever-present and people being encouraged to view working as the norm, there was very little need for welfare. Our schools were safe, clean, well supplied, and considered by many to provide some of the highest-rated academic instruction in the state. Our streets were clean, and trash was collected regularly and free of charge. Public transportation would be both readily available and affordable, and buses ran on time. Community parks were spacious and well maintained, and pollution was minimal despite all the industry. Crime was practically nonexistent, and people had no need to lock their homes or cars as neighbors mostly knew one another and were given to helping one another when problems arose rather than victimizing one another. During the twentysome years I spent growing up in Columbus, I recall only two homicides—and one of those was an attendant working at a gas station located along the nearby interstate outside the city limits. Finally, while many still considered it outrageous, the sales tax was 2 percent during the time I was a youth. To this day, this tax is only 7 percent.

Cummins Engine Company Inc. was founded around 1919 by Clessie Cummins and one W. G. Irwin. Following W. G. Irwin's assuming leadership of the family-owned Irwin's Bank, he became wealthy enough to hire Clessie Cummins as his chauffeur. In his spare time, Clessie experimented with building diesel engines. So with W. G. Irwin's financial backing, the two eventually cofounded Cummins Engine Company Inc.

Cummins Engine Company Inc. was originally known for having built the first diesel-powered passenger car in America. I'd also be told that much of the success of Cummins during the 1940s could be traced to the engines it manufactured for trucks and other heavy equipment used by the US military during WWII. Years later, under the leadership of W. G. Irwin's great nephew, J. Irwin Miller, Cummins would become the worldwide company it is today. During the latter half of the twentieth century, Cummins would gain an international reputation for powering both commercial and passenger trucks, as well as backup generators for many of the world's largest medical facilities and corporate factories. Then upon moving into the modern era, Cummins would be touted as a "global power technology leader" credited with, among other things, creating the world's largest PEM electrolyzing system to generate green hydrogen in Quebec, Canada, and with powering a hydrogen fuel cell train in Austria.

In addition to being the CEO of Cummins Engine Company Inc., J. Irwin Miller was also a philanthropist and visionary. He believed that elevating the attractiveness of the city would further entice individuals he recruited to assure the ongoing growth and success of Cummins. Accordingly, J. Irwin Miller and the Cummins Foundation set about investing in world-renowned architects to design churches, libraries, banks, schools, government buildings, etc. in little Columbus. And these structures would forever alter the landscape of this small town, eventually leading it to be called Athens of the Prairie by the *Saturday Evening Post* magazine. Recently, Columbus was ranked sixth in the nation for innovative architecture design by the American Institute of Architects. Not bad for such a small community.

Finally, Columbus has gained some notoriety for being the home to both sixteen-term US congressman Lee Hamilton and Congressman, Indiana governor, and Vice President Mike Pence. Several professional athletes, including INDY and NASCAR race car driver Tony Stewart, would also hail from Columbus. Most agree that Lee Hamilton was a respected congressman, that Mike Pence was a good governor and vice president (as well as a decent and caring man of strong personal and religious values), and that Tony Stewart was a fierce competitor.

My family was not wealthy by any means. My parents had been born and raised in the even smaller, mostly farming community of Linton, Indiana. They would marry shortly before Dad joined the Navy and was shipped overseas to serve in the Pacific arena during WWII. Mom continued living with her parents while Dad was away and while pregnant with my eldest brother, David Anthony. Dave would be born in 1944, while Dad was still serving in the Navy. My parents would then relocate to Columbus upon my father's return from the war, sometime around 1945. Four years later, in 1949, my other brother Kevin Lee would be born. I was born in 1951, followed by my sister Regina LouAnne some four years later in 1955.

In Columbus, my father took a job as a draftsman for Arvin Industries. Arvin's was a manufacturing company based in Columbus that, at that time, produced a variety of household products ranging from portable radios to toasters to electric space heaters, etc. Arvin's also specialized in making such automotive parts as car mufflers. Growing up, I would never be quite sure what a draftsman was. But over time, I'd come to believe it involved a certain degree of artistic ability used in the designing of items for production. My dad had always been artistically inclined, a talent he would seemingly pass on to my brothers Dave and Kevin but not to me. Dad would work for Arvin's some fifteen years. So while we lived by very modest means, my father was consistently employed outside the house. Like many families of the 1950s, my mother raised the children and took care of the home.

Much of my earliest childhood is remembered as uneventful. I would be told that we lived in an area called Tellman's Camp the first year or so of my life. Apparently, this camp con-

BEGINNINGS

sisted of a smattering of homes built on stilts along the banks of White River (near Columbus). Most of the homes have since been torn down, with some of the property being incorporated into what is now Mill Race Park. But at the time we lived there, the camp was known as a lower-income-level area where river-flooding was a common hazard, thus the need for homes to be built on stilts. It was also during this time that my father got into crafting small speedboats.

Hydroplane racing was and is one of the many forms of racing popular in the state of Indiana, in addition to the open-wheel racing of the Indianapolis Motor Speedway every May and, more recently, the NASCAR racing held in midsummer. Drag racing, sprint car racing, stock car racing, go-cart racing, even lawnmower racing can also be found by those so interested. As the saying goes, if it has a motor on it, someone in Indiana will race it. And every summer, the Unlimited class of twin-engine "Monster" boats would come for a weekend of high-speed fun along the Ohio River separating Indiana from the state of Kentucky—Thunder on the Ohio, they called it.

My father had always loved racing, and living along White River apparently made building speedboats an enticing hobby. His boats weren't as big as the Unlimited series, but they were fun for him just the same. And while I was very young at that time and don't actually remember seeing Dad building his boats, later on, I would come across a photograph of him proudly standing next to two of the boats he had purportedly built. Over time, the stories of my father's boatbuilding, and other such pursuits, would become somewhat legendary within our family.

I think we moved around a fair amount during my early years. I'm not exactly sure why. But as I recall, when I was about three years old, we moved into a small farmhouse located in the nearby community of Elizabethtown. We didn't live there long, and my memories are sketchy. But I do recall the house being a two-story, yellow, wooden structure that came with a handful of chickens in the backyard. And I remember my brothers and me going into the coop and collecting the eggs regularly or until such time as the rooster took offense to my pestering it and got ahold of one of my fingers. Blood was everywhere. I would never venture near him or the chicken coop again. I also recall my brother Kevin having had a small dog named Laddy. Sadly, she'd be struck by a car while running loose one day, and we'd bury her under a large tree in our front yard. While I didn't fully understand what Laddy's death was all about at the time, I understood that she was gone and that her death made Kevin sad.

Perhaps my best memory of this time was that of awaking early one Saturday morning to find a half dozen goats meandering around our front yard, eating grass. It seems the goats had escaped from a neighbor's farm and made their way down to our property. A few hours later, the owner would come down with his truck and pick them all up, but playing with the goats prior to the neighbor's arrival would be a memory my brothers and I would talk about for years to come.

When I was around four years old, our family moved into a small log cabin in neighboring Brown County, Indiana. Brown County is probably best known for its county seat of Nashville. This community is a small artisan village located some twenty miles west of Columbus that serves as home to painters, potters, leather crafters, woodworkers, and the like. From May to December, one finds the streets packed with tourists who come to shop and, especially in the fall, to experience the beautiful colors of the leaves that mark the changing of the seasons. We only lived there a short time, maybe one summer. The cabin was probably too small for our family. And while my father tried to characterize our living there as a family adventure, the location was quite remote. I think my mother generally felt cut off from civilization, given its rural setting.

A few months later, we'd move again, this time into a house on Lafayette Street (Columbus). If memory serves me right, we'd live there about a year. And I'd attend kindergarten at Jefferson Elementary School during this period. I also remember this being a time when our family had a black dog named Bardol. He was named after the oil additive used in some Indianapolis 500 race cars of the era, and I'd always recall Bardol as being huge, surely a Labrador retriever or some such breed. Later on in life, my brother Kevin informed me that Bardol was actually a cocker spaniel. I guess if you are five years old, a cocker spaniel might seem bigger than it truly is. Tragically, Bardol died as a young dog after ingesting something that made him ill. The story my dad told was that a neighbor had poisoned him, and this could have been true as it probably irritated some that Bardol was allowed to roam the neighborhood with no collar or supervision. But it seemed just as likely that Bardol had simply gotten into someone's trash and eaten tainted food. We'd never know for sure.

Another memory I have of this period is of it being the time when my dad got involved with the Indiana chapter of the Clockmakers Association of America. Yes, there really was (and may still be) such an organization. This was long before the invention of modern or battery/solar-powered clocks. And mechanical clocks were typically too valuable to be thrown out when they broke down. Consequently, Dad decided to learn clock repair as a way to generate additional income. As noted above, Dad was somewhat known for throwing himself into his pursuits, and he would eventually gain a local reputation for being the "go to guy" in our town when it came to such repairs. At one point in time, I remember Dad's work resulting in our having some twelve or more grandfather clocks and one blond "grandmother" clock, all lining the walls of our great room and in various stages of repair. At the top of the hour, when they all chimed in unison, it seemed to shake the entire house. I also remember how in the fall of 1956, my father dressed up in top hat and tails, complete with a moniker and pocket watch, and chaired the Annual Clockmakers Association's Convention at the Abe Martin Lodge in Brown County State Park. It was a bit of a treat following him around as he carried out his leadership duties. It kind of made Dad seem special in my eyes, although it was also a little embarrassing. Dad would continue repairing and restoring clocks for any and all who needed such work off and on for years to come.

The same year, two other events occurred. First, one evening, while carrying an old coffee can filled with Christmas candy up the steps of our front porch in the dark, I fell and seriously cut my chin and neck on the rim of the can. Apparently, blood was everywhere, although between the darkness of nightfall and my being a bit traumatized, I wouldn't learn of this until later on. Dad rushed me to the hospital, and some fifty plus stitches later, I was on my way home. Eventually, I would heal up, though I'd always have a noticeable scar (and story) as a reminder of the incident. Second, as fate might have it, this event occurred on the same evening as my mother was in the hospital giving birth to my sister Regina LouAnne. This probably explains why my mother was not present when I fell or was being stitched up (but not why my father was not at his wife's side while she gave birth to my sister).

My relationship with LouAnne, as we came to call her, would always prove a little distant, not the usual brother/sister relationship. I suspect this was due in large part to the fact that she was four years my junior, six years younger than Kevin. Accordingly, from a developmental perspective, none of us boys would have all that much in common with her. But equally important was the fact that Mom always seemed overprotective of LouAnne. True, we boys were a rather rowdy bunch. And LouAnne was always on the small side as a child, short in stature and a bit frail. But it might have been nice had we been encouraged to take her under our wings, so to speak, and to have had a real sibling relationship with her. As we all grew older, and especially after we boys moved out to find our own way in the world, the distance would persist. It wouldn't be until much later on that, as adults, we'd come to know and appreciate one another as siblings.

When I was six years old, my family moved once again, this time to a house on Indiana Avenue. I believe this to have been the first house my parents actually purchased. It was not an especially large house, but it was built on one acre of land. And I remember my parents seemed especially proud of being first-time homeowners. This house also had a chicken coop (no chickens this time) in the backyard, and I remember Kevin and I would occasionally catch Dave hiding out in there, sneaking a cigarette. He'd make us promise not to tell our parents, but the truth was I couldn't have cared one way or the other as I didn't even understand what smoking was all about at that time. While living there, I attended Clifty Elementary School for my first grade of school. And I remember this as the first time I ever became infatuated with a girl. Brenda C. was the cutest thing I'd ever seen—although, as I recall, she wasn't much taken by me. The following year, due to redistricting, I'd transfer to Booth-Setser Elementary School to attend the first half of the second grade.

Later that year, my father would have the first of what would wind up being several (possibly twelve or thirteen) heart attacks over the course of his lifetime. He recovered reasonably well, but shortly thereafter, it'd become evident that my parents were experiencing marital problems. Whatever the reason, their arguing would become increasingly troublesome. And from that time on, their relationship never quite seemed the same.

We probably lived on Indiana Avenue about a year and a half, as around 1958/1959, my mother filed for divorce. This would prove a confusing time for me and my siblings, and I'd long question why their divorce had happened. How could life suddenly become so uncertain, so scary? I'm not sure any of us kids would ever fully understand the reasons for the divorce. Clearly, my mother was unhappy in the marriage and, for the longest time, blamed my father for her unhappiness. My father, on the other hand, never wanted the divorce and was given to blaming my mother for her "sinful" way of abandoning him. There may have been some infidelity on my mom's part as well. But while Dad would hint at this over the years, Mom was never overtly accused. And to my knowledge, it was never confirmed. All I and my siblings knew for certain was that the divorce had greatly disrupted our daily lives and resulted in much animosity between our parents that lasted for years to come.

With our parents' divorce, my mother was awarded custody of the four children. This was common in the late 1950s. I guess the judge just believed keeping kids with their primary caregiver would be less traumatizing, even though my mother seldom worked outside the home and had no real source of steady income. We generally struggled by on food stamps and the meager child support money the courts had ordered my father to pay. As part of the divorce settlement, we also had to sell the house on Indiana Avenue. And this meant Mom and we kids needed a new place to live. We'd end up moving into a rental house at 1502 Union Street.

As a single mother of four who struggled to stay employed, Mom seemed persistently depressed, remaining in bed for long periods and showing very little in the way of happiness or enthusiasm for life. My father was granted three hours of visitation each Monday night, one weekend a month, and one week of vacation time during the summer months. He also boasted of being awarded one extra day of visitation each May so he might take us to the Indianapolis Motor Speedway time trials. But while my father would be forever faithful in keeping his visitation dates up until the time of his death in 1969, he begrudgingly paid the forty dollars of monthly child support.

Accordingly, the next several years were very difficult. This is often the case where divorce is concerned and especially in today's times when households sometimes run by two incomes are reduced to only one. But in our case, the situation seemed even worse. During the late '50s and early '60s, job opportunities for women were generally limited. From time to time, Mom would take in laundry from a neighbor in an effort to earn extra income. And I remember her trying to work once as a waitress for a small Chinese restaurant. But for whatever reason, this latter job only lasted a few weeks. Whether it was Mom's lack of confidence, limited work skills, or her depression, she just couldn't sustain gainful employment. Accordingly, by all accounts, we were poor. Our clothes were generally ragged or hand-me-downs that didn't fit. New shoes and haircuts were usually available only once a year. And during the most difficult of times, strangers, I assumed neighbors or people from a nearby church, would leave bags of groceries on our doorstep. It was as if they knew we had little to eat. The house itself was a roach-infested, three-bedroom dwelling renting for fifty dollars a month. There we were, four kids and my mother, all living together under the same roof with scarcely enough financial resources to go around. And the hostility between our parents continued.

I write these things not to sound melodramatic but rather to describe the situation that would contribute to my own growing sense of uncertainty and self-doubt. Later on, as I became an adult, I'd realize that even the poorest of people in the USA probably have life better than those in many other countries around the world. And later still, I'd come to see how these experiences probably laid the groundwork for my learning to empathize with the hardships and suffering of others, a capacity that would prove invaluable later on in my career as a psychologist. I remember a college instructor of mine once suggesting empathy to be something most probably learned through our worldly experiences rather than in a classroom setting. Maybe this is what he meant. But in any event, all I knew as a small child was that it was difficult going to school in a generally affluent community dressed in dirty, ragged clothes, having nothing to eat for lunch, being unable to afford even the most basic school supplies, and otherwise struggling emotionally to fit in with peers.

The divorce was probably hardest on my brother Dave. He had always had a hot/cold relationship with my father. And as the firstborn, he probably got the worst of my dad's demanding demeanor and inexperienced parenting skills. They just seemed to take a terrible toll on Dave, for try as he might, he never seemed able to live up to my dad's expectations. Dave just wasn't an especially good student, probably average but not "good." He wasn't an especially good athlete either. In fact, while growing up, Dave just didn't seem to excel at much of anything, at least not in my dad's eyes. There were stories of Dad's frustrations sometimes boiling over into physical abuse, striking Dave with a belt. But I never witnessed this. There would be times later on when I *did* experience Dad's anger bordering on episodes of rage. But I never witnessed any real signs of violence or clear physical abuse. Nonetheless, my dad's anger was enough to leave Dave anxiety-laden, fearful, and "gun shy" of ever displeasing him. Then as time went by, Dave would grow increasingly lacking in confidence and toward avoiding or withdrawing from Dad altogether. This seemed to anger Dad even more. Like many children, Dave probably would have responded better to a father who was more understanding, supportive, and nurturing. Unfortunately, that's not the father he got. Still, and in spite of it all, I think Dave looked up to Dad. And I've long suspected Dave would have preferred growing up with the presence of both parents in the home, even if one was unduly harsh and critical. Regrettably, the divorce effectively ended this as an option.

It was about this same time that I began to recognize my brother Kevin's artistic talents. As noted above, to the extent that artistic ability is inherited, both Kevin and Dave seemed to get some of our dad's gift. Even from an early age, Kevin was able to draw all sorts of things with far more precision, accuracy, and imagination than I ever could. He just seemed blessed with an uncanny talent for perceiving shapes, colors, dimensions, and the like. And he always had the ability for visualizing how parts went together to make a whole. So growing up in the home state of the Indianapolis 500, I guess it was natural that he'd get interested in drawing race cars.

He was also far more skilled than I at model building. Together we'd assemble model cars, ships, airplanes, even horror movie characters (Frankenstein, Dracula, Creature from the Black Lagoon, etc.). And his models always came out looking and functioning far better than mine. The wheels on my cars seldom turned freely, and the mechanics on my planes and ships never seemed to work quite right. Moreover, when finished, I'd always had pieces from the kits left over. Kevin's models wouldn't have these problems. Later on, I'd come to learn that he'd been reading the instructions when building his models. I, on the other hand, just looked at the pieces and tried to guess where and how they all went together based upon my skills for deduction. Who knew reading instructions might actually make a difference? Later still, after studying art at Ball State University, Kevin would actually become a rather accomplished local artist and respected high school teacher.

Also during this period, I came to recognize differences between how Kevin responded to Dad's expectations and anger versus how Dave and I responded. As noted above, Dave had become increasingly anxious, even fearful, of Dad's demeanor, at times seemingly cowering in his presence. I, on the other hand, took up Dad's criticism and anger as a challenge to do better. In retrospect, while Dave looked up to Dad, I'm not sure he truly felt loved by him, seemingly perceiving Dad's disappointment and criticalness as evidence of disdain for what Dave assumed to be his own deficiencies. I, on the other hand, always believed Dad loved me, even in his most critical moments. I just saw his intolerance and explosiveness as an extension of personal frustrations he couldn't manage and of his desire for me to become the best I could be. Kevin, by contrast, took up these issues differently still. Dad would get angry and order Kevin to do something, and Kevin would immediately agree to do it. Then Kevin would simply go off and do whatever he pleased. I never quite understood how Kevin could ignore Dad so easily, let alone get away with it. And I just couldn't comprehend why Kevin believed noncompliance would somehow be tolerated or why, for that matter, Dad seemed to overlook Kevin's apparent defiance. On more than one occasion, I tried to warn Kevin about disobeying Dad, to explain how Dad would probably make him pay dearly. But Kevin just continued doing that which he chose, and invariably, Dad seemed to let it slide. Over time, I think Dad probably grew to expect a little less of Kevin because of all this. But I knew for a "fact" that if I ever responded in such a fashion, I'd certainly get the worst of it.

Among other memories of our time on Union Street would be that of our having neighbors who were prone toward yelling at one another and, I believe, fighting regularly. I'd later discover their behavior was related to alcohol use problems, whether by one or both of the adults. Still, while they pretty much left our family alone and kept the squabbling to themselves, I found the entire experience unsettling and a bit scary. Our mother would warn us not to go anywhere near the family. But I always felt particularly sorry for the children who seemed like nice kids struggling to manage their fears and to hide the family secret from everyone they met. I think I also understood their shame and empathized with their plight, even if I wasn't yet sure what all these emotions meant. Years later, after becoming involved with treating substance-abusing individuals, I'd learn of the terrible toll alcoholism and drug addiction takes not only on the abusing individual but on their loved ones as well. Some reports suggest that the lives of nine people (parents, siblings, partners, children, etc.) are harmed for that of every one alcoholic or addict. It's truly tragic.

I attended McKinley Elementary School from part of the second grade through the fifth grade (1959 through 1962), and this was where I'd meet my lifelong friend Mike Sprague. For the next sixty-plus years, our paths would continue to cross in important ways, and our friendship would stand the test of time. While I was from an impoverished household and of divorced parents, an important distinction in the late 1950s and early 1960s, Mike's family was intact and decidedly more stable. He never seemed to struggle with the feelings of inadequacy, shame, resentment, and anger that I experienced throughout much of my childhood. Unlike me, he always seemed to have more confidence in who he was and to be unburdened by the need to prove himself in order to fit in. As importantly, he liked and accepted me for who I was.

I also remember meeting Mark Goff during this period. He, too, was from divorced parents, but his father had moved out of state and was seldom to be heard from. His mother, on the other hand, had remarried, so Mark still had two parents in the home. Unfortunately for Mark and his brother Phil, his stepfather (and two stepbrothers) were generally mean and abusive toward them. The stepbrothers, in particular, seemed to treat Mark and Phil as though they were generally less than or inferior, which would yield a rude awakening for the stepfather once the stepbrothers got arrested for burglary and were placed on probation. It seemed they had broken into a candy vending distribution business and robbed it of several cases of candy bars. Oh, the lessons of growing up.

Probably the fondest memories I have of my time spent with Mark were those Saturday mornings when we'd go scrounging around for empty soda bottles. Twelve-ounce bottles could be redeemed for two cents apiece at the nearby market, while the larger quart bottles yielded five cents each. Usually, the best place to find these bottles was along the railroad tracks winding through Columbus and in trash bins located behind various businesses. As Mark and I were both too poor to have any real spending money of our own, once we'd collected enough bottles to generate twenty-five cents apiece, we'd cash them in. Then we would go down to the Crump Theater and take in the double-feature horror movies showing from 9:00 a.m. till noon. *The Curse of the Mummy, Dracula, The Werewolf, The Bride of Frankenstein, The Time Machine*, all the original black-and-white films from the 1950s were shown there. What a treat!

It was around this same time that I started realizing just how poor our family really was. I noted above that from time to time, we struggled to have food or other basics of life. These were problems our family suffered through together, so early on, I'm not sure I understood this meant we were poor. But all that clearly changed once I started making friends my own age and came to recognize that other families didn't seem to have these problems. For the most part, when my friends wanted a candy bar or a pop or to go to the movies, they generally seemed to have money to do so—whereas I normally didn't. Sometimes I could talk Mom into giving me some change, or a friend would feel sorry for me and share some of their money. And once I got into junior high school, I'd learn to sneak into the movies or a basketball game or a school dance. But for the most part, these were all exceptions rather than the rule. Then as I moved up to high school and fitting in became even more important, I'd come to realize that not being able to afford a regular haircut or have clothes like many of my peers, let alone money for attending social events, created additional barriers to making friends. When I could, I'd try to do odd jobs to earn a little spending money. And once we were in high school, Kevin was able to persuade our dad to give us fifty cents a week for "allowance." But for the most part, there was no escaping the reality of our family being poor.

Other kids recognized the difference as well. We all know how judgmental and petty kids can sometimes be. And in my hometown, where so many families were of middle-class or upper-income levels, it was not uncommon for schoolmates to be particularly intolerant of those from lower-income families. This may well be true in school settings all across our nation. However much we try to raise our children to be caring and accepting, comparing oneself to others seems part and parcel of the growing-up experience. Unfortunately, for many, so too does looking down on the less fortunate.

Of course, my own attitudes and behavior probably were more negative, maybe more hateful, than those of many of my peers. Certainly, life circumstances had left me hypersensitive to being negatively judged. I'm sure I reacted defensively when feeling inferior to or slighted by others. And I know now that responding in this manner probably contributed to my struggles. In some ways, it might have made sense that other kids would treat me as though I were somehow "less than" or be reluctant to include me in many of their activities. I probably wasn't the easiest or nicest person to be around. In many ways, I probably didn't fit in. Nonetheless, as a young boy, it was still difficult to understand. And I still questioned why it seemed to hurt so much.

Another thing to emerge from these struggles was the ever-present drive to fight back against the world, against the lack of control I experienced as going hand in hand with being poor and struggling to gain acceptance. It just seemed like there wasn't much else I could do about my circumstances and the obstacles they created. Consequently, for the longest time, the need to willfully overcome my apparent fate would push me in a host of self-defeating ways. I learned to lie and, occasionally, to steal to get what I wanted. I also learned to fight others if I felt judged or put down by their attitudes or actions. And rather than assume responsibility for my own demeanor and behavior, I'd choose to blame others when frustrated over not getting what I wanted or not having things work out the way I believed they should. Later on, as I matured *a little*, I'd try to find ways of pleasing or impressing others in hopes of gaining their acceptance or of getting what I wanted. And as already noted, I'd try working to earn a little spending money when I could. I'd also try achieving in sports, improving my schoolwork, and excelling on the job, all in the hopes of fitting in, of "proving myself," and not feeling so inadequate. But all these efforts were driven more by the need to rise above my perceived plight in life than by healthier and more caring motives. And while these actions occasionally yielded some relief of my discomfort, because they were primarily fear- or anger-driven, the relief would only be temporary. It'd be years before I realized the folly of all this, that as the saying goes, "True happiness in life comes more from wanting what you have than from having what you want," more from "being who you are rather than from trying to be someone you're not." Early on, fighting against (or running from) all that which I had learned to dread just seemed the only answer.

I'd never enjoyed reading. This is probably why I wouldn't read the instructions for the models I built. Sometimes I wonder how I ever completed my doctoral studies given my generally poor reading skills. In fact, later in life, I'd come to suspect I probably qualified for a formal reading disorder. Because of this deficiency, perseverance and a strong capacity for memory would prove my only real hope for academic success.

Still, while I wasn't a good reader, I will never forget studying Indiana state history as a fourth grader. And in addition to other assignments, once a week for an entire semester, my teacher, Mrs. Tiemeyer, read chapters from a book titled *The Bears of Blue River*. The book described the struggles of a frontiersman striving to establish his homestead in the wilderness of what was then unsettled Indiana. And of course, the story included the lead character's dangerous encounter with a giant bear. It would be another two years before I'd actually read a book on my own, but for the very first time, I was beginning to see the possible benefit of books. Between the author's descriptive writing and Mrs. Tiemeyer's expressive reading, I was fascinated.

When I was about eleven years old, in the spring of 1962, our family moved to 1447 Union Street. This house was only a few doors down from the house at 1502 but in a little nicer shape and a bit larger than our previous house. They were both owned by one Mr. Shanklin, and as I recall, he allowed us to move into the 1447 house with no increase in rent. I think he agreed to this arrangement because he knew we were poor and was sympathetic to our family's plight. I also suspect he thought we'd be better tenants than his previous renters. In any case, I don't remember much else about Mr. Shanklin other than his being pretty old (eighty-ish?) and a slightly built man with white hair. I do, however, remember two other things about the house at 1447. First, while it was just down the street from the house at 1502, it was located in what truly seemed the poorest section of town. The area consisted of some ten to twelve homes all lining a one-block area of Union between 14th and 15th Streets, and all the families living along this stretch (ourselves included) were of lower socioeconomic status. The second thing I remember about the 1447 house is that the house was located in what was otherwise a totally black neighborhood.

While moving into this area would prove my first real exposure to black people, being white in an essentially all-black neighborhood didn't really seem to matter much at the time. Everyone on the street tried their best to get along regardless of race, and we were all too poor to see ourselves as better than anyone else. Moreover, though our family was white, our mother never encouraged us to view our black neighbors differently. In fact, as best I recall, I don't remember anyone in Columbus ever making a big deal of race one way or the other. Admittedly, this might have been because of the limited number of black families (and other ethnic minorities) living in the city while I was growing up. But for me, it just seemed more a result of the common bonds the people of Columbus all shared. Columbus was predominantly a Christian community, and in general, we all believed in the importance of family and a strong work ethic. As a result, these shared bonds seemed to make getting along and working together far more important than the color of one's skin. In retrospect, I truly do not recall experiencing any real prejudice or racism during that time. I guess there probably were certain individuals who were prejudiced, even racist. I just don't recall experiencing such people.

Now some might think growing up in such an environment would leave me ill-prepared for dealing with all the racial divisiveness and prejudice I'd encounter later on upon leaving Columbus. No doubt, it would be a much different experience than what I'd come to know while living in Indianapolis, Pittsburgh, Dayton, and Mobile, for example. But from my vantage point, growing up in this environment seemed to provide an alternative, if not healthier, perspective on black/white relations than that which I'd find in many of the larger cities where I'd eventually come to live. Because of my upbringing, I'd grow to view racial strife *not* as the result of a minority race being victimized by an oppressing majority race. I know some would argue this point, but I just never came to see racial problems this way. Rather, my experience of racial conflict would be that of its representing something *both* sides, if not our society as a whole, seem to create and to be responsible for, and that the real source of racial conflict is actually about something far greater than differences in the color of one's skin.

From my perspective, when people undertake productive work that bolsters self-worth, maintain commonly shared cultural values, pursue a foundation of love, and develop a unifying sense of purpose, then differences like ethnicity, race, religion, gender, etc. all seem to become somewhat less important. And when family systems and the society at large foster such an environment, the ground for peaceful coexistence seems to prevail. It may be much like differing kinds of flowers flourishing alongside one another when planted in healthy soil, provided abundant sunlight, and nurtured by adequate rain. On the other hand, when people dismiss or reject the value of work, of giving back to the community of which they are a part, then their self-worth and personal value are diminished. When people decide to chase their own desires and pursue their own individual wants and needs at the expense of family systems and social institutions, then they risk becoming estranged from all those relationships needed to help them feel a part of the culture at large. And when individuals become so absorbed in their own individual lives that long-standing traditions and customs are ignored or no longer believed important (much like when we as individuals fail to agree on even the most basic rules and laws by which to live), then inevitably the structure of daily life itself breaks down. And this, in my opinion, represents the source for much of the racial anger, divisiveness, and conflict we as a nation are facing today. I am not trying to say that individual and ethnic differences aren't real or don't matter. Just that when we as a people no longer share common bonds, no longer hold common values, and no longer work toward common goals, then our tendency is to focus more on our differences and on blaming one another for our struggles than on identifying with all those things that might otherwise hold us together.

Again, the house at 1447 was a little nicer than that at 1502. There were no roaches here as I recall. It had a coal furnace, which I and my brothers soon learned to stoke and operate on a regular basis—or at least when we could afford the coal. As I remember, in the mid-60s the price of coal was about twenty dollars a ton. But keeping us in regular supply would prove difficult because, as already noted, Mom struggled to work outside the home or otherwise earn enough money to meet all our needs, pay a babysitter, and justify her labors. This meant we had to get by on child support, food stamps, and the charity of others. Again, if you figure it out, you quickly realize there wasn't enough money to make ends meet. And when the money dried up, coal/heat would usually be the first to go. Of course, this made tolerating the Indiana winters difficult to say the least.

In the summer of 1962, my father, bless his heart, decided he would take us on a vacation trip to Florida. Yes, we were poor,

BEGINNINGS

but nothing could stop him from realizing a lifelong dream. So we loaded up his 1957 Volkswagen Beetle, and off we went. By this time, Dave had left home to join the Navy, so it was just Kevin, LouAnne, and I, along with Dad. We spent nine days driving South from Indiana to the Gulf Coast, across the Everglades, down to Key West, up the Atlantic Coast, and back home. We took our own food or bought groceries because we couldn't afford to eat in restaurants. Gas for the car was about fifteen cents a gallon, as I recall. Hotels were six dollars a night, but of course, we didn't have money for a hotel room, so the four of us slept in the Volkswagen Beetle. We swam in the Gulf/ocean, ran out of gas along Alligator Alley in the Everglades, slept in the car on Daytona Beach, and (at Kevin's prompting) visited Ripley's Believe It or Not Museum. This was our one recreational expenditure, and I'll never forget the Ripley's infamous two-headed goat. LouAnne got eaten up by mosquitos as we had to sleep with the windows down because of the summer heat and humidity, and we all got sunburned. But we would talk about this experience for years to come.

Although only one block from the house at 1502 Union Street, the house at 1447 would also be in a different school district. As a result, I was again attending Jefferson Elementary School in the fall while completing my sixth grade of schooling. The teacher there was a Mr. Roush, and he would be one of the first teachers I ever recall as having taken a personal interest in me. More than any other teacher I'd had to date, he encouraged me to believe in myself. He would, for example, sign me up to be a patrol boy (crossing guard). Never before had anyone given me an opportunity to prove myself or to take on any such responsibilities. He also encouraged me to focus more on my schoolwork and learning. And under his guidance, I would become a little more social—joining the school basketball team that he coached. This would end up being my only attempt at playing organized basketball as I was not especially talented for the sport. But the experience would pave the way for later social development and for my playing football and running track once I moved up to junior high school.

Mr. Roush would also require each of his students to present book reports at various times throughout the school year. He was quite struck by the fact that, although I could read words, I had made it to the sixth grade and *never* read a real book. Under his guidance, I found a Hardy Boys mystery that I could both read and found interesting. That year, I read three other Hardy Boys mysteries—until Mr. Roush realized I was limiting myself to one genre. Then he helped me pick a book titled *We Thought We Heard the Angels Sing* (by Charles Major). The story was of a war plane shot down over the Pacific Ocean during WWII and the crew's harrowing tale of survival in shark-infested waters while awaiting rescue. At long last, I was beginning to read.

When I was about twelve or thirteen years old, my mother began dating the man who'd one day become my stepfather (Marcus Merriman). This would prove another confusing experience as, prior to this time, Dad was the only father figure us kids had ever known. Moreover, the hostility that existed between my parents immediately following their divorce would only worsen once Mom began dating. I always suspected my dad was just jealous over Mom dating another man, even though he behaved more like he was offended. But whatever the case, for the next few years, he and Mom continued to express their disdain for each other. And all too often, this left Marcus in the middle. Marcus (or Pop as we came to call him) was obviously sympathetic toward Mom's hurt and anger, but he also knew the hostilities were tough on us kids. So eventually, he suggested she not vent her anger in front of us. But while this helped me and my siblings, it would not totally protect Pop from the strain their bitterness created. For example, I remember clearly how

Dad would go out of his way to inform us that Marcus was *not* our father. Now I'm sure we all knew this, but Dad's constant reminders left us feeling as though we needed to make sure that Pop knew it as well. So unfortunately for Pop, we made it a point of telling him every chance we got. Still, we couldn't really hate Pop because of all the stability he had brought into our lives. For the first time since the divorce, we now had regular food and heat.

Pop was a large, strongly built man who was generally quiet. But when he did speak, everyone knew to listen. He too was a bit authoritarian and serious in his manner, but he worked consistently, was a good provider, and was less anger-prone than my biological father. I can honestly say he never mistreated us or our mom. And because of this, I'd be forever grateful that he'd assumed the responsibility for raising me and my siblings when he truly didn't have to do so.

Like many in our town, Pop worked for Cummins Engine Company Inc. And by all accounts, he was a dedicated worker. I can remember him working six to seven days a week, sometimes double shifts, for as many as fifty weeks out of the year. And he'd work in this manner for years and years, eventually accumulating some forty-six years of service for Cummins before retiring. I also remember Mom saying Pop had served as an airplane mechanic during WWII. And as a result, I quickly learned that he was quite mechanically inclined. Never had I known anyone so adept at repairing cars, trucks, anything with a motor. And he was also a jack-of-all-trades around the house. He could repair plumbing leaks, roof damage, electrical problems, just about anything that was broken. On many such projects, Pop would enlist my support as his helper. And while I was usually a reluctant participant, later in life, I'd come to appreciate the benefits of all this instruction.

My mother would continue struggling with depression, off and on, throughout this period. I haven't spoken a lot about my mother. She was diminutive in stature, probably 5'1" tall and 115 pounds when she was younger. From a collection of modeling photos taken during her early years (lying on a blanket in a bathing suit, surrounded by books and the like), she was an attractive and shapely young woman, with beautiful, long dark hair and fair complexion. I remember well how, in the photos, she looked happy, self-confident, and full of life. But by the time I had gotten old enough to know her as a person, and especially from the time immediately following her divorce, she seemed but a shell of her former self. As a youth, I understood very little about depression or other mental health issues. But I clearly recall her being chronically sad or irritable, when she wasn't crying or staying in bed. She seldom laughed and tended to isolate herself from others, except for her occasionally attending church. Even after remarrying, she seemed lonely much of the time. Over the years, she'd get involved with canning vegetables or crocheting. And she liked gardening and caring for roses or other flowers when the notion struck her. And much later in life, she even developed some talent for painting (with oils, pastels, and watercolors). But throughout my teenage and early adult years, she seemed beset by self-doubt, low self-esteem, and depression. And I can still recall the feelings of helplessness associated with my inability to fix her problems.

Again, I am not exactly sure why my parents divorced. I know Mom regularly accused our father of having been "abusive." But while I don't recall witnessing any battering per se, I sometimes thought I understood where she might have been coming from. Dad was clearly critical by nature and difficult to please. So maybe it was more about emotional abuse than physical. Still, over time, I'd also come to believe that Mom may always have struggled with a lack of confidence and what some call dependent-laden traits. She just seemed burdened by self-doubt, anxiety, and a need for somebody strong to lean on, to make decisions for her, maybe even to take charge of her life. These same qualities were also present throughout much of her marriage to Pop. My father, on the other hand, always seemed driven to personal insecurities and a need to disguise his fears of failure through being strong-willed, demanding, and controlling. And his own deep-seated, if not so carefully hidden, self-doubt seemed to yield an equally strong need for someone else to need him, as if this would make him feel stronger, more complete, or more important. In truth, Mom and Dad probably "found each other"—and what they found in each other probably worked for both during the early years of their marriage. Unfortunately, with time, I suspect my mother's neediness and my father's dominance just took a toll on them both. As already noted, my father could be lavish with praise, even though he was also critical and easy to anger. I guess my mother just became increasingly submissive to my father's more authoritarian style, until she eventually grew resentful of the arrangement and came to view this cocreated state of affairs as abusive.

Probably my mother's greatest strength, as well as her greatest gift to me, would be her unwavering commitment to spirituality and her compassion for others. We didn't necessarily attend church regularly, but we always had a Bible around. And she taught us to pray, to care about others, to treat others as we would want to be treated, and to never give up hope—in short, to keep the faith. It may be because of my mother that I've committed much of my own life to seeking answers to my most troubling questions, to understanding life, and to striving to live in God's spirit.

As noted above, upon advancing through school I'd try to improve my academic focus, get more involved in athletics, and work toward becoming more social. All this pleased my father greatly. But while his praise would be increasingly important to me, my desire to avoid his occasional wrath would define my character even more. Again, my brother Dave had *never* been successful at staying out of Dad's crosshairs. And it was only a short time after the divorce that Dave dropped out of school to join the US Navy. The years that followed his leaving home would result in a long series of poor choices—eventually leading him into alcoholism and despair. Upon completing basic training at Waukegan, Illinois, he was reassigned to the Boston, Massachusetts, area. There he met and married a woman struggling with family and emotional issues of her own and who was anger/violence-prone. Shortly thereafter, he'd be sent to the New Mexico area, and while there, his alcohol use progressed, and his marital problems worsened. Eventually, he became the father of four children. He may have served a stint on a gunboat in Vietnam before being discharged, but I write "may" because questions always remained about his time away from home and the truthfulness with which Dave was reporting things during that period. Prior to his being discharged, his wife was charged with battering their children (one in particular). This resulted in my mother and Pop traveling to New Mexico to take custody of the most seriously battered child (my nephew, Brian). Shortly after that, upon being discharged from the Navy, Dave divorced his wife and returned home to Columbus. Clearly he'd struggled throughout this time, and I always suspected that my father's demanding/critical parenting, in conjunction with our parents' divorce and their ongoing hostility, had contributed largely to Dave's problems. But while I would never know this for sure, what I *did* know was that I wanted to avoid a similar fate. So this meant working diligently to escape the pain of my father's disapproval while creating a future of my own. As a sidenote, some years later, Dave would remarry, achieve sustained sobriety, and become involved with his church. And this would help him realize a semblance of inner peace.

> My guard stood hard, when abstract threats,
> Too noble to neglect,
> Deceived me into thinking, I had something to protect.
> Good and bad I define them both;
> Quite clear, no doubt, somehow.
> Ah, but I was so much older then
> I'm younger than that now.
>
> —B. Dylan

From *My Back Pages*, words and music by Bob Dylan (1964), Copyright Columbia Records

FAMILY, FRIENDS, AND THE GIFT OF MUSIC

Between ages twelve and fifteen, I attended Central Junior High School (CJHS). My brother Kevin was a ninth grader when I entered the seventh grade and generally disliked me hanging around with him. But at Mom's prompting, he agreed to our walking to and from school together the first few weeks so I could learn the route. Traveling the mile or so on foot may sound old-school, but it was really not that big of a deal. In Columbus, lots of kids walked to school, and it was generally safe.

My social skills remained limited during this time, and connecting with others would be an ongoing struggle. But eventually I'd make a few more friends. One such acquaintance was Donnie Moore. Again, Donnie's family was intact, and he seemed to have less self-doubt and more self-esteem than I. He also had the social skills that I was lacking. On the other hand, what Donnie lacked was physical stature—a real shortcoming, so to speak, when it comes to dealing with the occasional bully one finds in junior high. I on the other hand was taller and physically stronger than many of my peers. Add to this the fact that I was from a poorer section of town and familiar with the occasional need to fight in order to "defend" myself, and I'd prove a good choice to be his buddy and protector. Donnie and I would spend the best part of two years hanging out together; walking to and from school, riding bicycles, and swimming in the public pool at Donner Park during the summer. In winter, when I could come up with the money, we'd go ice skating at the local rink, to basketball games, or to school dances. These were the hot spots for meeting girls, and Donnie helped me feel less anxious in their presence.

Upon entering the eighth grade, Donnie would also talk me into joining the CJHS football and track teams. I always loved sports but lacked the confidence necessary to try out for a team on my own. In fact, I probably would never have played on the Jefferson Elementary basketball team had my teacher not also been the coach and pressed the issue. But with Donnie's encouragement, I'd join the CJHS teams, and this helped me with some of my social deficiencies. Still, apart from everything else, my most lasting memory of Donnie will always be his sharing tips on playing the drums. As I recall, Donnie had a beautiful set of Rogers drums and was taking lessons at a local music store. So occasionally, he'd show me a few of the more basic techniques he'd learned along the way.

This was right around the time the Beatles first came to America, and the "British Invasion" would be huge during the '60s. The arrival of the Beatles was followed by the Rolling Stones, the Animals, the Yardbirds, the Kinks, the Zombies, Cream, Led Zeppelin, and countless other musical groups from "across the pond." Later still, the movement would lead to the emergence of such American groups as the Byrds, the Doors, Creedence Clearwater Revival, Steppenwolf, the Young Rascals, and so on. Earlier generations might have been enthralled with the big band sounds of the Tommy Dorsey Orchestra or the crooning of Frank Sinatra and Nat King Cole. The late fifties and early sixties had rockabilly, Elvis, and surf music. But for me and many others my age, it was the music coming over from England and the bands that followed in their wake that would forever be imprinted on our delicate brains.

Of course, in addition to the music's creative sound and distinctive style, the "British Invasion" was also responsible for ushering in the slew of so-called garage bands that eventually popped up all across America—including in Columbus. If you were a teenager who sang or played an instrument of any kind (guitar, bass, drums, organ, etc.), you could dream of forming a combo and one day becoming a star. It was many a small-town boy's fantasy during the time, or at least it was mine. And I wanted to get in on the action. So any exposure to playing music, even in such a limited fashion, provided hope that I too might one day be able to join a band and "make it big." Eventually, of course, I'd give up the dream. But I'd still use some of the drumming tips Donnie showed me later on when adding percussion to music I'd record in my home studios in Kentucky and Alabama. And the friendship we created served us both very well as we remained the best of friends until my mom remarried a couple of years later and our family moved some four miles south of Columbus to Bethel Village.

A year or so after meeting Donnie, I also met a lad named Don Smith. I was riding my bicycle one day and happened upon him near his home in the East Columbus area of the city. Don also attended Central Junior High School and was in the same grade as I. And much like me, Don was from a family of limited means. As we struck up a conversation, I'd soon learn that both Don and his father played guitar. As importantly, Don's father had a stash of musical gear that would be the envy of many a musician. In addition to a Fender Precision bass, a large Silvertone bass amplifier (with two twelve-inch speakers), another guitar amplifier, and assorted other instruments, his father owned a brand-new, 1965 Rickenbacker 360 model guitar with the Fireglow finish.

Rickenbacker guitars had been around for decades, and they continue being made to this day. They're probably not as well-known as those made by the Gibson and Fender companies, primarily due to the fact that Rickenbacker has always been a small, family-owned business that refuses to mass-produce its instruments. Still, Rickenbacker guitars and basses are considered to be of very high quality, and they would become increasingly popular with the emergence of the Beatles in the mid-'60s. At different times, John Lennon, George Harrison, and Paul McCartney of Beatles fame all played these instruments, and many aspiring teenagers wanted to emulate these "stars." Later on, artists such as Roger McGuinn of the Byrds, Pete Townshend of the Who, Tom Petty of the Heartbreakers, John McKay of Steppenwolf, Susanna Hoffs of the Bangles, and others would also find the jangly Rickenbacker sound inspiring. When Don asked if I was interested in learning to play, given my interest in music, and never one to shy away from a challenge, I immediately said yes.

Now the Rickenbacker guitar owned by Don's father had to be one of the very first 360 models with the rounded horns ever made. It was quite a special instrument at the time and beautiful by any measure. And the impact this guitar had on me would prove long-lasting (as some thirty plus years later, I would buy one of my own). Don, however, wouldn't let me play his Dad's Rickenbacker out of concern I might damage it. What Don did agree to was showing me how to play his father's Fender bass, and I took to playing bass like the proverbial duck to water. Within a matter of minutes, we were playing the Van Morrison tune "Gloria," me on bass and Don on guitar and vocals. And it was a breakthrough moment for me. I had previously seen my older brother Dave strum chords on a cheap acoustic guitar he'd once borrowed. And again, Donnie Moore had shown me a few techniques on his drums. But this was my first real shot at actually playing an instrument for myself. And this was rock and roll.

From that moment on, music would be an important part of my life. From that time forward, in all but my darkest of moments, playing music always seemed to give me a sense of hope and a feeling of not being quite so alone in the world. Later that year, with the help of my father, I'd buy a Japanese-made Teisco bass and a small amplifier through the local Sears & Roebuck Store. As I recall, the entire package cost one hundred dollars (give or take), and my dad signed for me to buy it at five dollars down and five dollars a month. Now I'm not sure where Dad got the bright idea that an unemployed fourteen-year-old could ever come up with the five-dollar monthly payment. And I would end up having this bass for only about a year before Sears repossessed it for nonpayment of the note. But playing that bass for the year I did have it was pure magic. To this day, the bass remains my favorite of all the instruments I'd learn to play.

Clearly, making a few new friends and being introduced to playing music would be important to my self-esteem and personal development. But during this same period, I'd also be touched by another important event of the times: the assassination of President Kennedy. As I recall, I was actually in the seventh grade when he was killed. I was in art class, and we were just wrapping up the school day. That was when the principal came over the loudspeaker to inform students of the president's having been shot and that he was being taken to the hospital. At the time of the announcement, he was not yet being reported as having died. I think that news would come a little later.

Initially, I couldn't fully understand the full importance of the president's being shot. I was still so very young and, for the most part, scarcely knew who the president was or his role in running the government. Moreover, I had no real idea how his death might affect our nation's place in the world, let alone my own life. Still, I was able to sense the shooting to have been a bad thing. Maybe it was something in the tone of the principal's voice or something in my teacher's nonverbal response to hearing the news. But whatever the case, I knew something was wrong. I guess it was much like the circumstances surrounding the death of Laddy or my parents' divorce. At first, I just felt confused. There were just so many questions. As for other recollections surrounding the president's death, most remain foggy. I do recall watching some of the news coverage, particularly Walter Cronkite's accounts of the shooting and the swearing in of President Johnson. And I remember watching the funeral procession. But I guess my mother protected us kids from watching too much of the television footage. Only later would I realize how this experience would be my introduction to such things as human frailty, social change, and political upheaval.

In the summer following my eighth grade year of schooling, my path would again cross with Mike Sprague's. I hadn't seen Mike since after the fifth grade when our family moved to 1447 Union Street and I left the McKinley school district. Upon completing the sixth grade at Jefferson Elementary, I would go on to Central Junior High School while Mike went to Northside Junior High across town. This meant we wouldn't see much of each other for the next few years. All this was about to change.

As luck might have it, both of my brothers, Dave and Kevin, had worked as soda jerks for a place called Zaharako's Confectionary. Zaharako's was the brainchild of three brothers, Lou, Pete, and James (whom we knew as Manual), who had all migrated from Greece. Another brother, George, would go on to start up a separate restaurant (the Olympia Dairy), before relocating out West to California some years later. But each of the brothers were members of a proud, hardworking, traditional Greek family that opened the original confectionary business around 1909.

Zaharako's was (and is to this day) a notable landmark in Columbus, Indiana. Step inside the front door off Main Street, and you are greeted by a beautiful, fifty-foot long marble counter, lined with evenly spaced barstools. Behind the counter are gorgeous mahogany cabinets, brass fixtures, and large mirrors, all serving as decoration. The rear dining room area is equally opulent: marble, brass, and mirrors everywhere. But the crowning jewel of it all is the Welte Orchestrion (circa 1907), reportedly first heard at the 1904 World's Fair. This Orchestrion is a ten-foot-tall, self-playing pipe organ imported from Freiburg, Germany, and located near the rear wall of the dining room. I've been told it was one of only two such organs ever built, and it continues to operate to this day—vibrating throughout the building whenever customers ask to hear it play. At one point, the brothers were known to have made all their own chocolate candies and ice cream by hand and from scratch, hence it being known as a confectionary. Later on, these items would be obtained from outside vendors. But by then, the brothers had added an assortment of sandwiches and carbonated drinks to the menu, with the drinks all being mixed by hand from syrups and carbonated water. Most would say that dining there was (and is) a memorable experience.

Dave had quit his job at Zaharako's when he left home for the Navy. But one day, while still working there, Kevin came home and told me the Zaharako brothers were looking for more help. This would be my first paid job. I'd make sixty cents an hour, food not included. And shortly after I went to work there, so too did Mike Sprague. We both started out bussing tables and washing dishes. This was standard for new workers, until such time as they could memorize the prices for the food listed on the menu board up front and learn the order of the drink syrup dispensers located in the two huge marble cabinets behind the serving counter.

Again, at that time, all the carbonated beverages were made by hand from combining the appropriate amount of syrup (Coca-Cola, Green River, Sarsaparilla, root beer, orange, lime, grape, etc.) with carbonated water. Nowadays, restaurants have machines that combine these ingredients automatically. But at that time, we did this by hand, and as one might expect, if the combination of ingredients was off, so too would be the taste of the drink. In this regard, mixing the drinks was truly as much of an art as a science. Mike would be amazingly quick at learning the order of the syrups and can recite them in the correct order to this day. For me, memorizing their order took a little longer, and I am not certain I ever learned them *exactly* right. But once we achieved this goal, proved we could take direction, and demonstrated we could be counted on to show up when scheduled, we were allowed to work behind the counter and start serving customers. The Zaharako brothers were stern, but fair, employers. And under their supervision, I would learn much about being responsible and working with the public. As they would frequently remind me, "this job builds character."

Throughout that summer, Mike and I worked for Zaharako's. We didn't make much money, barely enough to cover the cost of the food we ate with a little spending money left over. But working there bolstered my self-confidence and helped me become a little more socially adjusted. It also helped Mike and I to stay busy during our time off from school and kept us both out of trouble. Between shifts, we'd hang out, looking for ways to entertain ourselves, although clearly there were few options for two fourteen-year-old boys living in a small town and lacking transportation. Occasionally, we'd make our way down to the local Murphy's Five & Dime store to buy some candy or to the Sears department store to check out the latest Silvertone guitars. Once in a while, we'd duck into Schiff's Shoes and try on the latest Converse sneakers. Still other times, we'd simply ride the city bus on its loop around the town. At that time, one could ride the city bus all the way around town, nonstop, for the price of a single ticket (ten cents, if I recall correctly). And the bus always brought you back to where you first got on. Usually we'd wear out our welcome with the driver, but what else was a couple of boys supposed to do with very little money and extra time on their hands?

Mike has always had what I consider an unusual sense of humor and a seemingly endless list of ideas for new things we might try. I, on the other hand, whether because of my need for affiliation or my gullible nature, was more prone to be a follower. Consequently, I tended to go along with most anything Mike proposed. While this never got us into any serious trouble, it did result in our creating a nuisance of ourselves on more than one occasion. For example, I remember an incident whereupon Mike and I were asked to leave Sears because we had been playing their guitars so loudly we'd aggravated some of the customers. Truth is, neither of us were very good on guitar at that time, and the salesman probably knew we didn't have enough money between us to ever buy one of their instruments. So moving us along probably made good sense.

On another occasion, I remember the two of us going into Murphy's and Mike approaching the counter where new keys were being made. He nonchalantly asked if he could get a key made for his father's boat. When the lady behind the counter asked to see the key from which the copy might be made, Mike responded, "Why would I need you to make me a key if I already had one?" As the lady tried to explain how new keys were made from other keys, Mike continued questioning the process for what seemed like several minutes. He was just so sincere in his questioning that the lady behind the counter actually began questioning herself. It was much like a skit from a *Seinfeld* episode.

Finally, I recall yet another incident around Easter when Murphy's was giving away a free baby chicken if you purchased a small box of chicken food. Such a special would probably only be common in rural Midwestern communities, but it was a big deal for us. Under Mike's direction, we raced through the store, yelling, "Free chickens, free chickens, where are all the free chickens?" He then proceeded to confuse the unsuspecting clerk by insisting that the chickens were supposed to be free, independent of any food purchase. I'm sure these stories sound like childish antics to the reader, and they were. But for two fourteen-year-old boys trying to find their way in a small rural town, they were forming the bonds of a lasting friendship.

It was during the summer before my ninth grade year of schooling that my mother married my stepfather. A month or so later, we'd move into a three-bedroom, one-bath, ranch-style house in Bethel Village. The house cost some 12,000 dollars, which was a decent price for a home in the mid-60s, although scarcely worth mentioning in today's housing market. My mother had come up with the down payment through a settlement of her family's estate in Linton, Indiana, and the inheritance she had received. The mortgage was made possible by Pop's good credit rating and steady employment history. And I remember one of the more exciting features of this house, apart from it being only six years old, was that it had both a gas furnace and central air conditioning. Clean, reliable heat would be a first for our family in many years. And while we couldn't always afford to run the air conditioning unit, the air conditioning we did have on the hottest of days of the year was a real treat for our family. Finally, for the first time in some years, life seemed to be settling down.

Bethel Village is also where I'd meet another childhood friend, Dennis Steele. Dennis and I had much in common from the start. We were the same age, and physically, we were the same size and stature. We also shared an interest in sports. Moreover, his family lived only five doors down from ours, and we were both "trapped" in the village. We rode bikes together, played basketball together, and when school started, we both played on the CJHS football team (I as a quarterback/defensive back and he as a receiver). At one point, we even dated sisters who also lived in the village, next door to Dennis. And although Dennis would occasionally get frustrated by my interpersonal shortcomings, we generally got along well. I'd always feel lucky to have him as a friend.

During that same summer, my biological father began dating the woman who'd eventually become my stepmother. At no time in my life had I ever imagined Dad would date someone other than my mother, let alone think of getting remarried. He'd always swore that marriage was "forever." So how was I to understand *forever* being a relative term? But in any event, now that Mom was remarried, I guess Dad had just decided to get on with his own life. Whatever the case, this was also the time when Dad started letting go of his anger toward Mom.

Dad had met the woman after leaving his job with Arvin's and taking a position with Sarkes-Tarzian in Bloomington, Indiana. I think this company was primarily a communications entity as, among other things, it operated a regional television station (Channel 4, WTTV) and the local newspaper (the *Bloomington Herald-Tribune*). The television station was best known for its broadcast of Indiana University basketball and football games—as IU was located in Bloomington, Indiana. It was also home to Sammy Terry's Friday night horror show and

FAMILY, FRIENDS, AND THE GIFT OF MUSIC

Big Time Wrestling with Dick the Bruiser, Cowboy Bob Ellis, and the Sheik. As a regional station, it would never be as big as CBS, NBC, or any of the other national networks. Still, it had a local following in south central Indiana and continues to prosper to this day.

After a year of commuting back and forth to his work in Bloomington, Dad officially moved there. A short time later, he'd marry my stepmother. Then about a year or so after that, my stepmother gave birth to my half brother (Karl). I remember how Karl's being born seemed to reenergize my dad and how he took particular pride in being a new father. It was as if Karl represented a second chance for him to become the kind of father he'd always wanted to be. Unfortunately, Dad also seemed to favor Karl over the other children my stepmother still had living at home. Favoring one's own "blood" child over stepchildren is probably more common than any of us would like to admit. Still, I considered it a bit unfair to my stepsiblings as they didn't really have much input into the decision to bring a new brother into the family (let alone to their getting a stepfather). My dad also tended to be a bit overprotective of Karl, keeping us older boys at a distance from him. This contributed to Karl and me never really being close. Of course, there was also the rather significant age difference between Karl and myself, as well as the limited contact brought about by his living in a different city and our only having overnight visitations with my father once a month. My dad and stepmother would remain married until my father's death some five years later. I only recall seeing Karl and the rest of my stepfamily on one other occasion following my father's death.

My three stepsiblings were essentially the same ages as me, my brother Kevin, and my sister LouAnne. This gave us much in common and would make for some interesting times when we'd get together for our monthly visitations. And in general, we all got along very well. Unfortunately, Dad seemed to have particular difficulty parenting my stepmother's youngest son (Fred). He was my age but, in some respects, seemed somewhat less mature at the time. He was also noticeably less receptive to my dad's strict and unforgiving brand of discipline. My oldest stepbrother (Phil), on the other hand, always seemed more responsible and mature than most teenagers, and this caught my dad's favor. My stepmother's youngest child (apart from Karl) was named Betty June, and we boys had little contact with her as she was several years younger than us and spent most of the visitation time with our sister, LouAnne. Overall, the infrequent nature of our visits and Dad's untimely death meant we'd never be close with our stepsiblings.

As suggested earlier, junior high was when I also got more active with sports. This was when I joined the CJHS football team and tried my hand at running track. In addition to being a little larger and stronger than many kids my age (even more so than Kevin, two years my senior), I was probably more athletically inclined. Moreover, because of my dad's love for sports, from an early age, he and I had spent long hours together watching both college and professional football games on TV. And all this time spent watching football had helped me develop an understanding for the nuances of the game that many kids my age lacked. Thus, by the time I started playing for an organized team, I already knew the responsibilities of the various positions and how different plays were intended to unfold in order to achieve their designated objective. This knowledge, combined with an ability to process information quickly, would allow me to recognize happenings on the field and to respond with little hesitation. Playing football just seemed to come naturally. I'm sure it also helped that I had grown up in a poor family on Union Street and been left with very little fear of getting hurt (not to mention the ever-present need to prove myself). I was competitive. And these talents, as mentioned earlier, would lead to my playing quarterback and defensive back. Admittedly, I'd only be an average football player on what would be very average teams. My passing arm wasn't strong enough for me to be a good quarterback. And I lacked the necessary interpersonal skills to be an effective leader. I also wasn't quick enough to be good at running the ball or very effective on defense. Still, I loved playing the sport, and my father was very proud of my participation.

In addition to football, I'd also try my hand at running track. I wasn't fast enough to run the hurdles (my first love), but I'd have a little success with the half-mile and one-mile runs. This again pleased my dad greatly. Unfortunately, as time went on, I realized my limited football and track talents would never lead to my having meaningful success with sports. And Dad's praise for my participation and limited achievements was always matched by his criticism. Again, disappointing him had grown increasingly intolerable.

My freshman year was when I'd first come to realize an interesting fact about my academic skills. While my reading skills had always been generally poor, it'd turn out that my capacity for memory was better than that of many of my peers, and my analytic skills were in some ways superior. At my brother's recommendation, and against my school counselor's advice (who believed my math skills were more suited for basic math), I signed up to take ninth-grade algebra. And much to everyone's surprise, I was a bit of a wiz. I could seemingly figure out the most advanced algebraic problems with very little effort and faster than nearly all my peers. In my entire life, I had never found schoolwork so easy. Unfortunately, after getting As for the first two six-week periods, my teacher noticed that I wasn't able to explain the process for achieving my answers (I couldn't "show my work"). As a result, he presumed I had been cheating or copying answers from other students. Finally, after drilling me in private, he came to recognize I did have a bit of a gift, that for some unknown reason, my brain simply knew how to process algebraic problems, even if I wasn't able to verbally explain how this occurred. This would clear me of suspicions I'd been cheating. Unfortunately, he remained a stickler about my being able to reveal the *process* as well as the correct answer. So he insisted on tutoring me until I could develop the ability to explain my steps for solving problems to his satisfaction. In retrospect, this was probably my first introduction to the distinction between *process* and *content*. And later on, when studying psychology, this distinction would prove even more valuable as it would help me gain a deeper understanding of human behavior and mental processes and of how to better help others with resolving personal struggles and conflicts.

In the winter of my ninth grade year, Mike Sprague and I would again work together—this time selling magazine subscriptions. Mike had answered an ad in the local newspaper seeking boys to go door-to-door to get people interested in buying magazines. The character overseeing the project had a whole script prepared for us to recite upon meeting the homeowner (and again, to this day, Mike has the script memorized). Our boss would take us from neighborhood to neighborhood in teams of two, and upon someone answering the door, one of us would say something like, "Hi. I'm one of the boys in the neighborhood taking a survey of magazines you like to read…" Then we would hand the person a card with a long list of magazine titles (e.g., *Sports Illustrated, Newsweek, Saturday Evening Post*, etc.) and ask them to circle a few of their favorites—"no obligation to buy." For every card we got completed (including the name and address of the homeowner), we would be paid five dollars. As an incentive for us to show up to work for five days in a row, something young kids were not especially prone to do, the boss would pay us an additional five dollars at the end of the week (whether we had been successful in getting leads or not). The boss was the closer, and he would follow up with our leads once we made the initial contacts. As I recall, neither of us was especially good at this job. And walking around the cold streets of Columbus, Indiana, at night in the dead of winter would be almost unbearable. But I enjoyed making a little spending money and spending time with Mike, so we worked this job until spring.

Finally, before moving on from CJHS, I'd meet a girl named Teresa O. Eventually, Teresa would become my first wife, although at the time we met, she was just a cute little girl, some 5'0" tall and 100 pounds ("soaking wet" as they say) with long, curly auburn-colored hair. She too had come from a family of divorced parents, and much like my own mom, her mother also struggled with mental health concerns. As a result, she seemed to understand some of the problems I had with being poor, having a difficult homelife, and not always fitting in. Still, socially she was better adjusted than I.

While Teresa had caught my eye, so to speak, we'd end up having only limited contact during this period. We went to a couple of basketball games together, and she was my first kiss. I remember walking her home from one of such games and our sitting on the stairs leading up to her family's second-floor flat. We must have kissed for some fifteen minutes. It would prove the most exhilarating and terrifying experience I'd ever known. Unfortunately, the level of intimacy proved so scary for me that I'd scarcely speak to her again for the next few years. And it wouldn't be until I returned from my freshman year of college and we actually started dating that we'd kiss again.

The summer following my ninth grade of school, I'd take a job as a stocking clerk and grocery bagger for Fritchie's Country Market. Fritchie's was a small, privately owned grocery store in Walesboro, Indiana, half a mile south of Bethel Village. And much like before, I worked for sixty cents an hour. Ms. Fritchie would prove an intriguing woman. She was probably in her late seventies and both owned and operated her store with very little assistance from others. I think she may have had another woman who helped with running the cash register and a part-time butcher who ran the meat department. And again, I was hired to stock shelves and bag groceries. But basically, Ms. Fritchie did everything else, including ordering all the grocery items, monitoring the inventory, and managing all the finances—and this during the middle 1960s when women seldom ran their own businesses. I also remember her having been a caring and compassionate woman who was easy to work for. Again, this job would provide a little spending money while also helping me learn a little more about being responsible. But more importantly, working for Ms. Fritchie would be the first time I'd come to experience work as actually important to my self-image. Working this job, showing up on time, and earning something for myself seemed to give me a sense of value and purpose I'd seldom known before. In the years to come, there'd be many times when I'd find working difficult, even distasteful. But from this time onward, I would always consider work to be meaningful and an important part of who I wanted to be. I would ride my bicycle to and from the grocery store each day for the best part of three months and until I entered high school in the fall.

For the tenth grade, I'd attend Columbus High School (CHS). This school was much larger than any I had ever gone to before and, by comparison, probably bigger than most high schools today. I think we had some 2,700 students across three grades. My brother, Kevin, would be a twelfth grader by this time. But again, like many older brothers, he didn't want to be seen with me. This pretty much left me alone and fending for myself. Again, it'd be a difficult time to say the least.

While I still tried fitting in with others, the lasting impact of my parents' divorce, their hostility toward each other, my mother's depression, etc. had all hindered my emotional and social adjustment. I don't think I actually blamed anyone in particular for my problems. I just felt like I'd been cheated by life. And there were just so many things I didn't understand, so many questions to which I couldn't find answers. This, in turn, resulted in my carrying around a generally irritable disposition along with an attitude of resentment. Moreover, by this time, I'd also become overly sensitive to the difficulties faced by other disadvantaged kids. And given that teenagers tend to be rather egocentric and impulsive, I often struggled when it came to being patient with the sometimes childish and immature behavior of my peers, especially when it came to their mistreating those less fortunate. Unfortunately, my intolerance only made things worse. For in addition to my negative attitude and surly manner, getting frustrated with others only further undermined efforts toward making friends.

Certainly, getting involved in sports during junior high had helped me with being a little more social. And had I continued playing football once I moved up to CHS, getting by might have been a little easier. But between my ongoing confidence issues, my troubled homelife, persisting fears of disappointing my dad, and a lack of any means for getting back and forth to practice (given that we lived so far from town), there just didn't seem enough support for my continuing with sports at the high school level. Consequently, I struggled to get by as best I could. Dennis Steele and I would still ride the same bus to and from school, and we'd hang out with each other in the village. And I was grateful Mike Sprague and I were once again attending the same school. I felt truly fortunate having him around. But these and a few other companions would be my only real friends to help me through what was otherwise a hard time in my life. Eventually, I'd turn to focusing more on my studies and becoming more involved with music. But that wouldn't occur until sometime later. Early on, I just felt alone.

As remains the case for nearly all high schools in the state of Indiana, the sport of basketball would be king at CHS. Perhaps the movie *Hoosiers* (with Gene Hackman and Barbara Hershey) best highlighted the culture and values and the hopes and dreams of so many residents of our small state in its depiction of basketball, and the importance this sport held for the many small communities spread out across Indiana. This movie would speak of the pride Hoosiers took in the tradition of a season-ending, statewide basketball tournament wherein all schools, no matter their size, had an opportunity to compete for the championship. And this "David and Goliath" account of a high school team from a small Indiana town defeating one of the largest schools in the state was real. It was well-known by young and old alike (even though the name of the small-town school was actually Milan High School instead of Hickory). The victory, and the legend it created, would give hope to generations of Hoosiers for decades to come. And it would encourage many, myself included, to believe in the possibility of overcoming the obstacles of life, no matter what the odds. Accordingly, basketball games would be the place Mike Sprague and I would spend many a winter's Friday night.

Because of the relative wealth of our town, Columbus High School would also be fortunate enough to have a gymnasium that, to this day, would rival those found on the campuses of many smaller colleges. I think it held 7,200 seats all total, and nearly every seat in the house was good. And its size also allowed our school to host the sectional and regional tournaments held every year as part of the overall statewide tournament. Moreover, at the time I attended Columbus High School, our basketball teams were among some of the best in the state. We regularly won these sectional and regional titles and, on many occasions, traveled to Indianapolis (to Hinkle Fieldhouse, on the campus of Butler University and of *Hoosiers* fame) to participate in the semifinal and state final championships. We also had several players selected to Indiana's All-State teams and one player named to the 1964 US Olympic team. And so it was that, during the course of my time at CHS, Mike's encouragement and support for attending these games would be yet another opportunity to help with my personal growth.

Then as my sophomore year was coming to an end, my dad bought me a used six-string guitar. I think he paid twenty dollars for it. I hadn't had an instrument of my own since the bass was repossessed a couple of years earlier. And though I'd never liked playing a six-string near as much as I liked playing the bass, over the years, I had learned how to tune a six-string and knew a few guitar chords. So I was happy to again have an instrument to play. Moreover, those who play music regularly would probably agree that music played on a six-string guitar actually sounds more like real music than that played on a bass—more melodic. Even amateur musicians know what I am talking about. It's just hard to sing along with the thump, thump of a bass. At long last, I'd have an instrument that would allow me to both play music and sing along at the same time.

As might be expected, at twenty dollars, it wasn't really much of a guitar. It was an electric, and I recall it being shaped like a Fender Stratocaster. But it was a little smaller than a standard guitar, maybe 3/4 scale. And I think it was labeled Holiday on the headstock and made in Japan. In any event, it worked. And in an attempt to personalize it, I recall stripping all the finish off and painting it pink (of all things). I also recall decorating it with assorted green-and-blue polka dots, after being inspired by the Stratocaster George Harrison was pictured playing on the Beatles' *Magical Mystery Tour* album. These modifications would officially make the guitar mine. And once again, music was back in my life.

Eventually, having this guitar helped me meet a few other guys who also played music (Steve Dobbs and Gary Galbraith), and together we would try playing as a group whenever we could. They too played six-string guitars, so I'd try to play bass lines on the bottom strings of my six-string. Still, as a band, we never amounted to much. I think we played at a couple of small parties over the span of two years. But with my living out in Bethel Village and having no reliable means of transportation, getting into town for practice would be a struggle. And it's difficult for any group of musicians to improve without playing together regularly.

Playing music would also introduce me to one Billy Moffett, who was a *very* good guitarist. Story has it, he was once invited to audition with John Mellencamp, a recording artist of some fame during the '70s and '80s who was born in Seymour, Indiana. Seymour is a small town located some twenty miles south of Columbus. And obviously, Billy's local reputation had made him known to Mellencamp. Unfortunately, like many musicians, Billy reportedly had other priorities at the time of his invitation and missed the audition. Ah, the life of a musician.

As I recall, sometime during my junior year of high school, the son of a local music store owner had given Billy a Univox bass (similar to the Hofner bass played by Paul McCartney of the Beatles). It seemed this boy had a penchant for taking instruments from his father's store without permission and passing them on to peers in hopes of encouraging their friendship. And because of my love for the bass, Billy passed it on to me with the understanding I could keep it as long as I liked. I remember using it while playing with a band out of Bloomington,

FAMILY, FRIENDS, AND THE GIFT OF MUSIC

Indiana, called the *Last Issue*. Unfortunately, I would end up playing it only a short period of time as one day, out of the blue, Billy (and/or the boy who had given the bass to him) suddenly said they needed it back. I'd never find out exactly what became of the bass, although I'm guessing the boy's father had gotten wind of its missing from the store and demanded its return. Nonetheless, again, having access to this bass for the time it was in my possession further reinforced my love of playing music. Apart from being something that just seemed to come naturally for me, music always touched my soul in a very special way. Then again, maybe it just gave me hope that one day I'd accomplish something meaningful in the world. Certainly, the time would come when I'd realize I was never going to be good enough to make a living as a musician. But nonetheless, playing music still brought me joy. It served as a distraction from all my questions, my worries, and my doubts. And during this period, it also helped me to connect with others.

As noted earlier, schoolwork never came easy for me. It might have helped had my homelife been more stable and my parents shown a little more interest in my studies. But in many ways, my learning difficulties were probably just as much the result of my overall poor reading skills and lack of self-discipline. In any event, I had never been a great student, maybe a little above average, but certainly not great. And this was particularly true during my sophomore year at CHS. Then during my junior year of high school, I happened to notice some of the other students talking about what they were planning to do once high school was over. Never before had I considered where I was headed once I left school or what I'd do with my life. I had always just put one foot in front of the other and done what I'd been told, what others expected. Suddenly, realizing that graduation was only a year or so away, I figured I too probably needed a plan. So in keeping with this realization, I decided to begin exploring my own options.

As it turned out, my options seemed limited. I could join the workforce and risk being drafted into the military, or I could consider attending college and pursuing a student deferment. At that time, life in the military probably meant a ticket to Vietnam. On the other hand, while going to college might keep me out of the military, I'd never really been a great student. To get more help with the decision, I decided to ask my school counselor for his thoughts on the matter.

Mr. Utterback, my counselor, was commonly referred to as the Gray Ghost by many of my peers. This was due in large part to his advancing age, gray hair, frail stature, and generally gaunt complexion. These features also left many students questioning his wisdom and, thus, discounting his advice. At times, I too wasn't sure he had a lot left in the tank. But I'd always found Mr. Utterback a caring and well-intentioned individual. Moreover, I wasn't sure where else to turn. So I figured I'd give him a chance.

In the end, Mr. Utterback would be firmly of the opinion I was *not* college material, that I'd be better suited for a manual-labor or factory-type job. Now he was probably correct in assessing my academic potential based upon my performance to date. Still, I wasn't convinced about his take on things, especially given that attending college and getting a student deferment seemed my only real hope for staying out of Vietnam. While I wasn't sure I could even manage the coursework and had no idea how I'd ever pay for college, I clearly didn't want to get stuck in a factory or resign myself to life in the military. Consequently, and in spite of Mr. Utterback's recommendation, I decided I should at least *consider* extending my education beyond high school. Of course, this meant getting more serious about improving my study habits and GPA, as well as coming up with a plan to pay for college.

Like most states, Indiana offered Pell grants to residents attending in-state universities. And I figured that would cover the costs of my tuition and books. As a result, all I really needed to come up with was the money to pay for my room and board. But while this might sound easy enough for some, I was pretty sure I'd never qualify for any sort of scholarship, and I knew the prospects of my family coming up with money for my living expenses while away at school were practically nil. What to do? Try as I might, I just couldn't see myself working in a factory, and being drafted into the Army was far too scary. Still, finding a way to pay my room and board while away at college would be crucial if I were to have any hope of attending. Thankfully, I still had time to work on it.

Sometime during that same year, as I was still trying to figure out plans for my future, Mike Sprague would take a part-time job as an intern for the local radio station, WCSI. There he'd host a Saturday morning segment called "Tune in to Teen In." And as the name implies, it was a one-hour program tailored to provide pop music to the young people in our community. Later that same summer, the Lovin' Spoonful pop group would come to Columbus to perform in our high school auditorium. All the kids were excited. And because of Mike's affiliation with the radio station, he had credentials allowing him to attend the group's press conference held in the ballroom of a local hotel following the show. As one of Mike's best friends, he agreed to take me along. Needless to say, I was in heaven.

The Lovin' Spoonful was a band formed by one John Sebastian out of New York. They may have had three or four top 10 songs during the latter part of the 1960s, with John Sebastian writing most of the tunes (although he may be just as well-known for having written the theme song to the television sitcom *Welcome Back, Kotter*, introducing a young John Travolta to the viewing audience). Following the Lovin' Spoonful's concert and press conference, and after much investigation, Mike and I located John Sebastian's hotel room. Mike knocked on his door, and when John answered (acoustic guitar in hand), he proceeded to tell John of his position with the radio station and asked if he'd record a promotional spot for the show. Mike had brought a portable tape recorder along (remember them), and his instructions were for John to say, "Hi, this is John Sebastian of the Lovin' Spoonful asking you to 'Tune in to Teen In." John proceeded to say things such as, "Hi, this is John Sebastian warning you about Teen In…no, no… This is John Sebastian asking you to Teen in to Tune In…no, no," etc. He must have attempted four or five takes before we realized he was messing with us. Then after everyone had a good laugh, John recorded the promo correctly. Mike and I will never forget the incident and how relatable John actually proved to be. Again, such were the misadventures of two small-town boys in the 1960s trying to grow up and find their way in the world.

That summer, my dad would decide to increase his involvement with photography. He'd been shooting family photos since the latter part of my junior high school days, but during this time, he started taking photography much more seriously. He'd take cameras and assorted wide-angle or telescopic lenses everywhere he went. And he'd stop at every car wreck or other interesting or catastrophic event encountered to take pictures he hoped might bolster his skills and one day prove profitable. He then signed on with the *Bloomington Herald-Tribune* as a freelance photographer. This allowed him to obtain press credentials and to have free access to all the Indiana University basketball and football games, the pit stalls at the Indianapolis 500, and any other sporting event he desired to attend. This was long before the age of digital cameras, computer chips, and/

FAMILY, FRIENDS, AND THE GIFT OF MUSIC

or modern printers. Then my father decided to create a darkroom in the basement of his home. The darkroom would allow him to process the film used in cameras of the day, develop negatives, and print his own pictures, all without ever leaving the comfort of his own home. And it would also allow him to do this faster than many of the other photographers in the area. Again, he'd pursue this hobby while continuing to work his full-time job with Sarkes-Tarzian. In the end, I don't think Dad ever made much money from taking pictures, probably not enough to cover his expenses. But eventually, he got pretty decent at it, and photography seemed to bring him a great deal of pleasure.

The summer before my senior year of high school was also when I'd meet my first love. Nancy B was the sister of a girl Dennis Steele had dated and the girl I'd briefly mentioned earlier. Her family also lived in Bethel Village, just up the street from me. And she and I would date for the next couple of years. It would always prove a rocky relationship as I needed her approval and affection to quell my own low self-esteem, while she was immature, impulsive, moody, and prone to intermittent outbursts of anger. I remember my brother Kevin trying to warn me of this relationship being a bad idea. But it's hard to reason with a young boy "in love." She and I eventually called it quits halfway through my first year of college. Some might say I got lucky, both because she came into my life and because I was able to get away without too much pain and suffering. Heaven knows, with all my other struggles, I didn't need additional problems. Still, I would always remain grateful for having known her.

During my senior school of high school, Dad would shift his focus to politics. He was a die-hard conservative of seemingly unlimited energy. So when he began volunteering with the Indiana State Republican Committee, they loved him. I remember Dad being especially proud of his involvement in

Edgar Whitcomb's gubernatorial campaign, among other things writing Edgar Whitcomb's campaign song. And once elected, as a way of showing his appreciation, Governor Whitcomb obtained tickets for my dad to attend one of president-elect Richard Nixon's inaugural balls. I will always remember the photo of my dad in his tuxedo standing alongside my stepmother on the dance floor. The governor also offered my dad a position in his administration, although Dad (probably out of concern for his increasing heart problems and the stress the job might create) turned the appointment down. By now I guess I've written a fair amount about my father's various exploits. And in some respects, I may have made him seem bigger than life. But he was never famous by any stretch of the imagination. Rather, he might best be seen as an aspiring "big fish in a little pond."

I mentioned above how my brother Kevin didn't much like my hanging around with him. Nonetheless, Kevin was only two years older than me, and throughout our childhood and teenage years, we would always be close as siblings. Dave was some five years older than me, and LouAnne was some four years younger. Thus, from a developmental perspective, we each had much less in common than Kevin and I. Moreover, throughout the years, Kevin and I often shared the same bedroom, attended the same schools, and had similar hobbies. We were also close enough in size to wear some of each other's clothes. Occasionally, people would even say we resembled each other enough to be twins—even though our dispositions were clearly different.

After graduating high school in 1967, Kevin moved to Muncie, Indiana, to attend Ball State University. Exactly where he got the money to go to college would always remain a mystery for me, but in any case, this was where he would study art and teaching. While Kevin had always been an average student, the Vietnam conflict was still going on, and Kevin clearly had no interest in being sent to war. Thus, he chose to enter college instead. Unfortunately, he quickly got involved with marijuana and possibly other drugs, and this, in combination with his general lack of interest in academic pursuits, resulted in a total absence of motivation for studying or attending class. He'd be dismissed from school by the end of his first year.

Shortly thereafter, as might have been anticipated, Kevin would be drafted into the Army. But although the Vietnam conflict was still ongoing, by this time, the social and political unrest in the US had become such that politicians were looking for ways to reduce the number of US troops being sent overseas. As a consequence, once he'd completed basic training, Kevin would be fortunate enough to get stationed at an Army base in Colorado. This was where he'd complete his military stint. Two years later, he was discharged. Upon being discharged, however, rather than return to Columbus, Kevin decided to marry the woman he'd dated while attending Ball State and relocate to Anderson, Indiana (near Muncie). This was where he would live out the remainder of his days. In many ways, Kevin became estranged from the family, and his and my relationship would remain forever distant. While we occasionally spoke by phone, we'd never be truly close again.

While Kevin was still in the Army, and upon graduating high school in May 1969, I'd go to work for a local company named Como Plastics. I hired on as a press operator but was soon promoted to a position as a materials handler. I am not certain how I learned about this job, but it would be my first real exposure to factory work. And it would be unpleasant to say the least. The factory produced all sorts of plastic products, ranging from toy farm animals to casings for portable televisions to automobile fan shrouds. And I will always remember the experience of slaving away at a hot molding press or working in the warehouse during the heat of summer. By the time

I dragged myself home, I'd be dripping in sweat and feeling exhausted. While I appreciated the money, the work seemed tortuous.

That would be the same summer I'd received my military draft card. For all eighteen-year-old American males, getting your draft card was considered a rite of passage as receiving your draft card meant you were now eligible for the Army and being sent into combat. So this immediately complicated my life. It was now painfully clear that if I didn't figure out a way to get into college that fall and qualify for a student deferment, I'd be drafted and risk being sent to Vietnam. While I had previously hedged my bet by applying to Indiana University at Indianapolis (and, by this time, been accepted), I still had no real idea how I'd pay for college. I'd been stashing the money I earned working at Como Plastics, but this would only amount to a few hundred dollars. And I knew that my meager savings and state grants wouldn't cover the entire costs of tuition, books, *and* room and board. I also knew I couldn't count on my parents for help. Fortunately, for me, fate stepped in.

In June of 1969, just a few weeks after receiving my draft card, my father would again be hospitalized for treatment of yet another heart attack. By this time, he'd been hospitalized multiple times for such problems, so even though my stepmother telephoned, saying us kids might want to come to the hospital to see him, I wasn't especially worried. We had all just grown to believe that no heart attack would ever kill our dad. Still, the next day, my mother took me to see him in Bloomington. As usual, Dad sounded reassuring about his recovery. So I returned home. Then the following morning, Monday morning, my stepmother called to say my father had died during the night. The news would leave me numb with disbelief. Not since my parents' divorce had I felt so confused and unsure of how to react. So given that I was scheduled to be at work within the hour of receiving her call, and not knowing what else to do, I simply went on to work. Halfway through my shift, the supervisor came to me and asked if I knew my dad had died. I responded that I did but that not knowing how to respond, I just came in to work. He advised me to go home.

My dad's funeral would be held in Bloomington. It was a somber affair, as might be expected. And I remember a very large crowd of people paying their respects, including Governor Whitcomb. My father's dynamic energy had clearly touched many lives. Still, for years after, I'd go about living my life speaking very little of him. I just couldn't explain how such a critical and negative voice might ever hold such a meaningful place in my life or why his passing would leave such a huge void inside that I could never seem to fill. I simply wasn't sure how to make sense of the importance he held for me. Then later on, I'd realize how my father had probably been both the best and the worst thing that had ever happened to me. He was the best thing because of all the encouragement he gave me to persevere, to never give less than my best, to never underestimate what I might be able to achieve, and to never quit believing in myself. He was the worst thing because no matter how hard I tried, no matter how much I gave, no matter what I achieved, it never seemed to be good enough in his eyes. In many respects, I both loved him dearly and hated him deeply. A part of me still wishes he could have seen me graduate from college. A part of me wishes he could have been there when I received my doctorate degree. And a part of me wishes he could have met my current wife. Maybe he'd have been pleased with the person I'd become. Maybe he would have been proud. Then again, maybe he'd still have found a reason to be critical. From time to time, I still miss him.

Over the years, I also came to understand that love them or hate them, our parents, our biological mother and father, will always remain the only mother and father we will ever have. Sure, we may have stepparents or adoptive parents who care for us. And we may even grow to love them deeply. But our natural parents are the only such parents we will ever get. Hopefully, we learn how to accept them as people, as human beings with strengths and limitations just like the rest of us. But whether that happens or not, we can never deny them as being an instrumental part of our lives. In existential writings, it is sometimes suggested that one can never escape their "thrownness," those elements of one's existence that are an intrinsic part of who one is, even if we don't choose them. I understand now that my dad did the best he could, even when doing so was not what I believed I needed or wanted at the time. I've also learned to give him credit for all the things he did right as a father. On balance, he was a good man. And I have made peace with him and his impact on my life.

If there was to be any upside to my father's dying, it would be that I now qualified for social security survivor's benefits. Again, while I originally had no idea how I'd ever be able to pay for college, or whether I really even wanted to go, I had decided to keep my options open. Now I'd finally have the financial resources needed to attend. And having the necessary resources for attending school, in combination with my increased desire for avoiding the military, would make the decision to attend college easier. I would enroll at Indiana University of Indianapolis that fall.

> To Every Day, There Is a Season,
> And a Time to Every Purpose under Heaven.
> A Time to be Born, a Time to Die.
> A Time to Plant, a Time to Reap.
> A Time to Kill, a Time to Heal.
> A Time to Laugh, a Time to Weep.
> —Book of Ecclesiastes (Adapt.)

Adapted from: Book of Ecclesiastes, King James Bible (1769/2017). Music by Woody Guthrie.

EXPLORING THE WORLD

WHILE DEALING WITH THE CHALLENGES OF MY childhood, the '60s had also introduced me to a decade of social, cultural, and political change unlike anything I might ever have imagined. In those ten short years, the evolution of events naturally occurring with the passage of time seemed to have spun all out of control. Perhaps the reader will think this an overstatement as I am sure there are people of every generation who believe their time to be one of dramatic change. But for those of us living through the '60s, the time certainly seemed tumultuous.

The possibility of a nuclear confrontation with the Soviet Union had existed since the end of WWII. Fortunately, wiser heads had always prevailed, and such a conflict had been avoided. It probably helped that the US and the USSR were the only nations having nuclear weapons at the time and that the two countries were separated by the Atlantic Ocean. Nevertheless, when the Soviet Union attempted to place armed missiles in Cuba, an imminent threat seemed to have finally arrived at our doorstep. President Kennedy's decisive action to establish an embargo around Cuba, after the failed Bay of Pigs invasion, effectively brought an end to the threat. Peace had again been preserved. And as might be expected, the president would be praised by young and old alike for his resolve in confronting the danger. But only a short time thereafter, the nation would be in mourning following his assassination. The senseless shooting of a president admired by so many seemed even more tragic given the confusing attempts to explain the circumstances surrounding his death. How many shooters were there? Were the Soviets involved? Was there a CIA plot? And these and other questions would remain unanswered for decades to come.

During this same period, years of advancements in modern technology had set the stage for a gradual decline in American manufacturing and a reduced need for that brute physical strength previously provided by males in what had previously been agrarian and industrial societies. As family-owned farms were being gobbled up by corporate entities having sophisticated machinery, and as factory jobs were increasingly being automated or sent overseas, the doors effectively opened for more and more women to enter the workplace. This meant increased employment options and financial resources that many women in America had never known. Now women would no longer need to rely on the limited career options defined by social custom so as not to interfere with their role as mothers and homemakers. And they no longer needed to remain in untenable relationships or rely on the income of their spouses for financial support. More than at any time in our nation's history, American women were making choices to define their own lives and to give those lives meaning.

The opened doors would become floodgates with advancements in contraceptive options. Prior to this time, sexual activity was commonly associated with pregnancy and, by social convention if not practical necessity, both marriage and the institution of family. Now for the first time, readily available birth control having minimal side effects allowed women to be sexually active with little concern for the "complications" sometimes associated with an unplanned pregnancy. It would also allow women to view sexual behavior as a viable option for pursuing interpersonal closeness and sensual pleasure with less of the emotional or practical stress typically accompanying a committed relationship.

Then the US Supreme Court handed down a ruling effectively legalizing abortion nationwide. While this decision effectively gave women new legal rights, it would also fuel a contentious cultural battle having no end in sight. Long-held religious values and social traditions were now being openly challenged by the new law and the emergence of abortion clinics all across the country. Pro-choice groups would praise the decision as upholding a woman's right to "control her own body." Right-to-life activists condemned the ruling as undermining society's moral responsibility for "protecting the unborn child." And as a result of all these changes, as a result of the expanded employment opportunities, the increased financial resources, the enhanced personal freedoms, and the newfound legal rights, a woman's liberation movement would emerge that would forever change traditional gender roles in America.

Drastic changes were also emerging for race relations. Slavery had been a small, if not meaningful, part of American culture throughout its history. Some of the earliest colonists owned slaves, including some very prominent citizens and signers of the Declaration of Independence. And while slave ownership would eventually become more prevalent in the South, it would probably be erroneous to describe it as ever having been widespread in the United States. Slaves were typically owned only by a select number of very wealthy plantation owners whose estates were large enough to allow for such an investment. Most Americans were either too poor or too preoccupied with making their own way in the world to ever concern themselves with having a slave. Thus, it would seem more accurate to say the vast majority of Americans, including those in the South, were indifferent to slave ownership.

This being said, slavery would become a bone of contention between many of those believing it to be morally wrong and plantation owners in the South who came to view it as essential to sustaining their way of life. And this dispute would eventually contribute to our nation fighting a civil war over these differences. Again, I think it an oversimplification to say the war was only about slavery. Many have suggested it to have been just as much about economic and political concerns. Moreover, many of those fighting and dying on both sides were only boys who had a very limited understanding of the relevance of slavery. Many may have seen going to war as a moral duty to "serve their nation" or to "defend" their farms from invaders. Many may have seen it as simply a way of earning a little money during a time when job opportunities were scarce and scratching out life on a farm was difficult. Many may have just done what their elders believed was expected of them or given into peer pressure or viewed being part of a group and wearing a uniform as a way of fitting in or feeling important. There were probably hundreds of reasons why people went to war, whether for the Union or the Confederacy. But whatever the case, for many, it was hoped that the war and freeing the slaves would eventually reunite our nation and make it stronger.

Unfortunately, while the war may have put an official end to slavery, many in the South continued believing there existed some very real social and cultural differences between blacks and whites. Consequently, integration of blacks into the society at large was inconsistent at best. For all intents and purposes, two separate societies emerged, one for blacks and one for whites, with each having their own churches, schools, business establishments, and essentially separate legal rights. Many communities, seemingly out of fear that their way of life, their cultural values, or their economic prosperity were being threatened, continued treating blacks as inferior and as second-class citizens. Vigilante groups would torture, even kill, blacks they deemed to have violated their social code. White shop owners would ban blacks from their establishments. Courts and judges were all too often inconsistent in their exercising of justice. And for decades, this would remain the norm. The animosity grew.

With congressional passage of the Civil Rights Act in 1957, many hoped an end to America's racial struggles might finally be at hand. But efforts to implement the law were themselves met with resistance. As a result, the '60s would witness a civil rights movement intended to rectify ongoing discrimination. Black Americans had clearly grown weary of waiting for change and were starting to *demand* it. And even though this would result in the 1964 revision of the initial law banning discrimination, all the activism only seemed to escalate hostilities. While politicians and leaders of both the black and white communities struggled to find workable solutions to the existing problems, race riots would break out, pitting neighbor against neighbor and community against community. Before it was all over, a pro-segregationist presidential candidate would be shot while giving a campaign speech, a civil rights advocate preaching peaceful resistance would be killed, and yet another presidential candidate and supporter of equal rights would be assassinated. In the end, while some would question just how much change had ultimately transpired, most realized race relations in America would never again be as they once were.

Amid all this social change and stress, the generation of baby boomers born following WWII would come of age. As teenagers and young adults, these young people brought new questions about the status quo and new ideas about how the world should be run. During the early '60s, the US government had decided to support the South Vietnamese resistance to military invasion by the North Vietnamese intent on reunifying a divided country. Unfortunately, this support put us smack-dab in the middle of a war that would rage on for years. South Vietnam operated under democratic rule, while North Vietnam was a communist regime. And many politicians were concerned that all of Southeast Asia would be vulnerable to communist rule should North Vietnam be successful in its efforts to over-run South Vietnam.

Initially, the US provided only military advisers and financial aid. But as American involvement in the war grew, some believed it necessary to send weapons and (eventually) troops. American soldiers consisted of seasoned officers who had served in the military prior to the conflict, those more recent enlistees seeing few other opportunities for earning a living as civilians, and those eighteen and older who were now becoming eligible for the draft. With the passage of time, tens of thousands of Americans would die, and the casualties would be primarily young boys or men. This resulted in many of the younger generation beginning to question our reasons for being there and the terrible cost it was having on the US in terms of dollars and the loss of life. Some conscientious objectors would flee to Canada to avoid the draft, while those having the academic skills and/or financial resources to continue their education would seek college admission and a student deferment. Unfortunately, many had no such options for avoiding military service.

This conflict would only further divide an already struggling nation between those who believed in supporting our government, our politicians, our young soldiers, and our more traditional way of life, on the one hand, and those "socially minded" young people opposed to the war and seeking political change, on the other. Eventually, a youth movement emerged, with anti-war protests erupting all across America, particularly on college campuses. Sit-ins would be staged, and some university administration buildings would be overrun. Occasionally, protestors even set buildings on fire. And all this happened at the same time as marijuana, LSD, and other so-called recreational drugs began flooding the scene. Now young people, some with legitimate concerns regarding the state of our nation, some striving to discover personal values by which to live their lives, some just struggling to survive in an ever-changing world, some wishing to avoid the responsibilities inherent in growing up, and a number of troubled souls caught up in the drug culture, all became part of a "generation gap" that would rise up to challenge "the establishment."

Most everyone felt the strain. Between the women's liberation movement, the civil rights movement, and the anti-war movement, some believed the nation to again be on the brink of civil war. But while many people had opinions about what needed to be done, in the end, there seemed to be few good answers. Times were changing, whether for the better or worse. Eventually, an exasperated sitting president chose not to run for reelection amid outcries he was destroying the country, and one anti-war protest at a university in Ohio ended with National Guard troops firing on protestors and killing four of the students. Still, the tensions raged on. In the end, all the social dissention seemingly accelerated the nation's decision to get out of Vietnam. Unfortunately, once the withdrawal was complete, the government of South Vietnam promptly collapsed. North Vietnam was victorious. And questions regarding the meaning of it all remained.

For the most part, I had been protected from much of the social, cultural, and political chaos described above. It was present in many of the songs I listened to. But I'd always been more attracted to the music and melodies of songs rather than the lyrics, so I wasn't really impacted by the occasional reference to violence, war, or drugs. I did see TV footage of women marching and burning their bras in acts of defiance or symbolic demands for change. And I saw coverage of blacks rioting in the ghettos of larger cities in hopes of achieving racial justice. I also remember hearing stories of protest marches on college campuses seeking an end to the war. And I saw news reports on the shootings of George Wallace, Martin Luther King Jr., and Robert Kennedy Jr. So I'd wonder about all the dissenting voices, the anger, and the hostile acts. But living in the rural Midwest, and especially in little Columbus, the commonly shared values and relative absence of diversity seemed to protect me from much of the craziness.

Moreover, on a personal level, I'd always been encouraged to respect others, be they men or women, black or white, young or old. I may have come to experience women and men as being different, but being different never meant being "less than." We all have different strengths and limitations, different talents, different abilities. Being different just never required a value judgment. Similarly, I had never been exposed to the racial strife and prejudices of the Deep South. Nor had I been taught to view blacks as inferior to whites. In the community where I grew up, people were judged by their actions, their character, by how they treated one another, their honesty, and their integrity—not by their gender, religion, ethnicity, or the color of their skin. Lastly, whether you agreed with your elders or not, I was always encouraged to respect their authority. And this included parents, community leaders, police officers, soldiers, and politicians. They might err in their assessment of a situation, and they might exercise questionable judgment in their decision-making. But if I disagreed with those in positions of power or authority, I needed to express this disagreement respectfully, as in many instances, they had knowledge and wisdom that I did not. Moreover, they were probably doing a job that others, myself included, were either less capable of performing or afraid of doing. Thus, because of my youthfulness, my environment, and my upbringing, I'd be spared much of the stress encountered by others during this time of upheaval.

Still, as a teenager dealing with my own developmental issues, all the turmoil of the times would contribute to my personal angst. For the first time in my life, I'd find myself questioning what was real and what was not. How was I to know good from bad or right from wrong? What was truth, and what was lies? Why did people experience pain, sickness, and death? And what was the deal with war? Why would people kill one another for the sake of ideology? As importantly, for the first time, I'd find myself questioning which values I should adopt to help me realize the person I was to become, to make my own life matter.

It has been said, "A journey of a thousand miles begins with a single step." To the extent this is true, leaving home to attend college would be one of the first big steps in my own life's journey. There would be other steps along the way, but this would be my first real attempt toward growing up, toward finding out who I really was and who I might become. And this step would mark the beginning of my efforts toward understanding and making peace with myself as well.

While I had enrolled at Indiana University of Indianapolis in the fall of 1969, this had not been my first choice. Since early on, I'd figured that if I ever went to college, it would be to Indiana University (Bloomington campus). My dad loved Indiana University and, as noted above, had moved to Bloomington following his and Mom's divorce. Again, we'd watch every IU basketball and football game possible, and I'd learned the names of many of the IU players of the era. I proudly wore IU sweatshirts, while my brother Kevin always favored Purdue University. So I never would have imagined going anywhere other than IU. That is, until my junior year of high school when I first began thinking about actually attending college. That was when my dad suggested I could live in his house while I went to school. Given my mixed feelings regarding his power and influence over my life, I could never have imagined living with him while attending college in Bloomington. Rightly or wrongly, I knew this would leave me so preoccupied with his opinions and judgments about what I was or was not doing that I'd never be able to perform at my best or be at peace. And heaven knows, I'd never have been able to *enjoy* the experience. On the other hand, once Dad proposed this idea, I also knew I could never enroll at the Bloomington campus and *not* live with him. This would have disappointed him greatly. Thus, while considering the idea of applying to college, I'd decided to go with what I considered the next best option: Indiana University of Indianapolis. After working for Como Plastics through the end of the summer, I'd move to Indianapolis and attend college there.

At the time I enrolled in college, Indiana University of Indianapolis was a little more than a handful of buildings located in the heart of downtown Indianapolis. It had been set up mostly as a commuter campus for those Indianapolis residents wanting to pursue college studies while not moving away from home or giving up their day jobs. Students choosing to extend their coursework and pursue a degree would eventually transfer to the Bloomington campus following their first two years in Indianapolis. Later on, IU at Indianapolis would build expansive new facilities out on West Michigan Street. And later still, the campus would join with Purdue University of Indianapolis on 38th Street to form Indiana University-Purdue University of Indianapolis (IUPUI). This allowed the university to begin issuing bachelor's and master's degrees on-site.

Unless something has changed of late, IUPUI is what the school is known as today. Unfortunately, for me, once the merger occurred, bachelor's degrees for majors in education, English, music, business, etc. would be issued through Indiana University, while bachelor's degrees for those majoring in the sciences of biology, chemistry, psychology, etc. would be issued through Purdue University. This meant I'd actually end up receiving my BA degree in psychology from Purdue University and would never realize my dream of graduating from Indiana University—regardless of how much I loved IU and considered myself a "Hurrying Hoosier."

Living in Indianapolis would be quite a change from living in Columbus. There was more poverty, more crime, more violence, more drugs, and more ethnic diversity than I could ever have imagined from growing up in my hometown. I knew no one, apart from one distant uncle and his family, who actually lived in the Indianapolis suburb of Speedway, Indiana. For the longest time, I felt isolated and alone. Eventually, I'd come to appreciate this experience as being one in which I became increasingly independent and gained a great deal of self-confidence. But initially, I just questioned my reasons for being there.

The only student dormitory for IU of Indianapolis was attached to the Student Union Building located on the West Michigan Street Medical Center Campus. This campus was made up of some five or six hospitals all grouped together, including a children's hospital, a VA hospital, the university hospital, and the Larue Carter Psychiatric Hospital (among others). The dormitory consisted of five floors of rooms set aside to house the medical, nursing, dental, and similarly trained students, attending classes and completing rotations at the nearby hospitals and clinics. I would end up being the only general studies student in the entire dorm. I was also somewhat younger than nearly all the other residents. Accordingly, early on, I felt quite out of place. Moreover, the dormitory was located nearly two miles from the downtown campus of IU where I attended classes. And inasmuch as I lacked the money necessary for riding a city bus to my classes, I'd end up walking this distance both ways four or five days a week for my entire first year. It was a real drag, especially in the dead of winter. Thankfully, my roommate (an X-ray technician student) had a car and would drive me to class on the coldest of mornings.

Probably the only real benefit from my being in the dorm was that of it being coed. The top four floors all housed females. And most of them were nursing students. Ours would be the only floor in the building with males. And I can still remember the general consensus among guys on our floor being that nursing students, and especially young nursing students, were a rather racy lot. Whether this continues to be true or not, it would clearly be an accurate description for those living in the floors above us. As a group, they liked to party. On the other hand, the nursing students also had a reputation for being caring toward those perceived in need. And my roommate and I were definitely in need. Eventually, we worked out an arrangement with a few of the girls to do favors for them in exchange for their preparing us "home cooked" meals or accompanying us to parties. They especially liked that my roommate had an automobile and would occasionally take them to the local mall. And they seemed quite at home treating me like a little brother. I loved the attention.

Once again, I wasn't an especially good student my freshman year. I hadn't yet figured out effective ways to compensate for my reading deficiencies, so I'd try to make do by attending lectures, taking studious notes, and trying to memorize everything I heard in class. As most college students understand, there really is no substitute for reading the assigned material. Consequently, my grades would only be a little above average. Then as the year wore on, I became increasingly disillusioned with taking such general studies courses like English composition, American literature, world history, etc. While I had no real idea what I wanted to be studying, I pretty much hated the courses I was taking.

I also found myself intimidated by the overall size and hustle of Indianapolis. And living away from home for the first time in my life, in a city many times larger than Columbus, proved far scarier than I might ever have anticipated. I was homesick most of the time and scratching by on fifty dollars a month for food and anything else I wanted or needed. And then between all the hours spent walking to and from school, attending class, completing assignments, and preparing for tests, there was really very little time left over for socializing. Occasionally, my roommate and I would go to one of the campus parties, but he was my only real friend in Indianapolis, and such opportunities were limited. It was good that he and I were well matched. But overall, I just grew more and more troubled about the direction in which my life was heading.

By the spring of my first year, I had started feeling depressed. Of course, again, the alternative to being in college was the possibility of ending up in Vietnam. The summer right before I left for school, a neighbor boy living only one block away (in the village) had been drafted. He was killed only a week or so after being sent overseas. So given all the social upheaval associated with our nation being in Vietnam, as well as the more pressing fear of my ending up dead, I was clear about not wanting to get sent there. Still, I didn't really want to be in school either. I definitely needed some time off.

Then just before wrapping up my freshman year, I would have an experience I'd never forget. At my roommate's prompting, I'd attend my first real rock-and-roll concert: *Three Dog Night*, live and in person at Market Square Arena. Three dollars and fifty cents a ticket (five dollars and fifty cents for the priority seats "up front") allowed twelve thousand screaming fans, my roommate and I included, to hear what I still believe to have been one of the greatest rock bands of 1970. The vocal harmonies were amazing, and the music was great. From the opening organ passage introducing "Chest Fever," all the way through the encore "Celebrate," it was spellbinding. I left school that year with renewed enthusiasm for the gift of music.

Upon returning home from my first year of college, I'd take a summer job as an attendant at a local Sunoco auto service station. The proprietor of the station was a hardworking and hard-playing guy named Herschel who took a liking to my work ethic. I pumped gas, cleaned restrooms, and learned such basic auto maintenance as changing oil, mounting tires, doing auto tune-ups, and the like. I also remember Herschel being famous for never missing work. He'd always say, "I can't afford to be sick because if I don't show up for work, I don't get paid." And true to his word, I'd never know him to take a day off, even when he didn't look well enough to be coming in.

I also remember two other things about Herschel. First, he liked to drink and fight. Every so often, he and one of the customers who worked as a slaughterman at the Stadler's Meat Packing Company in Columbus (when he wasn't to be found camping out and fishing along White River) would climb into the back of one of the U-Haul trucks the station rented and drink themselves drunk. Then they'd beat on each other until one succeeded in throwing the other out. Once this was done, they'd both laugh and go back to drinking again. A couple of weeks later, the whole process would repeat itself.

While I found all this a little intriguing, I never fully understood the attraction to substance use or, for that matter, fighting people you generally liked and got along with. Sure, like most teenagers, I was familiar with the peer pressure to drink and smoke marijuana. And I was also encouraged by some to view all this as part of the "growing up" process. But I guess I was simply too familiar with the pain and suffering people experienced in everyday life to understand why someone might voluntarily add the potential problems of alcohol or drugs to this mix. For me, the added risks always seemed to outweigh the benefits. Likewise, while I wasn't averse to fighting when I felt provoked, the idea of fighting someone for fun made no sense at all. Whatever the case, in general, I tried to steer clear of such foolishness.

The second thing I remember about Herschel was that his alcohol use resulted in a tendency to hang out in bars. This eventually led to his meeting and becoming romantically involved with a woman some ten or fifteen years his junior. Unfortunately, she would become pregnant. And when Herschel's wife found out, she confronted him at the station. I'll never forget her waving a finger in Herschel's face and threatening to take him for "everything" he was worth. When he responded, "You can't get blood out of a turnip," she retorted, "No, but I can put that turnip in jail." This statement was priceless and one I would always remember. Self-deception, especially when it comes to marital infidelity, almost always has its price.

At the time Herschel agreed to hire me, I didn't have a way to get around. But as soon as I got the job, it became apparent that I'd need a set of wheels to get back and forth to work. Luckily for me, by this time, my brother Dave had returned from his stint in the Navy and was living at home. Understanding my predicament, he agreed to let me drive his 1968 Ford Fairlane Fastback. This would turn out to be quite a car for a nineteen-year-old to be driving in 1970. And it proved crucial to helping me keep my job. I probably ended up driving Dave's car for a good year, until Pop helped me get my own vehicle—a subcompact Ford Cortina imported from Germany (does anyone remember these?). Apart from helping me get to and from work, Dave's car would also be instrumental to improving my social life.

That same summer, while working at the station, I'd become reacquainted with Teresa O. As mentioned earlier, Teresa and I first met in junior high school. I hadn't spoken to her since that time, but after spotting her in the department store where she was working, I decided to strike up a conversation. I quickly learned she had recently broken up with the guy she'd been seeing, and after talking awhile, I mustered up the courage to ask her about giving me another chance. She did, and we began dating.

Now during the Vietnam era, it was customary for the draft lottery to be conducted anew every year. Consequently, in the summer of 1970, my lottery number for the military draft changed. My new number would actually turn out to be higher than the previous one, and this, in conjunction with the US getting increasingly serious about reducing its involvement in the war, meant the risks of my being drafted and sent overseas would be significantly reduced. I've already mentioned how my fear of being drafted had been a big motivator for my going to college. But now, with the reduced chance of getting drafted and my dating Teresa, I no longer had any pressing reason to return to Indianapolis for my sophomore year of school. I'd stay in college but decided to take only twelve credit hours (rather than the fifteen required for a deferment) and take my chances with the draft board. Finally, as a result of my having access to Dave's car, I'd decide to remain living at home and commute back and forth to those classes I was still taking in Indianapolis.

I should mention that Dave's return from the military had not altogether been a positive thing for our family. Shortly after being discharged, he separated from his wife and moved back home. He then lived with us the next several months while trying to sort things out and get his own life back together. His wife, on the other hand, continued living somewhere out West (New Mexico or California, I think) with their remaining children. As Dave was still struggling with alcoholism and depression, he would have little contact with them for the next several years.

During this time, Dave could best be described as moody and prone to both anger outbursts and erratic behavior. And to further complicate matters, his relationship with Brian (again, his son whom Mom and Pop had taken custody of following the son being abused) would grow increasingly troublesome. Dave still considered Brian "his" child, while Mom was determined for Brian to see her and Pop as his parents. Consequently, Mom and Dave frequently argued over who was responsible for raising and disciplining Brian. Unfortunately, this left Brian stuck in the middle. As Dave's alcohol use and depression worsened, so did the strain of his living in our house.

Eventually, Dave would move out and begin staying with a woman whom he had met waitressing in a local bar. I think she understood that Dave was a genuinely sensitive and caring person with a good heart, even though he had a bad problem with alcohol and was depressed. Still, Dave's erratic behavior would cause her to pay dearly for the next several years—until Dave finally got sober, attended Alcoholics Anonymous (AA) meetings, and joined her church. As AA says, Dave came to "admit he was powerless over alcohol and that his life had become unmanageable." He also came to believe that "a Power greater than his own individual ego could restore him to sanity" and "became willing to turn his will and his life over to that Power." It is no exaggeration to say that his Higher Power, AA, his wife, and their two kids probably saved Dave's life. Nonetheless, and despite his loaning me the use of his car, getting along with Dave would not always be easy.

EXPLORING THE WORLD

Teresa and I continued dating for a year and a half, at which time we began talking about getting married. I was still trying to figure out where I wanted to go with my life...what might give it meaning. And though I was happy in my relationship with Teresa, I still couldn't decide what to focus on at school. Then as the months wore on, my decision to return to school and the stress of living under my parents' roof became increasingly troublesome. I just felt like I wasn't really getting anywhere. Finally, by the end of my sophomore year, and with the Vietnam War clearly winding down, I decided to drop out of college altogether and return to work at Herschel's service station. A few months later, I'd quit this job and take a position as a teller with the First National Bank of Columbus.

I've always considered working at this bank as my first *real* job. Certainly, I'd benefitted from my time at Zaharako's, Fritche's, Como Plastics, and the other places I'd worked. Those experiences taught me much about the value of self-discipline, of showing up on time, and of being dependable. They'd also helped me learn how to work alongside others and had been instrumental in bolstering my self-esteem. But working for the bank would be my first permanent, full-time job. It would also be my first job in an indoor, air-conditioned environment, where I could wear a dress shirt and tie and work with other semiprofessional people in an eight-to-five setting. Finally, this would be my first job with a regular salary, health-care benefits, and paid time off. I earned one hundred dollars per week, regardless of whether I made it into work or needed to call off sick. I had Blue Cross-Blue Shield insurance. And I received two weeks of paid vacation, with six paid holidays after the first year of employment.

For decades, the First National Bank had been one of two banks serving the residents of my hometown, the other bank being the Irwin Union Bank, overseen (if not owned) by J.

Irwin Miller. Like many banks of the era, the First National Bank had been founded by a local millionaire named Francis Overstreet. And as I was told, Mr. Overstreet had acquired his wealth through buying up vast tracts of property in and around Columbus at a time when the land was reasonably cheap. The bank would remain privately owned for decades and was in operation long after I had moved on.

Its main offices were located in a large, three-story, stone structure occupying the best part of a quarter block in the heart of downtown Columbus, right next door to Zaharako's Confectionary. Similar to Zaharako's, the furnishings consisted mostly of marble, brass, and dark, rich, locally harvested walnut or mahogany wood. Brass chandeliers hung from the ceiling, and on the south wall of the main lobby were three huge murals standing some twenty feet high and depicting life in rural America shortly after the turn of the twentieth century. It had one branch office at the time I was hired on, that was located in a shopping center at the corner of 25th Street and Central Avenue. Within a few years of my joining the bank, it had expanded to three branches.

Again, I started out working as a teller and seemed to catch on quickly to the daily routine of cashing checks, registering customer deposits, and the like. I was motivated to do well, worked hard, and was grateful for the opportunity I'd been given. And I especially liked that my employers seemed appreciative of me. Moreover, working for the bank gave me an increased sense of pride, while pleasing my family as well. My brother Dave seemed particularly proud of what he viewed as my having been the first in our family to have achieved some semblance of worldly success. Most of all, I felt like my life might finally be getting some direction.

A couple of other things worth mentioning would also happen during this same period. First, working for the bank made it possible for me to buy my first *real* guitar. It was a well-crafted, cherry-red Epiphone semi-hollow-body model, much like the ES-335 issued by its parent company, Gibson. I'd play this guitar for the next several years, and it even inspired me to try my hand at songwriting. Of course, nothing I wrote ever amounted to much. But once again, I was having fun playing guitar.

I purchased the Epiphone through Tom Pickett's Music Center on 25th Street. Tom's store had been a cornerstone of the Columbus business community since he first opened it in the late 1950s. He had just returned from serving in the Korean Conflict, and in addition to being an astute businessman, Tom was known for being a talented ukulele player and overall skilled musician. Over time, his store would become known for carrying all sorts of musical instruments, including guitars, drums, trumpets, keyboards, violins, etc. The store also sold sheet music and provided lessons for anyone wanting to learn how to play, in addition to selling both 45 and 33 rpm records. Finally, Tom would become well-known for his support of the many local musicians and rock bands in and around Columbus and for continuing to provide this support across many generations of aspiring musicians. Throughout the years, Tom's business would survive a fire that nearly destroyed the entire building and all its contents, one flood, at least two major recessions, and even the COVID-19 pandemic of 2020–2024. I'm pleased to write that Tom's store remains in operation to this day.

I know I've spoken a fair amount about my love for music. Again, part of the attraction was that playing music always seemed to soothe my soul. Furthermore, playing music had always seemed to come easy for me. Unfortunately, this, along with my dad's message about achievement of any kind being a direct function of hard work and willpower, would wrongly lead me to believe that anyone could learn to play an instrument if he or she only made enough effort. The older I get, the more I realize the fallacy of this belief. While hard work is usually necessary for one to become successful at almost any endeavor, most would agree that hard work alone is not the total answer. For example, people with lifelong blindness do not grow up to lead the Major Leagues in batting average or home runs. People with serious intellectual disabilities do not generally grow up to become CEOs of major corporations or president of the United States. And people with no sense of musical timing or possessing lifelong deafness seldom (if ever) become acclaimed musicians. Great achievement usually arises from a melding of innate ability, supportive life experiences, opportunity, *and* hard work.

In my case, I've never been able to learn to sight-read music. That's just not a talent I possess. But I could almost always watch other musicians play and learn from what I saw. I could buy music instruction books and memorize chord structures. And I could occasionally take lessons from those more skilled than I and benefit from their guidance. Probably my greatest strength was the innate ability to *hear* music. I truly believe I was given a gift to distinguish sounds made by differing instruments and to hear musical tones, melody, harmony, and tempo better than "the average bear." And in most cases, if I could "hear" the music clearly enough, I could usually learn to play it. Over time, I'd learn to hear notes on the lower register and to play bass guitar with a good deal of proficiency. I've also learned guitar chords and rhythm patterns, as well as some lead guitar scales and techniques. And my talent would also allow me to learn a little mandolin, some ukulele, some organ and piano, even some percussion. I'd never be great at playing any of these instruments. But my overall point is just that, for me, music just seemed to take less effort than is probably true for many people. And between my natural talent, the support of

EXPLORING THE WORLD

others, and hard work, I would learn to play music in a manner that would forever be rewarding. Music would just always be something I loved. And to this day, music helps me get out of my head (so to speak), out of my rational mind. Music allows me to be a little more spontaneous, a little more present with life. As already noted, later on, I'd get into recording music in my home studio. And here, I'd generally play all the instruments for the CDs I produced. In the liner notes for my first CD, I wrote, "Music is what keeps me sane in what can sometimes be a crazy world." The Epiphone guitar I bought in early 1972 would prove crucial to both advancing my skills as a guitar player and increasing my love for music.

One final note about the Epiphone guitar just mentioned. It was a used guitar at the time I purchased it, and as I recall, it cost 250 dollars—a decent price for a used guitar in the early 1970s. But some years later, I'd discover it to have been one of the very last such Epiphone guitars to have been manufactured in Kalamazoo, Michigan (along the same production line as the pricier Gibson guitars). Apparently, right after the guitar had been shipped, the Gibson Company discontinued building Epiphones in their Michigan factory and moved the production of these instruments overseas to save on manufacturing costs. The fact of this guitar being one of the very last Epiphone guitars made in America would ultimately result in enhancing its monetary value, as with time, it would come to be considered a desirable "vintage" item. So when I eventually got around to selling it, the guitar would yield nearly twice what I had originally paid for it. I guess I just got lucky. In any event, I'd use the proceeds from that sale to purchase my first high-quality acoustic guitar, a Martin D-18. Unfortunately, as fate would have it, when I left Columbus a year or so after buying the Martin, I found myself struggling to make ends meet and had to sell that guitar for less than a quarter of its value. Sometimes that's just the way things work out. Almost all guitar players have tales of woe about the "one that got away." The Epiphone was one such instrument for me. So too would be the D-18.

As I noted above, *two* meaningful events occurred shortly after I went to work for the bank. The other noteworthy thing that happened was Teresa's brother, John, returning from college. He came home around the same time Teresa and I started dating, and he too played guitar. John was a little more of an accomplished musician than I. But while he could play some stuff I had not yet learned, we were both clearly amateurs. Still, our guitar playing and personalities seemed to complement each other's. And having him around would further encourage me to spend time developing my own skills. Unfortunately, while John could play guitar, what he seemed to lack was a strong motivation for finding work. And this seemed to irritate Teresa greatly as she and her mother were the only ones bringing home money for buying food and paying the bills, and neither were in high-paying jobs. This meant I had to be careful about the amount of time John and I played together, lest Teresa become angry with me. All this aside, my friendship with John was meaningful. And the opportunity to play more music added much-needed balance to my life.

In the spring of 1972, Teresa and I married. Certainly, Teresa and I cared deeply for each other. But like many decisions made by young people, this one was probably not as well thought out as it might have been. On the one hand, I think Teresa and I both just wanted to get out from under our parents' roofs, wanted to spread our wings so to speak. I'm sure we thought we were all grown up, but so do a lot of twenty-somethings. On the other hand, getting married just seemed like the thing we were supposed to do. We had both graduated high school and were gainfully employed, me at the bank and Teresa as an office worker for a local furniture store. Moreover, many of our peers had already gotten married; some even had children. Then there was the fact that she and I had dated for a while and seemed compatible. She was easy to get along with, and she probably liked that I had a strong need to take charge of situations and a desire to better myself. She was also able to overlook my insecurities and occasional irritable/controlling disposition. Finally, we'd gotten engaged in December of 1971, and people were regularly asking about when we planned on getting married. Unfortunately, what Teresa and I didn't do was spend a good deal of time considering what getting married actually *meant*, the life struggles that lay ahead of us, or the spiritual and religious implications of making such a commitment. In retrospect, this was probably a serious error.

Our wedding ceremony would be held in the First Christian Church of Columbus. This was the church Teresa had been attending for some years prior to our getting reacquainted and the church in which I would eventually be baptized. The church had been built in 1942 and was actually the first of the many architectural masterpieces the Irwin/Miller family would bring to Columbus. It was originally named the Tabernacle Christian Church and had been designed by Finnish architect, Eliel Saarinen. To this day, the church remains a huge brick structure, with ceilings some 60 feet high and a sanctuary (including balcony) that seats several hundreds of parishioners. It has a freestanding bell tower some 166 feet tall and an independent chapel, office complex, even a gymnasium that included a full-size basketball/volleyball court. The organ was also massive and could fill the entire church with sound when cranked up. The complex covered a full city block and part of another. And later on, I'd read how *Time* magazine had reported it to have been the most expensive church of its style anywhere in the world at the time it was built. For a small-town church built in the 1940s, it is still something special.

As a youth, I had never been especially involved with church. My father had begun taking us to church shortly before my parents' divorce, possibly in a last-ditch effort to salvage their marriage. And my mother occasionally took us to church following the divorce. But for the most part, we never attended church regularly. Still, my parents tried to instill religious values into each of us children. And I remember always having a strong desire for making sense of life, in general, and for understanding the reasons for all the upheaval my parents' divorce had caused in our lives in particular. I can also remember praying, even at an early age, for God to bring me peace. Still, I didn't much understand the relationship between my desire for meaning, inner peace, and religion.

While I don't remember a great deal about our wedding, I do recall our colors to have been red and white. Mike Sprague was our designated photographer. Unfortunately, the pictures he took were limited. From the ones he did take, Teresa could be seen wearing a white gown, while I was wearing the off-white suit my father had given me some time earlier. The pictures also show me sporting a red tie and red carnation. I believe the wedding itself to have been small by most accounts, primarily just family and friends. Her mother would have been present, and the same for my mother and Pop. And I believe most of our siblings attended. But I don't recall her father and stepmother being there. And I'm pretty sure my stepmother did not attend. For some reason, Mike omitted the traditional family photos taken at most weddings. So I can't say exactly who all was really there. The reception would also have been small. It was held in a banquet room located in the basement of the church. And as I recall, our families made the cookies, punch, and any sandwiches we might have served.

Teresa's maid of honor for the wedding was her best friend, Diane L. My best man would be Diane's husband, Jeff. Diane's husband really wasn't my "best" man/friend. To this day, I consider him more of an acquaintance. But Teresa said I needed a best man, and at the time, Mike had gotten into photography and wanted to take the pictures for our wedding. So the arrangement would be for Jeff to stand in with me. I remember Jeff as one who had been raised in a very wealthy family and had grown up in a beautiful and spacious home on upscale Grandview Lake. His adoptive father was a vice president for Arvin Industries, and Jeff clearly had opportunities most kids didn't. I also remember that he too was into music and had a beautiful orange Gretsch double-cutaway guitar. It was similar to the one played by George Harrison of the Beatles, only Gretsch orange rather than walnut brown like George's. Clearly, Jeff and I were from opposite sides of town. He was a decent guy, but other than a love of music and his wife's friendship with Teresa, he and I had little else in common.

Teresa and I would honeymoon in Saint Louis, Missouri. It wasn't what you'd consider a glamorous or romantic place to spend our first weekend together as husband and wife. But I had worked at the bank for less than a year and had earned only three days of paid time off. So given that Saint Louis was close enough for a weekend trip, we made the most of it. We visited the renowned Saint Louis Arch and went to the Saint Louis Zoo. Then we returned home and moved into our small, newly built, ranch-style house at 2220 Indiana Avenue.

The house was a wood-framed structure of about 1,200 square feet, with three small bedrooms, one bathroom, white aluminum siding, and classic 1970s shag carpet. Mom and Pop had signed a bank note for the 20 percent down payment, and this allowed Teresa and me to secure the mortgage through a local savings and loan company. The house wasn't fancy, but it wasn't bad either, especially for two people who had known poverty most of their lives and were in their early twenties. In addition to being something we could call our own, it was of new construction and something we could afford. And the monthly payment was a meager fifty dollars. Now with my job at the bank, my marriage to Teresa, and a new home, my life truly seemed to be working...at least for a while.

Ms. O was (and is) a good person: caring, sensitive, honest, and attractive. As noted above, she too had lived through the divorce of her parents, as well as those struggles associated with her mother's mental health concerns. Consequently, we both understood the pain life can sometimes bring and clearly longed for a lasting marriage. As for our own relationship, it would be what many in the 1960s still considered "traditional." I was the primary wage earner, handled the household finances, and generally made most of the important family decisions. Teresa, on the other hand, also worked outside the home but assumed a more supportive role. Unfortunately, like many young people, neither of us was especially adept at communicating our wants and needs, our fears and hopes. Likewise, neither of us was especially good at working together to resolve problems or deal with conflict. Again, we were young, and due to my own insecurities, fears, and self-doubts, I was prone to arrogance and being controlling. Teresa, in an apparent attempt to avoid being argumentative, tended to acquiesce. Regrettably, as time passed (and much as was probably true for my own parents), this arrangement became burdensome for us both. For me, making the decisions and pretending to have all the answers, while hiding my fears and self-doubts, would create an insurmountable challenge.

As the stress of trying to "fix" all the day-to-day problems increased, my inadequacies would grow proportionately. I eventually came to feel resentful over having so much responsibility for our relationship and our lives and increasingly came to see myself as a failure when things didn't work out as planned.

Over time, I think Teresa probably became frustrated with the arrangement as well. And I also suspect that as the pressure to handle things grew and my ability to resolve situations waned, Teresa grew fearful of the lack of control she seemed to have over her own life.

Throughout our marriage, I'd work at the aforementioned bank. Again, I had always been pretty good with numbers, with analyzing data, and with making quick decisions, so success as a teller came pretty easy for me. Unfortunately, sometime during my second year on the job, my immediate supervisor left the bank and went to work for Cummins Engine Co. This left a vacancy in the head teller position, and given that I'd caught the eye of the vice president in charge of teller operations, I was moved into this supervisory role. The job entailed my opening and closing the bank, scheduling and supervising tellers for the main office, and balancing the bank's ledgers with accounts held at other banks—including the Federal Reserve Bank of Chicago, Illinois; the Indiana National Bank of Indianapolis, Indiana; the Fifth-Third Bank of Cincinnati, Ohio; and others. It also included my processing those checks written by customers on personal and business accounts having insufficient funds and operating my own teller window. I didn't get any extra money or benefits for all the additional duties I was assigned, just more responsibility and a little more prestige. But the new position gave me hope for an even brighter future with the bank.

Initially, I enjoyed the promotion into this new position and the responsibilities it entailed. And I anticipated that a raise in salary would eventually be forthcoming. But although I had been a pretty good teller and would be very good at managing the bank's ledgers, my skills for supervising others were woefully deficient. In retrospect, the vice president who had promoted me into the position might have anticipated I wouldn't have been up to the challenge. Yes, I was reasonably bright and eager to learn, but my limited interpersonal skills were bound to prove problematic. And managing people was simply never going to be my strong suit. At the very least, I needed much more training, supervision, and guidance than I'd otherwise end up getting. Unfortunately, I was pretty much left to my own devices. And over time, my interpersonal deficiencies would undermine my relationship with both subordinates and superiors alike. These problems only worsened a year or so later when I was promoted to a position of assistant manager for one of the bank's more recently established branch offices.

Seldom do people "crash and burn" without having some kind of early warning signs. Upon reflection, heart attack survivors usually acknowledge having had symptoms of fatigue, shortness of breath, or some other discomfort prior to the onset of those more acute problems necessitating medical intervention. Likewise, seldom does one look back on a failed relationship without admitting the existence of some kind of problems prior to the other party actually leaving, even if they had refused to acknowledge them at the time they were originally present. Countless are the times I've had (typically) men sitting in my psychology office stating, "I had no idea things were that bad," when in fact, their partner had been telling them for years that something needed to change. I too had warning signs of the growing problems in my own life, even if I was determined to ignore them.

As my job and life became increasingly troublesome, I tried supplementing marriage and work with recreation—coaching Little League baseball for two seasons (the first with Mike Sprague as my assistant coach) and playing softball for another. By now, Mom and Pop had adopted Dave's son, Brian. Unfortunately, since coming to our home, Brian had struggled with managing the trauma and abuse inflicted on him by his biological mother during his younger years. From the time he first joined our family, he would be socially awkward, lack confidence, struggled to make friends, and had trouble tolerating frustration. So in hopes that playing baseball might be a good way of helping Brian with his adjustment, I asked to have him assigned to the Little League teams I coached. Brian would actually excel at playing baseball. Moreover, being part of a team seemed to help him with his confidence and social skills. But like most of my undertakings, the coaching would be undermined by my perfectionism, my need to prove myself, and my own poor frustration tolerance. Simply said, I took the coaching way too seriously. My teams would have some success on the field, with my second year team going twelve for thirteen on the season. And I think the kids I coached generally seemed to have fun. But I worked them way too hard. And by the end of the second season, the intensity with which I approached coaching and my frustration over losing (even losing the one game in my second season) essentially robbed me of all the joy I might otherwise have experienced from working with the kids. I stopped coaching after my second year.

The following year, I'd join a men's slow-pitch softball team. But again, as might be expected, my competitiveness and the need to "be the best" kept me from enjoying the experience. I was also discouraged by the fact that several of my teammates appeared more interested in the beer parties held after the games than in what I considered the genuine fellowship of playing ball together. Softball just didn't seem to hold the answer I was looking for, any more than coaching had. In truth, I was just growing increasingly disenchanted with life, and nothing seemed to alleviate this. By this time, even music seemed to have lost its magic. As things progressively deteriorated, I developed more and more self-doubt, growing fears of being a failure, and (eventually) I despaired. And these problems only further undermined my daily functioning—both at home and on the job.

I eventually decided that returning to college and making a career change might be the answer. So while I continued working full-time at the bank, I also signed up for a full-time caseload (again) through IUPUI of Indianapolis. Coaching baseball and working with young children had encouraged me to think that studying elementary education and becoming a teacher might be the ticket. But while I enjoyed my studies, the academic caseload (in addition to working full-time) only exacerbated my increasing problems with sleep and energy. And in conjunction with my growing interpersonal struggles at work and home, returning to school only led to increased feelings of being trapped in a life I'd clearly grown to hate—a life seemingly devoid of meaning and, now, bound by feelings of hopelessness. I tried talking to our pastor about my despair, but while he seemed open to helping, our talking only produced limited relief.

About three and a half to four years into my marriage (and one year into my depression), Teresa suggested I might benefit from talking to a therapist. I'd resist this idea for a while, still hoping I could stubbornly *think* my way through the problems and solve them on my own. But over time, and scary as it was, it'd become apparent that my way wasn't going to work. I had tried everything I knew to sort out my situation rationally, and while my family and friends generally seemed of the opinion that I had my life all together, inside I felt like I was dying. When I started thinking about suicide, I finally realized I had to get help. This would be a watershed moment. It would be the beginning of the darkest time in my life and of a period of change that would ultimately lead to the inner peace for which I had long searched.

**Watch out now. Take care beware
Of thoughts that linger. Winding up inside your head.
The hopelessness around you.
In the dead of night. Beware of sadness.**
—**G. Harrison**

From *Beware of Darkness*, words and
music by George Harrison.
Copyright 1970 by Harrisongs Music Ltd. 3
Saville Row, London, W.1, England

OUT OF DARKNESS

Depression has many faces. Common symptoms include extended periods of sad or irritable mood; disturbance of energy, sleep, and appetite; and feelings of worthlessness and/or hopelessness. Other symptoms might include loss of interest in previously pleasurable activities (anhedonia), social withdrawal, even impaired cognition—most notably, attention and shorter-term memory. Finally, in the more severe cases, depression can be accompanied by auditory or visual hallucinations, false or delusional beliefs, and suicidal/homicidal ideation or tendencies.

While each of these symptoms can be experienced by one who is depressed, like most mental health syndromes, the actual manifestation of the disorder may vary greatly from one person to the next. The severity and duration of the depression, the etiology or suspected cause/trigger for the depression, and the confounding life circumstances or coexisting health factors—all these variables can affect one's experience with depression. Some forms of depression may be considered "major," while others may be designated chronic and low-grade or "persisting." Some may be endogenous or attributed to a genetic predisposition, while others may be triggered by the death of a loved one, loss of employment, substance abuse, the hormonal effects of childbirth, or other situational factors. Sometimes depression is recurrent, while at other times, it appears as a single episode.

While my own experience with depression seemed tortuous, in retrospect, it was probably not as severe or enduring as some. Certainly, the symptoms were similar to those most commonly found in clinical textbooks. I had extended periods of sad mood, accompanied by disturbances of energy, sleep, and appetite. I struggled with feelings of worthlessness and a loss of interest in activities that had previously brought me joy. Over time, I probably grew distant from others. But it's difficult to say just how much of all this might have been attributable to the depression and how much was due to the manner in which I'd been pushing myself to find a way out of my collapsing life. Again, I was working full-time at the bank and taking a full load of college courses. I'd get up early for work and go to class in the evening, sometimes drive to and from Indianapolis for lectures or tests and spend late nights studying. Clearly, my sleep and eating habits were taking a back seat to other matters, and my body was wearing down.

Moreover, even if I had so desired, there was little time for recreation or socializing. On one occasion, upon noticing my run-down condition, one of my college instructors encouraged me to think about what mattered most in my life and to spend more time attending to that. Unfortunately, I rejected the advice with strong-willed assurance that I had things under control. I guess some lessons just have to be learned the hard way. Nonetheless, as my depression worsened, it became impossible to ignore the reality that something was horribly wrong, that all my best efforts to control things were no longer working.

Probably my most troubling symptom was the overwhelming sense of dread and despair accompanying a belief that something deep inside me must be fundamentally wrong. I just couldn't shake the feeling that the inability to manage my own life was proof positive I was personally defective. And in some respects, maybe this *was* true. Again, my struggles growing up had all taken their toll on me. I'd long felt inferior to others, as though I always had to prove myself and that my best efforts were never going to be good enough. And I was clearly resentful and angry over not having had some of the opportunities with which many of my peers seemed to have been blessed. And all these feelings had undoubtedly contributed to problems with my relating effectively to others. On the other hand, under my father's guidance, I'd also come to believe that stubborn defiance and a willful attitude, combined with hard work and perseverance, could overcome most all of life's obstacles, shortfalls, and problems. As a result, I had also become an expert in masking my self-doubts, insecurities, and fears with an arrogant, know-it-all demeanor. Because I was bright and had problem-solving skills many others did not, when being arrogant failed, I could always *pretend* I had everything under control. And if faking it didn't work, then rationalizing my failures away as being someone else's fault would always provide an acceptable way out. All these gyrations, combined with the deep-seated need for gaining the acceptance of others, would feed the illusion that willpower alone could resolve any problem life might throw my way. Unfortunately, as my physical health, my intellect, my problem-solving skills, and my facade all began to crumble, I'd become increasingly estranged from myself and the world around me. Obviously, something was not working; my life was falling apart.

Just as symptoms of depression may vary widely, so too can treatment options. For example, available research actually suggests that as many as one-third of all depressed individuals seem to recover within six months from the time of onset with little or no formal treatment of any kind. This appears especially true when the depression has a clear precipitating trigger (e.g., unemployment, relationship problem, etc.) that resolves itself. Research has also demonstrated that many individuals with depression experience improvement of symptoms with six to nine months of interpersonal or cognitive-behavioral talk therapy alone. For those having more pronounced symptoms of depression, with recurring, endogenous depression, or for whom talk therapy proves less efficacious, psychotropic medication can also be beneficial. Finally, in cases where the depression is very severe or nonresponsive to other modes of treatment, even electroconvulsive therapy has demonstrated itself to have merit. Accurate assessment that correctly identifies the severity, duration, and pattern of symptoms, as well as the suspected cause or confounding factors, is crucial for helping a clinician choose the least invasive treatment option.

In a similar fashion, differing clinicians may approach talk therapy differently, depending on their training and personal life experiences. Some take an "analytic" approach, based upon the view that mental health symptoms arise from biologically based, psychosexual drives that become thwarted through harsh, critical parenting and other developmental experiences. Once this occurs, inner conflict arises, producing anxiety. And one's responses to this anxiety may manifest as "defense mechanisms," which are prone to becoming dysfunctional personality traits as the person enters adulthood. Loosely said, the therapy based upon this perspective involves a process of illuminating the underlying conflicts via the interpretation of dreams and a process of analysis. This is intended to help the individual free him or herself of the dysfunctional attitudes and behaviors, such that they might choose more effective ways of responding to the anxiety arising from present-day conflicts.

Other therapists may take a more "humanistic" approach, based upon the belief that people are intrinsically "good" at birth and possessing of an innate drive toward "actualizing" their full, unique human potential. Unfortunately, this actualizing tendency can become disrupted by parents or significant others possessing rigid social values. Once this occurs, people become estranged from their "inner self," which then leads to anxiety and related dysfunctional behavior. Here, the process of therapy becomes one of reacquainting the individual with his or her fundamental nature through an encounter with one (the therapist) who is "authentic, nonjudgmental, and accepting." Such an encounter may then allow the individual to reestablish a relationship with the true inner self and, once again, resume the self-actualizing process.

Still, other therapists take a more behavioral or cognitive-behavioral approach, based upon the belief that individuals are neither good nor bad but, rather, human organisms shaped (some might say conditioned) by the physical environment and/or experiences encountered while navigating the normal challenges or dangers of everyday life. For this approach, problematic behavior arises out of the direct impact one's environment or experience has on his or her behavior and cognitions and the reactions or responses associated therewith. These behaviors and cognitions may then become generalized to situations (including relationships with others) that, while different, appear similar to or resemble those situations originally seen as threatening. Here, the focus of therapy tends to be on helping the individual *unlearn* (or extinguish) dysfunctional behaviors or cognitions and to replace them with new, more adaptive ways of reacting or responding to presenting stimuli.

In some respects, the differences between these approaches may seem subtle (if not confusing). And there are other theories of pathology and modes of therapy as well. Sometimes, skilled therapists will draw upon components of more than one therapeutic mode as, in many regard, psychological theories and therapeutic approaches tend to be more alike than not. Furthermore, the existing research generally suggests that each way of explaining psychological functioning has some merit and that each approach to therapy can be effective with differing populations. Perhaps the most important factors to therapeutic success are the therapist's authentic caring, clinical experience and conviction in the efficacy of the approach one takes. Clients of caring and experienced therapists, who believe in what they are doing, almost always have better outcomes than those of therapists who seem to operate from an instruction manual (so to speak), who are new to the field, or who are lacking in conviction that what they do will actually work.

My own therapist (Christopher W) probably favored the humanistic approach, but he also had a strong spiritual component to the therapy he practiced. Chris was a large, heavyset, mountain man of sorts hailing from West Virginia. None of this really mattered much except that, to me, it meant he seemed human in ways other therapists and many psychologists sometimes do not. I especially appreciated the fact that he didn't wear a suit or tie, that he didn't seem stuffy. I also liked that he didn't seem to just be "going through the motions" or practicing some new techniques he'd learned in school. Rather, Chris was a master's level trained social worker who, from the onset, revealed himself to be a good listener, empathetic, sincere in expressions, and nonjudgmental in his attitude (qualities I would later strive to emulate in my own work as a clinician). Chris was also authentic and easily relatable, matter-of-fact. And he was wonderfully patient. I, on the other hand, often felt the need to rush things or to act impulsively. This I'd always believed necessary in order to help me avoid anxiety and gain control over the unpleasant situations and emotions life brought my way. Chris seemed to understand the foolishness of all this. I also liked the fact that, during our first meeting, I'd observe a poster hanging on the wall of Chris's office that read, "I believe in the sun, even when it isn't shining." Given the despair I felt and the desperation with which I entered therapy, I truly needed to get this message.

From our first meeting, Chris made no pretense about being able to fix me or of his having all the answers I so desperately sought. He knew I was hurting, and this clearly mattered to him. But he also knew the limits of what he or any therapist might do to help. Furthermore, he seemed to know that, in many respects, much of the suffering I was experiencing was of my own making. This may sound confusing to the reader, even insensitive or uncaring. But in Eastern philosophy, there is an old saying that goes, "For humans, pain is inevitable, suffering is optional." In other words, many times, our suffering is directly related to the *choices* we make, or don't make, when responding to those unpleasant or painful experiences that naturally arise as a result of living a factical existence.

As many have suggested, being human is, in and of itself, inherently difficult. Being human, we can experience such pleasant emotions as joy, happiness, peace, and love. But being human also means experiencing sadness, fear, pain, grief, and all the other painful emotions sometimes associated with being socially connected to others and with having a physical body that is vulnerable to disease, injury, and death. As humans, we are, each and every one of us, all those things that make up the human condition, the good and the bad. So when we strive to avoid any of these experiences, doing so only represents a hapless exercise in rejecting one's self. And in many respects, rejecting the self is the source for much of our suffering. For the longest time, all this would be something I'd struggle to understand. Thankfully, like most good therapists, Chris didn't.

More often than not, Chris would answer my questions with questions or redirect my needs for reassurance by encouraging me to believe in myself and to trust in my own ability to resolve problems and create my own life. I'm not saying he believed everything was solely up to me or that he wanted me to arrogantly ignore the counsel of others. Rather, he just seemed to have this steadfast conviction that, when everything was said and done, I (with the help of a Higher Power) was in the best position to know how to work through my own despair, to make the choices necessary for bringing about a more lasting peace, and to create a meaningful life. Of course, he also realized that making these choices would require I take responsibility for the consequences of them. Because when the choices you consciously make don't work out, there is no one else to blame but yourself. On the other hand, when the choices you consciously make *do* work out, you reap the rewards of knowing the life you are living is the one you helped to make.

I also remember Chris proposing three basic guidelines for me to consider as I worked through my struggles. First, he suggested I strive for staying in the present. Life, Chris would say, is meant to be lived in the "here and now." Yes, I might hold important memories from the past and be able to learn from earlier experiences, but for all intents and purposes, the past is forever gone, and the consequences of any decisions or mistakes once made are unlikely to be undone. Similarly, while I might have plans or hopes for the direction in which my life is presently moving, the future isn't here yet. So preoccupying myself with trying to control things that may never come to pass is generally a poor use of time. And in either case, dwelling on the past or worrying about the future only distracts one from focusing on the present and making the best possible decisions when striving to meet the challenges of today. If I ever wanted to look back at some future date and be pleased with the decisions I had made and the life I had created, staying in the present and making mindful choices in the here and now offered me the best chance for success.

Chris's second guideline was for me to listen to and honor my feelings, including those unpleasant feelings of fear, guilt, anger, sadness, even depression. This principle would encourage me to embrace my feelings without judging them and to recognize that, try as I might, I need never (indeed, *can* never) run from my feelings—only experience and learn from them. Prior to that point in time, I had viewed feelings, be they pleasant or unpleasant, as something external to myself, something irrational that influenced my life from beyond. Chris helped me recognize that my feelings, be they good or bad, were an integral part of my being fully human—and that fighting against them meant fighting against a part of myself that might be just as valuable as my logical mind.

Now clearly Chris wasn't suggesting I listen *only* to feelings—to the exclusion of my logical mind. He understood that feelings can also be misleading at differing times. Sometimes people even experience conflicting feelings, as when we love a child or spouse or sibling but feel like we just can't stand to be around him or her at any particular moment. And just about everyone has had the experience of *feeling* attracted to someone whom you knew, in the end, would only bring you heartache and pain. Likewise, most of us have known times when thoughts making logical sense actually represented rationalizations that made no sense in the practical world of day-to-day life. One might, for example, rationalize that sleeping with the spouse of another is justified when feeling lonely or neglected by one's own partner, even though, in truth, such infidelity typically results in feelings of guilt or shame or hurts others for whom we care deeply. Chris clearly understood the importance of listening to both our feelings and our mind as each can provide valuable input when deciding how to respond to the challenging situations life brings us. Chris also realized that both our feelings and our mind are fundamental components of who we are and that finding serenity in the world can only come about through making peace with all of oneself. Unfortunately, and this was especially true for me, sometimes people rely predominantly on one or the other. And this almost always causes problems.

Chris's final guideline was that I strive to treat others as I myself might want to be treated. This probably sounds familiar to most of us. But this rule of thumb is not intended as some type of psychological trick designed to manipulate others or get one what he or she wants, if only because treating someone in a particular way offers no guarantee the other will respond in kind. No, treating others the way I myself want to be treated means treating them in accordance with my own values, in accordance with what I believe to be right, fair, and just. And the benefit derived from treating others in this fashion is that it allows me to avoid those unpleasant feelings that, all too often, arise from treating someone in a manner I know to be wrong. Certainly, I might hope being honest with others encourages them to be honest with me, and often it does. But if the other responds accordingly, then this is simply good karma. If they don't respond in kind, then at least I don't have to carry around the guilt or shame of knowing I misled or deceived another. Either way, I will be more at peace.

These three guiding principles, basic as they may sound, would be the jumping-off point for steering me through my battle with depression, my struggles with relating meaningfully to others, and my efforts toward managing many of the other hardships I would face in the years to come. I would always value their simplistic wisdom. And as importantly, these principles would be instrumental in encouraging me to undertake the never-ending process of reflecting on how I really wanted to live my life.

My time with Chris would be instrumental in other ways as well. For example, he helped me to understand that I didn't need the approval of everyone I met in order to be at peace with myself. Prior to this time, going along with others to gain their acceptance seemed my only real ticket to avoid feeling inadequate and inferior. Still, striving to always please others never really worked. There were always times when others would be disappointed in me and times when people wondered if I was being sincere or just trying to appease them. Moreover, seeking the approval of others only served to undermine my own sense of worth by leaving me feeling as if my personal beliefs, needs, or feelings didn't matter. Chris helped me understand that by always seeking the approval of others, no one ever got to know the real me; no one really got to know where I stood or in what I believed. And I'd also never know for sure if others valued me for who I truly was or were only pretending to do so because I was being agreeable. I remember Chris suggesting, "Ken, you can't be all things to all people. You can't please everybody. Someone is always going to be disappointed. On the other hand, if you are genuine with others, a third of the people will probably like you, a third of them probably won't, and a third of them probably won't care. And whatever the case, at least people will know where you stand, and you'll know if they actually appreciate you for who you are."

Chris also helped me with realizing that life is seldom black and white, all or nothing. Over the years, I had become rigid in my belief that there was a correct or incorrect answer to every question, a right or wrong solution for every problem, a good or bad choice in every situation. And all too often, I thought I knew better than most which was which. Such was my arrogance. Unfortunately, such an attitude couldn't help but set me up for endless disappointment, frustration, and suffering. Chris, on the other hand, understood that most situations have shades of gray between the black and white, that while I might think I knew what was right or wrong given any specific situation, there was no *one* answer or solution for dealing with the multitude of ever-changing challenges or problems life might present. Rather, we must always remain open to exploring new possibilities, new options, and new perspectives. At times, as we shared what Chris referred to as the "road of life," he'd metaphorically suggest I think about moving left to deal with certain obstacles. At other times, he'd suggest I think about going right. For the longest time, these suggestions seemed contradictory, even absurd. Gradually, I'd come to understand their wisdom.

Finally, the most important thing I learned from Chris, and one for which I will always be grateful, was the conviction that inner peace may best be found from undertaking a spiritual, rather than psychological, journey. My depression and a loss of faith seemed to have gone hand in hand. By the time I entered therapy, I had pretty much exhausted any hope of ever finding meaning or peace through my Christian upbringing. Prayer and the teachings of my well-meaning pastors seemed to have all but failed me. But Chris still believed that spirituality could hold the answer. So not knowing where else to turn, I decided that if I was going to undertake a spiritual journey, I would devote my time and energy to studying Oriental philosophy and the religious teachings of the Far East. Later on, I would regain an appreciation for the teachings of Jesus, but for now, I would begin practicing meditation and strive to live my life with renewed spirituality more in keeping with Eastern traditions.

As a result of the decision to explore spirituality anew, and for the first time in my life, I'd start meditating and dedicating real time to being with nature. I had long considered meditation as esoteric and time spent in nature as wasted. This was probably because, for me, both of these things seemed unproductive. I'd always been driven, task-oriented, goal-focused. But now I'd find myself sitting for extended periods along the banks of White River, just focusing on my breath or listening to the water. Other times, I'd go for long slow walks along trails in neighboring Brown County State Park. For the unfamiliar, Brown County State Park is located some 18 miles west of Columbus and consists of some 15,800 acres of rolling, tree-covered hills which include 20 plus miles of hiking trails, a horse stable with 70 miles of bridle trails, and two lakes. Some might consider it heaven on earth. But all I knew for sure was that the more time I spent there, and the more time I gave to meditating and being in nature, the more I felt rejuvenated.

In retrospect, this time spent with meditation and nature probably seemed to others like I was isolating myself from people. And during this period, I'm sure Teresa felt I was withdrawing from her as well. But I was really just learning how to settle my mind, to get back in touch with my inner self, to rediscover my spirit, my soul, and to hear what some refer to as "that wee small voice within." And while it may have seemed confusing to others, doing these things, getting further away from the chatter of crowds and spending more time and energy quieting my mind, and listening to my inner voice all helped me to become more at one with life.

I remember reading a passage attributed to Lao Tzu that went, "Those who know, do not talk; those who talk, do not know." The latter portion of this passage seemed a good reflection of how I had lived much of my life prior to this time. I'd always had an opinion about everything, always believed I knew the answer. And so I spoke way too much. Learning to talk less and to listen more allowed me to begin understanding just how little I actually did know. It also helped me realize that acting as though I had all the answers only masked the anxiety I felt regarding all those things I didn't know. And thus, not only would meditating and being in nature give me a newfound appreciation for the gift of solitude, but it'd also give me the time and space to begin questioning many of those things I previously had thought to have been of such importance, those things I had once valued most. I started reflecting on what I really wanted out of life, my life. And gradually, I began making changes in the way I thought about my place in the world and in the way I chose to go about living in it. I began taking a more honest look at who I was as a person, both my strengths and my limitations. And I made a commitment to striving for being less judgmental, both of myself and others. I started examining the willful way I'd always confronted the challenges of my day-to-day existence. And I began changing the ways I dealt with frustration, disappointment, even success. Finally, I began making changes in how I approached others and how I responded to them. And all these changes, over time, would lead me to discover greater balance, greater peace, and greater love. Slowly, I would begin to heal.

In addition to the time spent with meditation and nature, I started listening to audiotapes of workshops given by spiritual teachers such as Ram Dass (a former Harvard psychology professor who'd also studied Hinduism). I began attending lectures by such noted speakers as Swami Rama of the Himalayan Institute in Chicago, Illinois (and later on, Honesdale, Pennsylvania). And Chris had already introduced me to the books of Alan Watts (an Anglican minister turned Eastern philosopher), as well as to writings attributed to the ancient Chinese philosophers Lao Tzu and Chuang Tzu. I'd study these works for months before picking up on books by authors such as Hermann Hesse, Aldous Huxley, Robert Pirsig, and others. I would eventually come to identify each of these as teachers of my own.

Probably the most enlightening book I ever read was that collection of six small essays written by Alan Watts titled *This*

Is It: And Other Essays on Zen and Spiritual Experience. These essays spoke of a vision wherein life is best discovered and understood by mindfully and consciously living in the present moment. And much like Chris, Alan Watts spoke of the value of living genuinely and of *meaning* not being something that just happens to us or something we discover outside ourselves but something we *create* through the choices made in each and every waking moment of our lives. Watts also spoke of the importance of seeing ourselves as intrinsically connected to God rather than as a separate entity existing distinct from God. He spoke of the value of living in harmony with one's existence rather than fighting against it or trying to impose one's will on it. And all these ideas stood in stark contrast to the willful, rational, analytical, controlling, and self-centered ways by which I had approached life prior to this time. These writings would speak to me in a very *personal* way. And I probably read passages of this book over and over for months, even years, to come. I have a copy to this day.

Books by other authors that proved inspiring included *Doors of Perception, Be Here Now, Steppenwolf, Zen and the Art of Motorcycle Maintenance*, Alan Watts's *The Book: On the Taboo against Knowing Who You Are*, the Bhagavad Gita, and the *Tao Te Ching*. Pirsig's book on motorcycle maintenance, the account of one struggling to regain inner peace and rediscover a life of meaning following a psychotic break, was probably one of the more challenging books I'd ever read. I remember it requiring multiple readings, but with each one, I seemed to gain new insights both about life and my own life experience.

Then there was the novel *Siddhartha* by Hermann Hesse. Siddhartha was born the son of a great king who, at Siddhartha's birth, would be told that his son was destined to become either a king like his father or a wise, spiritual teacher. The father, desiring his son to follow in his own footsteps, tried to protect his son from all the worldly distress commonly found outside the castle and from all those things that might influence Siddhartha to become spiritually inclined. But one day, Siddhartha slipped out of the castle and began mingling with the "common folk." This introduced Siddhartha to human pain, suffering, and despair and to the many questions about life that he'd never before considered. These questions then led Siddhartha to undertake a journey of self-discovery "amongst the people." At one point in the story, young Siddhartha sought instruction from another deemed wise in the ways of world and of spiritual enlightenment. And when the teacher asks what talents Siddhartha had to offer in exchange for her wisdom, Siddhartha stated his only talents were his ability to "think, fast, and wait."

Again, throughout much of my youth, I'd been impulsive, acting without contemplation, without thinking through the consequences of my actions, and seeking no one's counsel but my own. And for a while, with the possible exception of decisions regarding interpersonal relationships, my above average intellect and decision-making abilities seemed to have gotten me by. But over time, this approach had become less and less viable. Acting willfully and trying to solve problems on my own could never prove sustainable. And acting impulsively, acting out of my anxiety, my fear, my self-doubt, was bound to reach its limits. The idea that *thinking, fasting, and waiting* just might be the answer to so many of life's problems offered a whole new perspective. Later on, I would translate "fasting" to read "praying" because I had always considered fasting as yet another way of seeking a closer connection with one's Higher Power. And as a result, the possibility that *thinking, praying, and waiting* might be the only things one truly needs to resolve the real troubles of life and find inner peace has remained with me since that time.

I imagine spiritual growth can be realized in many ways and by a variety of disciplines. Regarding such a journey, and in response to a devotee searching for a spiritual guide, Ram Dass once suggested, "Spiritual teachers can be found anywhere. You can be walking along a road and trip over a rock and become enlightened." I guess this might be true. But, for me, there would be no rock, no one teacher. And inner peace would not come about from any single moment of revelation or enlightenment. There would be no flash of light that would forever change my experience of the world or my place in it. I do remember a time when I realized a change needed to be made. And I remember a time when I unequivocally knew that, even if I wasn't sure to where the change might lead, I could never go back to living as I once had. But my own transformation, if you will, would come about more as a gradual unfolding, more as a *process* marked by many ups and downs, by many starts and stops, and by many moments of faith and doubt. In many respects, it continues as an ongoing process to this day. Thus, it is that I still see myself as a never-ending work in progress.

Teresa and I would never have children. Early on, we put this off that we might get our own lives settled: our marriage, our home, our jobs, and so on. But I've always suspected our not having children was also due in part to both of us coming from broken families and to our both growing up with the instability our parents' divorces created and our family struggles with poverty and mental illness. It just seemed like we were uncertain whether either of us could really be good parents or provide a stable homelife for a child. I know this to have been true for me. And I knew I never wanted to bring children into the world to experience the difficulties I had known. Later in our marriage, Teresa would express a desire to become a mother, but as my own efforts toward self-discovery had grown increasingly important, my commitment to my job, my marriage, and the way of life we had created had all begun to wane. Thus, at that point in time, becoming a father was something I simply couldn't fathom.

The fact of our not having had children probably made the decision of redirecting my life elsewhere somewhat easier than might otherwise have been the case. In any event, the decision to make change included the decision to quit my job at the bank, leave our home, and ultimately leave Columbus in hopes of my returning to school in Indianapolis. Regrettably, the prospect of making all these changes, especially in light of the increasing distance arising between Teresa and myself, seemed to have left her feeling confused and afraid.

After some three months of talking and crying together, and trying to work out a plan of transition, and after repeated efforts to reassure Teresa of my love and my conviction that things would be okay, the time for change had arrived. I decided to walk away from my job at the bank and move out of our house. Teresa could not come with me. She felt abandoned. I tried to remain in touch with her over the next few months, but she continued to struggle with understanding my choices. Eventually, she became reluctant to taking my phone calls or talking with me. And with the passage of time, we grew further and further apart. Finally, she would file for divorce.

I never wanted to be divorced. I remembered all too well the pain my parents' divorce had created for them and for us kids. And yet there I was, on the threshold of repeating all that which my own parents had experienced. Upon receiving the divorce papers, I realized the prospects of returning to my former way of life were gone. There was little else I could do to save the marriage. The only decision left was that of making sure the love we once shared would not be destroyed by my turning to bitterness, anger, and regret. I would sign the divorce papers without contesting any of the conditions listed therein. My sadness was great. For the longest time, the loneliness seemed unbearable. I questioned myself and my decision repeatedly. But eventually, I came to realize the die had been cast. Our divorce would be final in October of 1977.

Upon leaving Columbus, I initially rented a sleeping room in Franklin, Indiana, a small community located halfway between Columbus and Indianapolis. I lived there a brief time while sorting through the wisdom of my decision and initiating efforts toward regaining my footing in Indianapolis. And during this time, I would take a job as an aide at Central State Hospital in Indianapolis. Central State was a large, state-run psychiatric hospital serving those from the greater Indianapolis area having chronic mental illness. I would commute back and forth to work daily for the best part of that summer. Times were tough. Financially, I struggled to make ends meet. Emotionally, I felt alone. And it was during this time that I would part with one of the last remnants of my life in Columbus: my Martin guitar. To the reader, this may not seem especially important. But for several years, during times of doubt, music had been my lifeline. And giving up this guitar only compounded my uncertainties over the decisions I had made and the direction my life was taking. In some ways, selling the Martin represented an end to my former way of life.

Some months later, I'd finally resettle in Indianapolis. Again, my ultimate goal had been a return to school at IUPUI, and I viewed the job at Central State as a way of facilitating this transition. But after working there for three or so months, I quickly realized I couldn't continue managing my own loneliness and despair while also being around those struggling with major psychiatric problems. Consequently, I left that job and once again took a job as an attendant at a gas station, this time in uptown Indianapolis.

Here I worked for a man named Van Vo. Van had relocated to America from South Vietnam during the airlift ending our involvement in the Vietnam conflict. The station was located in a part of Indianapolis that was poverty-ridden and violence-prone. And I was hired on to work the midnight shift (11:00 p.m. to 7:00 a.m.). I suspect Van hired me because I needed a job and was willing to work this shift when most others probably knew better. And I think it is no exaggeration to say that very little good ever happens after midnight. Sure, good people may sometimes need to be out during the early hours of the morning for any number of reasons. But a whole lot of angry, violent, and criminal types also seem to prowl about under the cover of darkness. And this was particularly true in the uptown area of Indianapolis at that time. Every sort of bad character one might imagine seemed out and about during my shift. And occasionally, one of them would come by the station. I would work this job some five or six months, and I probably stayed on longer than I should have because I liked working with Van. He was an honest, hardworking, and caring person, who always treated me fairly and pretty much let me do my work with very little grief. But after being robbed at gunpoint on two separate occasions, I decided the job might not be my best option.

 I then went to work providing janitorial services for a local building maintenance company. Here, my attention to detail and willingness to show up regularly resulted in my becoming a pretty good janitor. In addition to learning the basics of emptying trash cans, cleaning toilets, vacuuming, washing windows, etc., I was also trained on stripping and refinishing floors. To this day, I consider these skills useful, and I was grateful to again have a job where I could earn enough money to pay my rent as well as buy my food and clothes, without the risk of being shot. I also appreciated the fact that in this job, I didn't have to think a lot and I didn't have to deal with very many people. Many of us probably think too much when we are distressed. And during such times, dealing with people almost always becomes more difficult. Moreover, I was a dependable worker who seldom missed work. And because of my work ethic, I didn't require much supervision. These were all traits my bosses appreciated. Soon I would be assigned buildings where I was the only janitor on duty. I'd have my own key and could pretty much come and go as I pleased. Still, the job wasn't providing enough stability or income for me to return to school. I barely scratched by (floundered).

About a year later, while still working as a janitor, I met another spiritual teacher. Takor Patel was founder of the Kripalu Yoga Clinic and Ashram. The facility was located in Indianapolis (if you can imagine that)—not what you might consider a hotbed for yoga ashrams in the 1970s. And at that time, it was on the smaller side. Apart from Takor and his family, only three students (myself included) lived on the premises. As one might guess, Takor was of Indian descent, small in stature, not unlike many people hailing from India, dark-skinned, and of a very mild and unassuming nature. Upon occasion, I had the impression that his wife, also from India, was probably less than enthusiastic about living a life of spiritual austerity. Nonetheless, she remained steadfastly supportive of Takor (though she was known to get quite outspoken if she felt their lifestyle produced problems in caring and providing for their children). I would live at the ashram with Takor, his family, and the devotees for the next year or so.

I'd continue my meditation and spiritual readings while living at the ashram, and I still traveled to Brown County off and on to spend time in nature. But while it was nice to be living in a supportive, communal-type setting, truthfully, I can't say I learned a lot from my time at the ashram. It did provide a safe environment in which to pursue my own spiritual reflection and growth. And maybe I actually learned more than I realize. Sometimes that happens. But what probably impressed me the most about Takor was just his overall manner. Being near Takor and observing how he went about dealing with life taught me much about patience and the importance of letting go of my need to control. I will always remember the occasion whereupon Takor and I were having a discussion about spiritual values, and in his kindest voice, he said, "Ken, there is no arguing with the truth." I guess this was his not-so-subtle way of reminding me that "if you need to argue an issue, you have already missed the point." Life is not about forcing your opinion on others as pushing your opinion on another usually represents a lack of conviction about that which you purportedly believe. Said another way, trying to control or coerce others into believing as you do is usually done in hopes you won't feel so alone or anxious about your own beliefs. If that which you believe is really true, then there will probably be no need to force it on others; they will usually see its truth in the way you live your life, be drawn to it, and be open to your sharing it.

Some thirty years later, I and my wife (Pam) would again visit Takor and his family. As might be anticipated, his children were fully grown, and like myself, he and his wife had both aged. But they immediately recognized me, and we enjoyed sharing stories of earlier times. The ashram had expanded with the addition of a newer and much larger meditation hall, and this expansion was clearly a source of pride for Takor. He was hosting a meditation clinic on the weekend we were in town, and Pam and I would attend a two-hour meditation seminar with other guests. Takor still struck me as the same caring and gentle spiritual soul I had met years earlier.

It was also during my time at the ashram that I'd get involved with leather crafting. This was intended to help keep my mind focused, a kind of moving meditation if you will. And it would prove especially rewarding in other ways as well.

There is a reason psychiatric facilities often have residents doing crafts, artwork, gardening, and the like. Again, troubled souls are prone to rumination, to thinking too much. And it's simply much more difficult to obsess or worry about things when engaging in a practical, hands-on project.

As an added benefit, the leatherwork would eventually lead to my opening a small leather crafting shop in Nashville, Indiana (the small arts and crafts community located some twenty minutes from Columbus that I'd mentioned earlier). The name of the shop would be *Dharma Place: Works of God*. And I would use the leather shop to craft and sell book covers of various scriptural texts (the Bible, the *Tao Te Ching*, the Bhagavad Gita, the Dhammapada, the Koran, etc.) and other small gift items (wallets, checkbook covers, and the like). In keeping with my focus at the time, all items would be inscribed with religious symbols corresponding to various spiritual orientations. In the end, the shop actually generated very little income—barely enough to cover my expenses. Consequently, I had to continue providing janitorial services and commuting back and forth from my job in Indianapolis in order to make ends meet. And because I couldn't afford rent on two separate locations, on many occasions, I'd end up sleeping in my car. Nonetheless, during this time, I continued my spiritual work. And despite my persisting loneliness and the financial hardships, I'd still find this to be a period of growing peace.

Finally, this would also be the time I'd get serious about studying the Bible. As already mentioned, I was raised around Christianity throughout my youth but always found the Bible difficult to understand (if not downright confusing). And during my greatest time of need, my Christian upbringing had seemed to offer very little comfort. So as my life began falling apart in Columbus and I became increasingly depressed, I also began questioning the Bible and the teachings of Jesus. Finally,

I was in a place where I believed I could give the teachings of Jesus another chance. So I purchased some three or four different translations of the Bible and began cross-referencing these writings. To this day, I do not consider myself a biblical scholar by any means. But after much investigation, I have come to believe that my problems with Christianity might not so much have been with the scriptures or the teachings of Jesus as with the particular pastors to whom I had been exposed as a youth and/or my interpretations of the messages they shared. I've also come to believe, much as Alan Watts once wrote, that scriptures or religious doctrines of any source are but a road map pointing one toward a greater destination and that if you remain fixated on the map without ever traveling to where it points, you might never reach the destination you desire.

After operating the leather shop for about a year and continuing my spiritual endeavors, I again found myself thinking about college. Previously, I noted how I'd always struggled with having any clear direction for my life. Consequently, when I first attended college, it was more for the purpose of avoiding the military, of wanting to prove my self-worth, or of trying to please others. Now that I'd finally garnered the necessary resources and personal focus to return to school, I decided to do so with the sole intent of finding a course of study that might help me continue learning about myself and my life. Toward this end, I would choose to major in psychology. Hopefully, studying psychology would further my search for inner peace. Maybe it would bring me closer to God. And if studying psychology also led to a career wherein I could one day pay my bills and be of help to others, then so be it. If not, then I still hoped studying psychology would advance my own personal journey.

Walked out this morning, I don't believe what I saw.
Hundred billion bottles, washed up on the shore.
Seems like I'm not alone in being alone.
Hundred billion castaways, looking for a home.
—Sting

From *Message in a Bottle*, words and music by Sting. Copyright 1979 Virgin Music (Publishers) LTD. Ladbroke Grove, London W11.

STUDYING PSYCHOLOGY

Psychology has been variously defined as the scientific study of human behavior and mental processes. Strictly speaking, psychology is not a philosophical undertaking, not an artistic undertaking, and not a spiritual undertaking. It is a *scientific* undertaking pursued by humans. It utilizes the scientific method and attempts to verify its findings within certain degrees of statistical probability such that these findings can be replicated by other scientists. The process of replication is the scientist's way of trying to assure that findings are reliable and not unduly influenced by the personal biases of any given researcher. Despite this attempt at safeguarding results, however, the *findings* of psychology are not absolute. Rather, by their very nature, these findings are limited by those understandings and instruments devised by humans committed to such scientific work.

Alan Watts attempted to highlight this point when suggesting how, as humans, "we may see things with our eyes, but our eyes can never look directly at themselves; we may grasp with our hand, but the hand can never grasp itself." His point was simply that human endeavors are always limited by our own human capacities. And so it is with psychology or any scientific endeavor for that matter. As something human beings do, scientists can never move beyond their own capacities for experiencing or understanding anything other than that which our own capabilities allow. Once upon a time, very wise men sincerely believed the world to be flat. It was not a topic for discussion because humans *knew* nothing to the contrary. Eventually, as humans developed new instruments of study and became introduced to new knowledge, a paradigm shift would occur, allowing humans to believe (or hypothesize) the world to be round (or oval/egg-shaped). But who is to say that even this newer information won't be proven wrong at some future date, thereby dispelling our current understanding? Humans, psychologists included, can never know with any certainty that of which we speak because we can never demonstrate or prove knowledge that is beyond what we are capable of understanding at any given point in time.

All this is not to say that the information or findings which psychologists (or, again, other scientists) propose is useless or meaningless. Rather, it just means that our information or findings are necessarily limited in scope. Psychologists might, for example, be able to hypothesize *how* a person comes to be anxious around dogs, depressed by the death of a loved one, or traumatized by combat. But they cannot say with any certainty *why* people experience anxiety or depression or trauma in the first place or, for that matter, what it definitively *means* that people experience what we call anxiety, depression, or trauma. It is much the same conundrum as saying that while we may identify what caused a person's death, we can never know with any certainty *why* people are given to die (or, for that matter, live) at all. This is the problem psychology and all of science faces. And this problem should matter to the discipline of psychology in particular because these same concerns frequently matter to those people psychologists strive to understand, explain, and help.

STUDYING PSYCHOLOGY

Training in psychology, like all professions, usually starts with remedial instruction. Such education is designed to provide the foundation for that more advanced learning which comes later on. One would not, for example, think of attempting algebra, geometry, calculus, etc. without first understanding the basics of adding, subtracting, and so on. Psychology is no different. At IUPUI, I would study theories of personality, principles of development, research design, statistical analysis, theories of psychotherapy, and the like. And each of these courses would provide valuable information. But the information was usually rudimentary in nature. Students were provided the information and, in many regards, expected to accept it at face value.

I loved studying Freud's psychoanalytic theory, Skinner's theory of behaviorism and operant conditioning, Rogers's theory of humanism and person-centered therapy, etc. And I found all these teachings to be worthwhile. But the more I studied these various perspectives, the more I found myself questioning how these theories came about. What were their origins? They all seemed to be saying something meaningful, to be of value in promoting an understanding of how humans might think, feel, and behave. Still, in other ways, their views seemed limited in scope and (in some regard) mutually exclusive. That is, if you believed one such theory, how were you to make sense out of the others? Surely they couldn't all be right. And none of these or similar theories seem to adequately address the question of human existence in a more global sense.

As my interest in spirituality had progressed, I'd increasingly found myself concerned with this bigger picture. And this, of course, included the question of how the science of psychology meshed with what it meant to be human. Yes, psychological theories and principles were impressive and useful, but how were they relevant to questions about the *meaning of life*? This led me to wonder about where Freud, Skinner, Rogers, and all the other famous writers in psychology had themselves come from. What experiences had shaped their lives? How did they come to postulate their beliefs and develop their theories? And how might their beliefs and theories further one's understanding of their own existence in the world? In search of answers to these questions, I decided to return to the author's original writings.

As the reader may know, these theoreticians were prolific writers. Each had authored many well-respected books over the course of their lifetimes. But as I read through some of their original writings, I came to recognize that, while each wrote eloquently about their theories, none seemed to write about the larger picture. Freud was exquisite in his explanation of innate or biological drives, psychosexual stages of development, conflict and anxiety, defense mechanisms, and so on. B. F. Skinner was equally adept at explaining his theories of learning, operant conditioning, and behavioral modification. And Carl Rogers devoted his entire life to explaining how humans naturally strive toward self-actualization when provided a nurturing social and physical environment. And each believed their theory to best explain the human condition. So too has it been with all the great minds in psychology: Erik Erikson, Carl Jung, Karen Horney, Albert Ellis, Jean Piaget, and others. They all believed in what they were proposing or explaining. But none of them seemed able to recognize (or address) the limits of their vision. And each seemed to avoid the real question of what it meant to be a human being. Try as I might, I could not ignore this latter question and what for me were the very real and meaningful implications of the question. My decision to study psychology was proving rewarding. And I was finally learning to discipline myself such that my grades more accurately reflected my true academic potential. But if I was going to continue studying psychology, I needed to understand how this discipline related to the bigger question of life.

Toward this end, and as a practical exercise in applying my somewhat idiosyncratic views to studying psychology, I decided to approach my research design class differently than most of my peers. A course in research design is typically required by most regionally accredited universities for those seeking a bachelor's degree in psychology. The same would be true for those attending IUPUI. The course is intended to teach one to construct and carry out experiments so as to promote scientific findings that might be useful in understanding human phenomena from a psychological perspective. In research design classes, for example, subjects (as they are called) of experimental study are typically treated as objects to be manipulated in hopes that the researcher might learn some new knowledge or understanding about how the subject functions and how to influence this functioning. Out of ethical concerns, strict limits are usually placed on the use of human subjects for these experiments. Thus, animal subjects are often used as substitutes. Because of certain physiological similarities between the brain functioning of rodents and humans, rats are often the animal of choice.

For the practical, hands-on component of most research design courses, a "rat lab" is therefore utilized. As the name suggests, this lab experience is intended to teach students the principles of behavioral learning or conditioning through observing and training a rat. In my class, students were paired up, with the ultimate goal being to teach or train a caged rat to press a bar in order to access water from a dispensing tube. Rats, like all living things, require water to live. But pressing a metal bar to access water when thirsty is not typical rat behavior. For this experiment, the idea was to teach a rat the novel behavior of pressing a bar in order for water to be dispensed such that the rat would gain satiation. The rat would ultimately get no water if it failed to press the bar and, thus, eventually become dehydrated. So if the rat seemed confused by the task or unsure how to access water reliably, then the researcher would train the rat by rewarding successive approximations of the task. If the rat never demonstrated interest in learning the task of pressing the bar, the student was instructed to keep the rat from receiving any water whatsoever until such time as the rat became desperate enough to explore its environment in search of the triggering mechanism. This last-resort measure was supposed to be "foolproof." And again, all this is intended to show how the rat might *learn* a novel behavior associated with the task of accessing water. It was also intended to teach the researcher an important lesson in *how* to help subjects learn behaviorally.

For me, this approach to the study of behavior seemed out of step with my own values: too detached, too clinical, and too uncaring. Rightly or wrongly, it just seemed cruel, especially the idea of depriving the rat of water in those cases where learning the bar-pressing task proved confusing or difficult. As a result, I decided to take a different approach in working with the rat. With the agreement of my lab partner, I would take full responsibility for getting the rat to press the bar by the end of the semester (so we would achieve a passing grade in the course), but I would make no direct effort to train or manipulate the rat to press the bar for water per se. Instead, I would go to the rat lab every day, take the rat out of its cage, and walk around with it for thirty to forty-five minutes, all the while talking to and interacting with it. I made no attempt to ever deprive the rat of water. Instead, I tried to form what I viewed as a relationship with the rat, to allow the rat to get to know and hopefully trust me. As the semester eventually came to an end, I took the rat to the Skinner box, and with very little provocation, it went straight to the bar and began pressing it. The rat was rewarded accordingly. Maybe I just got lucky. Maybe my rat was special. But correctly or not, this exercise in psychology seemed to further reinforce my belief that being caring, respectful, and collaborative—being human—might achieve just as much (if not more) as being clinical or manipulative. I have continued trying to live this belief in all the clinical work I have pursued throughout my career as a psychologist since that time.

While I was still completing coursework toward my bachelor's degree, I also happened upon a reference to work being done through the psychology department of Duquesne University (Pittsburgh, Pennsylvania). Unlike the natural science approach to psychology taught by IUPUI and most other schools, Duquesne's program emphasized what was called a "human science" approach based upon existential and phenomenological principles. Again, by this time, I had come to believe the psychology instruction I was receiving through IUPUI was meaningful but incomplete. Yes, it was stimulating on one level. I was learning about human development, personality formation, psychopathology, and the rest; I was learning research design and the use of statistical measures necessary for conducting experiments; and I was learning how the natural science approach and its methods of study contributed to overall theory development and practice within the field of psychology. But this approach just seemed deficient; it simply didn't address the essence of what it meant to be human. And again, for one studying psychology and interested in learning more about people, myself included, this latter understanding seemed crucial. After reading about the "human science" approach being taught at Duquesne University, it occurred to me I might not be the only person sharing this concern.

In an effort to learn more about Duquesne's approach, I decided to take a short trip to Pittsburgh and check the program out firsthand. Over a three-day period, I'd visit the Duquesne campus, talk with some of the professors from the psychology department, and sit in on one of their lectures on the "theory of man." I also purchased a copy of Amedeo Giorgi's book *Psychology as a Human Science: A Phenomenologically Based Approach*. And after returning to Indianapolis, I concluded this might be the answer I'd been looking for. With the discovery of this new approach, I could finally contemplate extending my studies beyond those received through IUPUI. Of course, first, I needed to finish up my bachelor's degree.

Toward this end, and prior to graduating from IUPUI, I decided to pursue an independent study project to help me further clarify and integrate my ideas about spirituality and the field of psychology. The title for the thesis would be "For What It's Worth: An Inside Look at Psychological Explanation." And therein, I'd strive to record some of my thoughts and observations about the underlying assumptions for and limitations to psychological thinking. I wasn't trying to be critical of the discipline per se. Rather, I was just trying to explore the possibility that something might exist beyond what was commonly being taught through the standard curriculum of psychology and that this "something" might also be of value when working to help people.

The proposal was accepted by my psychology adviser, who agreed to oversee the project. He also seemed supportive of my efforts. Ultimately, I would be given high marks for its content. Unfortunately, I never really felt that he fully understood or appreciated what I was trying to say. Oh well. It was meaningful to put my own thoughts down on paper, and it allowed me to finish up my degree. A few months later, I would apply for admission to Duquesne's master's degree program.

In retrospect, even though the program had its shortcomings, I would always be grateful for my time at IUPUI. Yes, their teaching did promote a natural science approach to psychology and the study of human behavior and cognitive processes from a quantitative perspective. But while it may have had certain limitations, the instruction would also give me a foundation for all the advanced learning I would receive later on in graduate school. It also motivated me to improve my reading skills and to understand that *reading* the assigned material would not only facilitate my learning but improve my GPA as well. And perhaps most importantly, in a roundabout way, my studies through IUPUI reinforced many of those things I'd previously come to believe while also bolstering my belief in self and God. Upon graduating from IUPUI, I and some forty-nine other students would be accepted into the Duquesne University psychology program as master's level students. Much as I had hoped, this decision would prove another important step along my life's journey.

At the time I enrolled at Duquesne University, its official name was Duquesne University of the Holy Ghost. I would not learn this piece of information or the fact that it was touted as the only "Catholic University in the Spiritan tradition" in the US, until much later on. Still, the information probably wouldn't have mattered to me one way or the other. By that time, I felt strong enough in my own spirituality as to not be threatened by the beliefs or doctrines of others (Catholics included). More importantly, the description and focus of their psychology program seemed to fit perfectly with what I had long been seeking. So Duquesne University it would be. Unfortunately, attending Duquesne also meant moving to Pittsburgh. And for me, this would be a whole new experience.

When I relocated to Pittsburgh in 1982, that once majestic city in western Pennsylvania resting at the confluence of the Allegheny, Monongahela, and Ohio Rivers seemed but a shadow of its former self. I suspect things have improved greatly since the early 1980s. But at the time I was there, the steel mills that for decades had served as the lifeblood for tens of thousands of blue-collar workers and their families had all but disappeared. Overreach by the steelworkers unions, excessive governmental regulations intended to improve air quality and preserve the environment, and the importing of cheaper steel from overseas had pretty much decimated the steel industry in America and, with it, the thousands of middle-class jobs of all those whose very livelihoods had depended on them.

In addition to the loss of steelworker jobs, so too would there be a decay of the many small towns located along the rivers that had once relied almost solely on incomes generated by the mills. Grocers, clothing shop owners, gas station attendants, teachers, and a host of others depended on incomes generated by the steel mills for their own livelihoods. And once the steelworker jobs were lost, so too would many of these individuals board up their shops, homes, office buildings, etc. and move away. If I believed Indianapolis had more poor and disadvantaged people, more crime, more violence, more drugs, and more ethnic disputes than Columbus, Pittsburgh was even worse. Crime seemed to be everywhere. Shootings and killings were an everyday occurrence. Homeless people slept in downtown doorways. And in Pittsburg proper, both the traffic and crowding were almost unbearable.

Northern cities often boast of their diversity and how this yields more tolerance and less prejudice, bigotry, and racism than those down South. But this would not seem further from the truth based upon my experiences in Pittsburgh. Here, entire neighborhoods of ethnic populations existed separate from one another: Jewish, Italian, Polish, Black, Irish. And they'd all carved out their own areas of the city, complete with grocery stores, clothing stores, pharmacies, barbershops, doctor's offices, etc. In some instances, individuals and families reportedly lived their entire lives without ever venturing outside these circumscribed areas. And in addition to their own ethnic pride and cultural differences, these groups often held genuine and deep-seated animosity toward one another. While adults might have *tolerated* their differences, in most instances, they didn't like them. And warring gangs were common among the youth. It was well-known by young people that venturing outside one's own ethnic neighborhood was a risky proposition at best.

When I think of all the ethnic upheaval existing in today's society, all the protesting, rioting, and violence occurring across cities in modern-day America allegedly in the name of what some call confronting economic disparity and systemic racism, I am sometimes reminded of my experiences in Pittsburgh. While most all of us would probably like to see a time when people of different backgrounds, races, religions, and cultures live together in harmony, my time in Pittsburgh left me wondering how this might ever come to pass. Maybe it is as the old Buddhist saying goes, "A ducks legs, though short, cannot be lengthened without discomfort to the duck. A cranes legs, though long, cannot be shortened without discomfort to the crane." Maybe racial and ethnic harmony is possible. Maybe differing groups of people can *learn* to work and live together, even to love one another in due time. But it seems quite unlikely that such a vision will ever come to pass by any one group trying to *coerce* another into relinquishing deeply held values, beliefs, and cultural traditions. To the contrary, self-righteous anger, threats, and intimidation usually begets the same. Thus, the idea of trying to *force* such change seems misguided. *If we truly want the world to be a more accepting and loving place, it seems we'd probably best be served by starting with ourselves, by making ourselves more accepting and loving individuals, not by trying to bully others.* Were it not for the presence and hope offered by Duquesne University and its psychology department, I would have had little reason to ever wind up in Pittsburgh. But Duquesne University and the program were there, and as a result, so was I.

At Duquesne, I'd meet Drs. Bill and Connie Fischer, Rolf von Eckartsberg, Amedio Giorgi, David Smith, Richard Knowles, Edward Murray, and others; these would be my guides through the world of psychology as a "human science." While these professors are probably long since gone, they were the ones who'd introduce me to the writings of such authors as Edmund Husserl, Martin Heidegger, Maurice Merleau-Ponty, Jean-Paul Sartre, Søren Kierkegaard, and others. They would challenge me to think critically and creatively, both about my own existence and about what it meant to be fully human. And they'd encourage me to explore my own personal beliefs, biases, prejudices, and perspectives on the world and how these variables necessarily influence my interactions with others. At Duquesne, I'd come to question long-held assumptions about the so-called natural science of psychology while also learning to approach this discipline from a phenomenological perspective. And finally, I'd be taught to investigate such phenomena as consciousness, mind, language, emotions, values, and culture and how all these decidedly human phenomena both emerged from and contributed to one's daily life and worldly experience.

In addition to my academic instruction on existentialism and the principles of phenomenology, I would also learn to approach psychological research, assessment, and therapy from a whole different perspective. Here, I'd be taught never to view the so-called object of my work as just another research subject or client but as a *person*, unique in every aspect of his or her being. As simple as this might sound, it would prove a significant deviation from what I had been taught at IUPUI or what is frequently taught in other programs. Now rather than having me be a detached, independent observer of quantitatively measurable data, I would be instructed to actively engage with the participants of any research study, assessment, or therapy I was conducting. And I'd be encouraged to have these individuals actively engage with me as well. Here, the emphasis was on being *collaborative* rather than objective, to *dialogue* with the person rather than treat him/her as a patient or a diagnosis. And I was taught to have them be *meaningfully* involved in any psychological endeavor we might jointly choose to pursue. Here, I'd be encouraged to always remember the work I was doing directly affected the life of another human being. To this day, while I might use the words *subject* or *client* when discussing my work in more general terms, being trained to remember the subject or client as a *person* remains an essential focus of my practice.

As a practical example, when conducting research, rather than relying solely on scientific instruments for collecting objective data that might be statistically verified to provide *quantitative* facts, the "human science" program at Duquesne emphasized a *qualitative* approach to research. While still scientifically based, this approach frequently utilized personal diaries, journals, self-report inventories, and interviews as a basis for findings. And such an approach would allow me as a researcher to access valuable information that might otherwise be omitted or not be identified when relying solely on objective measures.

With this approach, I'd also be able to understand *how* any data obtained was actually being perceived or understood by the specific person I was trying to study, *how this particular individual made sense of the data within the context of his or her lived experience*. Yes, documenting the stimuli responsible for a person's fear of elevators might be useful in a general sense. Understanding these triggers might lead one to develop techniques for alleviating some of an individual's anxiety so they can grit their teeth and go on functioning despite their distress. But such information does little to help one understand what the fear of riding in an elevator actually *means* for the person, how the given individual understands this fear, how it impacts his or her daily existence, or what the fear means regarding his or her perception of self. Does the person run from the fear or view it as a challenge to fight against? Does the fear imply a personal defect, weakness, or inadequacy, or does the fear represent an opportunity to grow or become stronger? Does the individual respond to the fear by seeing themselves as a failure or as too fragile to pursue a particular job or career or to initiate a new encounter or relationship? Or does the fear reveal an inner strength that helps the individual pursue those things that might otherwise give his or her life deeper meaning? Helping people means more than simply working to alleviate troublesome symptoms. It means helping people in accordance with where they are in life and in keeping with what matters to them as individuals. It means enabling them to rise up and achieve those things in life that make their particular existence worthwhile. The "human science" approach to research would clearly emphasize that people are more than just subjects in an experiment. It would teach that people are unique in how they make sense of the world, purposeful in their everyday actions, and forever in search of that which makes their lives meaningful.

The human science approach to assessment would embody similar principles. While objective tests such as the MMPI, the Weschler scales, etc. would commonly be used, I was also encouraged to think outside the box when administering such instruments. This would allow me to gain not only objective data but also subjective findings regarding how the client approached the test-taking experience as well. And this kind of information would give me insights into how the individual experienced and moved through life. These findings, in turn, could reveal the *meaning* a person's life experience might hold for him or her. They could disclose one's personal goals and dreams, his or her stresses and struggles, and the strengths and limitations available to the person for attaining goals or confronting obstacles keeping him or her from realizing dreams. And over time, I'd come to realize this information to be crucial when helping a client manage real-life problems or when helping one to strive toward a life perceived as being of value.

As regards sharing findings of any assessment, it too would differ from those taught by most programs. In this regard, psychological reports were intended to be *descriptive* rather than clinical, to show the individual as actively engaged with their world rather than as static objects one might label or objectify. Wherever practical, I'd be encouraged to utilize direct quotes of the person to reveal his or her own unique perspective on life and the struggles associated with living it. Assessment reports were also designed to be written in a language the person could easily read and understand (as opposed to the technical jargon commonly used when speaking with other professionals). And the reports were to include recommendations specifically tailored to help the client with resolving identified problems. Finally, I was taught to always invite the person to both read the final report and to attach an addendum to it citing any findings they believed might be incorrect or invalid or ways they felt the assessment recommendations might prove useful. All these would represent significant deviations from the instruction most psychology programs offered when teaching psychological assessment. But these deviations were all ways of emphasizing respect for the humanness and value of the person being evaluated.

Finally, consistent with the above was Duquesne's "human science" approach to therapeutic intervention. Like most programs, Duquesne emphasized the importance of being authentic and genuinely present in my interactions with clients—as opposed to being distant, detached, or artificial, relying only on theories or techniques learned from books. And of course, I'd be instructed on such skills as active listening, therapeutic reflection, and the like. But my instructors also reminded me over and over that it was the *relationship* that heals, not I—that therapy was to be a collaborative process, wherein I and the client would work jointly to identify both the concerns he or she was struggling to manage and the goals for treatment. I'd also be trained to solicit the client's input on any interventions implemented. And lastly, I would be taught to periodically consult the individual regarding the effectiveness of our work, even to have the client rate the meaningfulness of this work (on a scale of 1 to 10) in terms of its usefulness in helping him or her reach expressed goals. I do not mean to imply that the client was to be solely in charge of the therapeutic process. Clearly, there would be times when, as a psychologist, I might be aware of a problem the individual did not recognize. And certainly, there would be times when I might have ideas for resolving a given concern that the person may not have considered. Over the course of my career, there would even be occasions when I would undertake unilateral actions so as to protect an individual from doing serious harm to self or others. But at Duquesne, I would learn unequivocally that the person I was there to help should always be viewed as the one having the inside track on what might give their life meaning and on what constituted therapeutic success. Again, the "human science" approach schooled me well on the value of actively engaging the person so I might clearly understand their worldly experience and find therapeutic solutions that were both meaningful to the individual and practical within the context of their own lives.

I have now practiced clinical psychology through a variety of hospital, clinic, prison, and private office settings for some forty years. But I have never forgotten the instruction I learned through my experiences at Duquesne University. To this day, these teachings continue to shape my interactions with others, both personally and professionally. And after all my years as a practicing psychologist, I have come to believe that I am at my very best as a clinician when my scientific training is used in service to, rather than instead of, my spiritual values. Said another way, I am best able to help others when I take my ego out of the equation and allow God's spirit to work through me.

Financially, I would again need outside employment in order to remain in school. Therefore, much as was true while attending IUPUI, I'd take a job providing janitorial services (this time for a ServiceMASTER group). Initially, I'd work refinishing floors, cleaning restrooms, vacuuming, and emptying trash cans, etc. for a Mercedes-Daimler dealership near inner-city Pittsburgh. And my meager salary, in conjunction with student loans, would make it possible to buy gas for my beat-up, outdated American Motors car, to pay for my sleeping room, and to keep me from starving while I pursued my studies. Again, this employer seemed to value my work, so I would continue working for him a year or so after I completed my master's degree. And during this latter period, I'd add a local bank to my schedule of buildings to clean. Occasionally, I'd even take on a "special assignment" (if a particular customer was dissatisfied with another janitor's work or if the company was short-staffed).

My sleeping room was a twelve-by-fourteen-foot room located on the main floor of a two-story home owned by an aging couple. Though they seemed to have been married to each other for many years and to be committed to their marriage, they were also given to bouts of screaming at each other and calling each other the foulest of names. Shortly after moving in, I happened to meet their daughter and came to learn that both of her parents had long histories of alcoholism. This provided me with some context for their behavior. Still, I wondered how any two people could ever live together under the same roof with so much animosity and while treating each other so badly.

I also remember how the home had plumbing problems and that toilet backups were an all-too-common occurrence, thus creating quite a stench about once a month. Renting a room in such an environment while pursuing my master's degree would make studying almost impossible. So I quickly learned to hang out at the campus library or in the university commons. In retrospect, I will say the couple generally treated me well, although I was still glad when my time at Duquesne was over, and I was able to increase my work schedule such that I could afford to move out.

At Duquesne University, I also met my dear friend Tony Salinski. Much like me, Tony was somewhat older than the other students in our program. We were both in our thirties and had some life experience behind us—for better or for worse. We had known some of life's struggles and were looking to better understand both ourselves and our place in the world. Tony had also played drums in a rock-and-roll band (along with his brother) during his younger years, and his interest in music gave us something else in common. We would support each other throughout the twelve months of our master's program. And where some of the younger students often struggled to understand the teachings of Duquesne's existential phenomenological curriculum, Tony and I could never seem to get enough. This shared zeal created many an opportunity to discuss our assignments and share personal insights, oftentimes following class lectures and over a beer in the local pub. While I'd lose track of Tony after he and I had both moved away from Pittsburgh, some years later, we'd reconnect, and I'd learn he had finished up his doctorate degree and was teaching at a small college in northeastern Ohio. I will forever be grateful for his friendship.

While completing my master's work, I also met one Sharon W. Ms. W was a twice-divorced mother of three (and foster mother of three), struggling to raise the children in her care and manage her homelife while also completing her graduate studies through Duquesne. On balance, she probably did a pretty fair job handling everything and far better than I could have. Still, she was given to intermittent episodes of emotional outbursts. Eventually, I'd come to see these outbursts as more character-based than situational. Unfortunately, by the time I realized this, I had already made a decision to date Ms. W.

At the time, I had not dated anyone for some or eight years, not since my relationship with Teresa. The divorce had just been so painful that I was reluctant to risk experiencing such pain again. Moreover, I didn't want to repeat the mistakes leading to my divorce so I might one day have a more lasting relationship. Thus, I felt I needed to better understand myself as an individual and figure out my own contributions to the marital failure. But while I believed I'd made some progress on this latter front, relationships still involve two people. Sharon and I would date for the next six years before I finally realized that, even with my improved understanding of self, this relationship was not a good match.

Again, I guess some lessons are just learned more slowly than others, especially when it concerns me and intimate relationships. In retrospect, being indecisive and failing to act promptly has probably caused me a fair amount of discomfort throughout my life. I'm sure it's cost me some opportunities that others would not have missed out on. Waiting meant I would never have children of my own, for example. And I am certain I could have achieved greater success in my professional career, generated more income, and most probably have built a better retirement plan for myself had I not moved so slowly on some of the career options that came my way. On the other hand, my desire for a life of peace, for living life mindfully, and for moving more slowly has also helped me avoid some of the mistakes others all too often make. For example, even though some might have felt I was missing out on all the fun, I was pretty much able to stay away from the alcohol and drug problems of some of my peers.

Truth be told, I probably wasn't mature enough to have been a good father at that time in life when many people become parents. For me, having children at a young age would likely have been harmful to all concerned. Likewise, working long hours, making a bunch of money, and/or shortchanging my family had just never seemed a high priority for me. Over time, I'd get better at learning from the teachers and mentors who came my way. I would learn to listen closely to their wisdom and to incorporate it into my life. And I would work diligently to live a life more in keeping with my own spirit and that of my Higher Power. And all this would speed up my decision-making process. But at the time, while I eventually recognized the need for calling it quits, all my indecision and moving slowly probably resulted in my staying in a relationship with Ms. W far longer than I should have. And while I have often considered the decision to get out of this "situation" as yet another example of my having "dodged a bullet," because of this relationship, I'd end up remaining in the Pittsburgh area much longer than might otherwise have been the case.

After graduating from my master's program, Tony Salinski, Sharon W, and I had all applied for one of the limited positions available in the Duquesne University doctoral program. But while both Tony and Sharon were admitted, I was not. Consequently, as noted above, I increased my working schedule with the ServiceMASTER Company for another year. I also began teaching part-time with the behavioral health department of the Allegheny County Community College (of Pittsburgh).

With the passage of time, and especially as a result of the work I'd done at IUPUI and Duquesne, my struggles with depression had become a distant memory. I had also gained enough confidence in myself as a psychology practitioner to try my hand at clinical work. So about a year or so after completing my master's work, and while still living in Pittsburgh, I took a position as an outpatient counselor for the Citizens Addiction Rehabilitation and Education (CARE) Center of Washington, Pennsylvania (a small community some thirty minutes south of Pittsburgh).

I'd take this job for several reasons. First, at the time, federal funding for the war on drugs had become abundant for substance abuse treatment centers, and both inpatient and outpatient programs were popping up everywhere. Many such jobs were available. Then there was the fact that it was one of the few positions for which I was qualified that was not in a community mental health center. I had minimal clinical experience after completing my master's degree, but word had long been out about the horrors of community mental health centers overworking master's level clinicians while giving them minimal pay. Accordingly, I knew enough to avoid such facilities. Finally, I'd had witnessed my brother Dave's struggles with alcoholism and the horrible toll it had taken on his life and that of our family. The possibility of helping others to avoid such a fate seemed promising. Little could I have known at the time how working for the CARE Center might prove to be another important step along my own life's journey.

From the lying mirror to the movement of stars,
Everybody's looking for who they are.
Those who know don't have the words to tell,
And the ones with the words don't know too well.
Could be the famine. Could be the feast.
Could be the pusher. Could be the priest.
Always ourselves we love the least.
That's the burden of the angel beast.
—B. Cockburn

From "Love Loves You Too," words and music by Bruce Cockburn, 1993, Published through True North Records, 23 Griffin Street, Watertown, Ontario.

SUBSTANCE-USE COUNSELING

CHEMICAL DEPENDENCY, IN ITS VARIOUS FORMS, IS a problem that has long plagued American society. Every year, alcoholism and addiction claim the lives of countless individuals involved in auto wrecks, accidental overdoses, violent altercations, and drug deals gone bad. Still others suffer from substance-use-related illnesses and/or the downward spiral of isolation and despair that all too often engulfs not only the alcoholic or addict but loved ones as well. In so many ways, chemical dependency is a cancer that robs everyone it touches of any hope for a brighter future.

In the mental health literature, alcoholism and other drug addictions are collectively referred to as substance- or chemical-use disorders. While the diagnostic symptoms for these syndromes have changed slightly over the years (as our culture and scientific research has evolved), common symptoms can include a pattern of increased use of the mood-altering substance, increased tolerance, use of the substance in greater amounts or frequencies than was intended, and continued use of the substance despite related legal, work, school, health, financial, and/or relationship problems. Other symptoms may include unsuccessful attempts to abstain from using the substance and the experience of withdrawal symptoms when the substance is no longer available. Not all these symptoms need to be present for alcoholism or addiction to be diagnosed as not all cases of alcoholism or addiction manifest the same severity of problems. Some alcoholics or addicts may dress in ragged clothes, be homeless, live in crack houses, etc. Others may work with some regularity and *appear* quite functional (at least for a while). Occasionally, one will meet an alcoholic or addict who is a business executive, physician, lawyer, or even a psychologist. Moreover, distinctions can be made between substance-use, abuse, and dependency. Still, in one fashion or another, the symptom patterns outlined above are what one generally sees when working with a person whose life is being trashed by alcoholism or drug addiction.

I'd work at the CARE Center for the next three or so years, and from the onset, I'd find the job a good match. The spiritual component of twelve-step recovery seemed a perfect fit with many of my own values and beliefs. Moreover, I'd find slogans such as "One Day at a Time," "Let Go, Let God," and "Progress, Not Perfection" (to name but a few) to be inspiring.

Because of my limited experience in working with substance-abusing clients, I would initially need to be supervised by a clinician previously certified through the state as a substance-use treatment specialist. This experience would provide my formal education on the dynamics of alcoholism, addiction, and recovery. It also introduced me to twelve-step support groups such as Alcoholics and Narcotics Anonymous (AA/NA) and helped me hone my overall clinical skills as well.

One of the first things I remember learning while working for the CARE Center was how *denial* tends to be a defining characteristic of chemical dependency. This may sound like an oversimplification, but in many respects, denial is often present for the alcoholic or addict. Sometimes it appears as intellectualization as when a person says they have to drink to be able to sleep or that they need to use drugs to deal with pain. On the surface, the statement may make sense. Alcohol can sometimes facilitate sleep, and certain drugs can sometimes alleviate pain. Nevertheless, many times, the coexisting problems (insomnia, pain, etc.) are as much a consequence of the substance-use problem as they are viable explanations for it. And in many instances, these other concerns may diminish or resolve themselves altogether once the individual stops using the addictive substances.

Denial can also show up as rationalization as when the person says they can't be an alcoholic or addict because they don't drink as much as their friends do or because they aren't homeless or because they don't "shoot" drugs. Again, to the alcoholic or addict, this might make rational sense. But when substance-use problems are truly present, the destructive consequences accompanying one's use are usually quite apparent to even the casual observer. And those closest to the alcoholic/addict almost always recognize the damage the substance-use is causing their loved one and the absurdity of the claim. So in one form or another, denial (or self-deception, if you will) is often present. Everybody else in one's world, one's spouse, parents, children, coworkers, employers, etc. might be aware the person has an alcohol or drug problem, while the alcoholic or addict continues to insist that alcohol or drug use is *not* the issue at hand.

Of course, denial or self-deception can arise for many reasons. In some cases, the individual might be caught in a pattern of oppositional defiance, as when a discussion turns to drinking or drug use, and one simply argues, "No one can tell me what to do" or "I have the right to drink or smoke dope if I want." These statements may be well and true, but this doesn't mean the substance use is necessarily good for the person or that the harmful consequences of the use aren't real and destructive. Other times, denial arises due to feelings of guilt or shame or simply out of not wanting to face the harm they know their substance use has caused themselves and/or others. Still, other times, the person may be in denial because they fear that admitting their problem means admitting their life has gotten out of control. AA and NA programs do emphasize the importance of an alcoholic or addict admitting they are powerless over alcohol/drugs in order to achieve recovery. But this does not mean the person is powerless over life. And it certainly does not mean they are powerless over their recovery. Finally, others might deceive themselves or deny their problem out of a simple lack of insight, as when they are just so impaired their brain has trouble recognizing the extent of the damage the substance use is causing.

On some occasions, denial can even be supported, if not encouraged, by friends or loved ones who unsuspectingly (or with the best of intentions) collude with the substance user in their self-deception. Such codependent behavior may be the result of one trying to protect the alcoholic/addict out of sympathy, shame, or even fear. But whatever the circumstance, in order to help an alcoholic or addict address their problem and get into recovery, I'd eventually discover it essential to acknowledge when and where denial was present. Again, Duquesne's teachings had always emphasized the importance of working with a client in terms of how he or she experienced his or her own reality. So addressing any denial would go hand in hand with learning how the individual viewed any existing problem: as whether or not a person him/herself believed a problem existed would be crucial to facilitating any change. Accordingly, all this would usually be done as part of a screening process and while determining an individual's need for treatment.

With guidance and experience, I'd also learn that helping a client face their denial might best be achieved by encouraging the individual to explore his or her pattern of substance use, the consequences therefrom, and what if anything he or she might like to change regarding the impact substance use was having on his or her life. Accordingly, I'd be trained to have the client write down how long he or she had been using the substance, how much was typically used, how often the substance was used, and how the amounts or frequencies of use may have increased over time. Next, I'd be taught to have the individual identify specific consequences of this use and how his or her substance use had affected work performance or attendance, relationships, his or her health, academic achievement, his or her financial situation, legal standing, etc. If the person truly had a substance-use problem, it would invariably show up in one of these areas. On the other hand, if the person's substance use had not increased appreciably over time or had not detrimentally affected his or her life, then it might be possible the person either didn't have a problem or that the problem didn't rise to a level necessitating treatment.

With the client's *self-evaluation* complete, I could then invite him or her to explore how any perception of the problem compared with that of others. Sometimes I'd find the real problem to be in the perception of whoever else had been complaining about their loved one's substance use. This might be true when prior life experiences had left the other person believing that even the smallest amounts of chemical use was a problem. One who grew up in a household where substance use was particularly destructive, for example, might be hypersensitive to *any* use of alcohol, pills, marijuana, etc. by another. On the other hand, if the majority of those closest to the person (partner, children, employer, parents, etc.) believed the substance use to be problematic, then it would usually be difficult to ignore the apparent truth of those combined observations. Whatever the case, as a coworker of mine once suggested, "an addict or alcoholic can lie to others about their situation, and they may be able to lie to themselves, but they can never lie to the disease."

If a substance-use problem actually exists (much like hypertension, diabetes, heart disease, etc.), it will not simply go away by denying or minimizing its presence. It will eventually get worse and make itself known.

Once the client and I had reached some agreement on the extent to which substance use might be a problem, we could then begin discussing what, if anything, the client wanted to change so as to resolve related concerns. If the client expressed ambivalence about making change, I might simply outline various treatment options for bringing about change at such time as the ambivalence was resolved or change *was* desired. If the client clearly didn't want to change, then it might still prove helpful to inform the client of my observations and any concerns I held for what could happen at some future date if the client didn't seek change (e.g., loss of a relationship, loss of employment, money problems, legal problems, health problems, etc.). *Above all else, as a clinician, working with alcoholics and addicts would reinforce two therapeutic principles: first, that lasting recovery always required change, and second, that it was the client who was in charge of his or her life, not I.*

As regards treatment proper, over time, I'd learn that such options could range from no treatment to twelve-step attendance alone to outpatient counseling plus twelve-step attendance to inpatient detoxification for those at risk of a medical emergency should they discontinue alcohol or drug use on their own. Treatment options might also include twelve-week intensive outpatient programs (where the client attends four hours a day, four or five days a week—usually in the evening, after work), thirty-day inpatient rehabilitation programs, or even longer-term inpatient treatment. The more serious and disruptive the client's substance-use problem was, and the less support the individual had for his or her recovery efforts in their home environment, the more extensive the treatment option might need to be for the person to achieve the desired or optimal recovery. Mild heart problems may be treatable with medication, exercise, and diet change. More severe heart problems may require open-heart surgery. So too would it be with chemical dependency. For recovery to have the best chance of succeeding, receiving the appropriate level of care would be crucial. But again, even if the client chose not to pursue change or treatment at a given point in time, providing information about the various treatment options available could still serve to guide the client in making a mindful choice for help later on.

When the risk of a medical emergency was present, of course, hospital detoxification would usually be encouraged so as to manage withdrawal symptoms and assure the availability of appropriate care. Detoxification, the process of helping a client to safely achieve abstinence, protects the client from organ failure or other medical complications arising with substance withdrawal. It also reduces physiological cravings and helps the individual's brain become free of the contaminating effects of the addictive substance. This, in turn, gives the person greater access to his or her full repertoire of reasoning abilities and coping skills and increasing the chances for sustained recovery.

Some clinicians, and some recovery programs, might take issue with the importance of promoting total abstinence. Some emphasize an approach designed to teach "controlled" drinking or drug use. But this latter approach is not the approach in which I would be trained, nor is it the one I believe to be best supported by clinical research.

In conjunction with detoxification, I'd also find it useful to have the person screened for any coexisting psychiatric symptoms. Sometimes, symptoms of depression, anxiety, even psychosis would be identified during the detoxification process. And while these symptoms might disappear once the detox was completed, on those occasions when the psychiatric symptoms would persist, it would usually be recommended to treat these comorbid condition simultaneously with the substance-use problem.

Once the screening process and detox (when necessary) were complete, I could fine-tune the assessment and establish a plan for those psychological and emotional interventions needed to support a successful recovery. While treatment might vary slightly between inpatient and outpatient settings, it would usually begin by educating the client on patterns common to the progression of the "disease" and practical strategies for maintaining abstinence. Once this was accomplished, I could begin helping the client restore self-esteem and develop those life skills necessary for addressing such areas as stress management, conflict resolution, assertiveness, anger management, etc. In many cases, building life skills would also include bolstering the person's communication and relationship skills as well. And this would frequently mean including spouses and/or family members in the rehabilitation process. As treatment progressed, therapeutic interventions could also be introduced to address any unresolved mental health concerns that threatened the person's recovery (e.g. histories of abuse/trauma, depression, anxiety, family of origin issues, personality struggles, etc.). Collectively, all these efforts might be seen as providing the tools needed for one to manage life's day-to-day challenges chemically free while establishing a foundation upon which lasting recovery could be built. Then upon nearing the completion of treatment, the individual would typically be educated on strategies for relapse prevention and encouraged to set up an aftercare plan. Usually, this phase of treatment included reinforcing the benefits of attending twelve-step support groups (Alcoholics Anonymous, Narcotics Anonymous, etc.) and scheduling the individual into an aftercare program.

All too often, years of coping with life by using mood-altering substances had left the alcoholic or addict trapped in a world bereft of meaning. Accordingly, as I'd learn, effective treatment usually meant more than just helping one become substance-free. It also necessitated helping the person put his or her world back together so as to again discover meaning in something greater than mood-altering substances or the individual's own ego. The emphasis on finding meaning through spirituality, reestablishing relationships, and becoming part of a community is what would make involvement with twelve-step groups so important to the recovery process. As you may surmise, to this day, I dearly love working with recovering people and witnessing what can only be described as the wondrous *miracle* that occurs when an alcoholic or addict succeeds in turning his or her life around and commits to achieving a life or recovery.

In addition to teaching me how to understand and help alcoholics and addicts (and their loved ones), working at the CARE Center also provided my first exposure to working with so-called criminal justice clients. In many ways, these clients would differ from people in the society at large, but early on, I'd struggle with acknowledging the distinctions. To me, people were people. We all have value, and I didn't want to be seen as discriminating against others. Still, as a drug and alcohol counselor, I'd soon realize that accurate identification of existing differences was crucial to devising treatment plans that worked for individuals having different problems. Oranges and apples, for example, may be different fruits, but acknowledging their differences doesn't require designating one as being better or worse than the other. Rather, identifying their differences is what actually distinguishes them from each other and gives each its own special identity. The same could be said of the criminal justice clients I'd seek to help. To effectively help these particular individuals with altering long-standing attitudes and behavior patterns responsible for undermining their relationships with others and resulting in their incarceration, I'd need to learn how to acknowledge and accept those differences responsible for such problems.

Toward this end, I'd be assigned to work with those alcoholics and addicts incarcerated at either the local county jail or those placed on probation/parole and released to live in the surrounding area. And while it would not always be true, I'd soon learn that many of these individuals had grown up amid poverty and come from violence-prone environments. During their developmental years, they may have received inadequate food and nutrition, lacked opportunities for education and learning, and/or had unstable role models. They may have been poorly supervised or inconsistently disciplined, had a punitive or authoritarian parent, and even been victims of abuse.

From an early age, they may also have developed problems with impulse control, with learning from the consequences of their behavior, and with acquiring effective skills for managing frustration and anger. Then by the time they became teenagers, they frequently demonstrated deficiencies in social functioning and struggled to form meaningful interpersonal relationships or healthy social support systems. And as a result of all this, they oftentimes had developed problems trusting others, while also lacking empathy for the pain and suffering their actions sometimes caused others. Many times, these individuals learned to approach the world with a "you gotta get them before they get you" attitude. This, in turn, would lead to their engaging in what's called antisocial behavior: behavior deemed outside of acceptable social norms and that, in many regards, ended up in their being incarcerated. Unfortunately, being sent to jail usually created additional problems as being jailed or imprisoned would frequently expose the individual to more maltreatment and victimization.

Needless to say, working with such individuals could be difficult in its own right as helping those with pronounced patterns of dysfunctional behavior to make change and learn to live within the norms of society can itself be challenging. Unfortunately, the incarcerated clients with whom I worked also had confounding substance-use problems, thus leaving them with two issues needing to be addressed for a successful transition back into society.

For me to effectively help these individuals, I'd first need to realize that their criminal behavior was not necessarily the cause of their substance-use problems, any more than their substance use was the cause of their criminal behavior. Yes, these conditions might have been coexisting, but correlation did not mean causation. Many criminal justice clients never abuse alcohol or drugs, and many alcoholics and addicts never engage in criminal behavior. Still, it is true that people who feel isolated or have trouble fitting in with society and who resort to criminal behavior oftentimes turn to alcohol and drugs as a way of coping with their social isolation and deviant behavior. Likewise, people who become trapped in a cycle of addiction frequently engage in criminal behavior as a way of helping them to either cope with or pay for their substance-use problems. So given that many jail and prison inmates also struggle with substance use, for me to help these individuals successfully return to society would mean helping them learn more effective ways of dealing with *both* those problematic behavioral patterns *and* their addictions.

This brings me to another important lesson. If I was going to be successful in truly helping a criminally inclined addict or alcoholic, I needed to learn not to participate in excusing him or her from the criminal behavior leading to incarceration. Doing this would prove just as unproductive as excusing the person from assuming responsibility for his or her substance-use recovery. Regrettably, when first assigned to working with addicted inmates, I'd make the mistake of recommending the judge award early release for inmates who agreed to enter inpatient addiction treatment. This seemed the compassionate thing to do. After all, I believed the individual shouldn't be "punished" for committing a crime while having a substance-use problem. Unfortunately, I quickly learned that inmates who were allowed to avoid accountability for the crime they had committed all too often returned to their life of crime. As was once wisely written, "Mistakes once made tend to be repeated until the lesson is learned." Moreover, excusing the inmate by helping him or her gain early release from jail seldom resulted in their following through with substance-use treatment and recovery. Because even if they had initially agreed to go to rehab, in many instances, at the earliest opportunity, the inmate simply took advantage of being released from the confinement of jail to promptly elope from the less-secure setting of the treatment program. Now they'd succeeded not only in avoiding any accountability for addressing their criminal behavior but for assuming responsibility to address their addiction as well. And again, this typically resulted in the individual returning to those same behaviors that had gotten them into trouble to start with.

As a result of these experiences, I came to realize that those engaging in criminal behavior were most successful with staying out of jail upon release when they were held accountable for and allowed to learn from those behaviors leading to their incarceration. Of course, as suggested earlier, this applies to alcoholics and addicts as well as recovery from substance dependence always requires change. Again, alcoholics and addicts are most successful with recovery when they acknowledge their addictions and take responsibility for their recovery process.

So whether one is speaking of criminal behavior or substance abuse, people who fail to take charge of their lives, who fail to learn from their mistakes or resist change, tend to repeat their actions.

This also explains why, in my estimation, recent attempts of so-called progressive politicians to address criminal behavior by defunding the police and releasing all but the most serious offenders upon arrest are doomed to fail. Clearly, we all make mistakes. And there are times when each of us needs forgiveness. None of us want to be defined by our worst possible moments. Everyone benefits from the understanding, empathy, and support of others. *But ignoring or minimizing long-standing patterns of dysfunctional behavior that harm one's self or victimizes others will not bring about meaningful or lasting change. It only perpetuates the problem.* And in a similar vein, this is also why government efforts to address the addiction epidemic that has long plagued America by providing addicts with the means to use drugs or creating safe havens for drug users will not reduce the problem. What those trapped in a vicious cycle of substance dependence, as well as criminal behavior, need most is help acknowledging their self-defeating behavior so they might undertake effective change and establish a more productive and meaningful life. And to bring this about, I believe, requires the multipronged approach of (1) limiting access to substances, (2) preventive education, (3) treatment/rehabilitation for the alcoholic/addict/criminal, *and* (4) incarceration for those crimes committed against society. Neglecting any of these components will likely prove of only limited value, thereby allowing the problems (and the individual suffering) to persist.

After three years of supervised experience working for the CARE Center, I sat for and passed the exam leading to my credential as a Pennsylvania-certified alcohol and drug addiction counselor. Successfully passing this test meant both presenting a case study of an actual client's struggle with substance dependence and the client's assessment and treatment plan we had devised and implemented. It also meant passing an oral exam revealing my knowledge of the "disease" of chemical dependency; comorbid conditions; the process of assessment, treatment, and recovery; and the principles of relapse and relapse prevention. The case study and oral exam would be overseen by a three-person panel of experienced and similarly credentialed clinicians.

Upon successful completion of this evaluation process and being certified, I would no longer require formal supervision in order to be a substance-use treatment specialist. Accordingly, after receiving my certification, I began exploring other options for continuing my work with substance-using clients and expanding my clinical experience. Having my master's degree in psychology and my drug/alcohol certification would eventually lead to my being hired as the psychology practitioner for the inpatient chemical dependency rehabilitation unit of the Saint Francis Medical Center (SFMC) in downtown Pittsburgh.

Much as had been true for addictions specialists, unlicensed master's level psychology practitioners in the Commonwealth of Pennsylvania were also required to be supervised by one fully licensed (in this case doctoral-trained) psychologist. And this requirement would lead to my meeting Dr. Bill Hawthorne, Chief of Psychology at Saint Francis. He was a seasoned psychologist with excellent clinical skills, who would agree to provide my supervision as a psychology practitioner. Not only would Dr. Hawthorne be instrumental in my continued development as a psychology clinician, a few years later, his encouragement and support would be crucial to my decision to pursue doctoral training and my career as a licensed psychologist proper.

Working at Saint Francis Medical Center would be my first experience working as part of an interdisciplinary treatment team. And it would also introduce me to my unit supervisor, Kathy Coleman. By the early 1980s, women supervisors had become commonplace—especially in medical and health-care settings. But *good* supervisors, be they men or women, were still a hit-or-miss proposition (much as is sometimes true today). Ms. Coleman would prove to be one of the best supervisors I would ever have. Most supervisors, most leaders of any kind for that matter, probably want the respect of their subordinates. But Ms. Coleman carried herself with respect. She was the consummate professional. And as a result of her integrity, her clinical expertise, her empathy for others, her supervisory style, and her superior communication and problem-solving skills, no one working on the unit ever questioned who was in charge.

Not only would I consider Kathy Coleman one of the best supervisors I'd ever have, but I'd also come to experience her as one of the finest people I'd ever know. Certainly, she helped me advance my knowledge of the addiction process and its recovery. But she also helped me expand my overall clinical expertise, my listening skills, and my communication skills. And all this would bolster my self-confidence as well. Under her guidance, I truly believe I became both a better addictions counselor and mental health practitioner and a better person.

Kathy would also encourage me to become affiliated with the Pennsylvania Office for Drug and Alcohol Programs (ODAP) as a statewide trainer of other clinicians. This, in turn, would allow me to travel throughout the Commonwealth of Pennsylvania providing one- and two-day educational seminars on various aspects of addiction assessment and treatment to other addictions and mental health professionals. It also helped me establish an ever-growing support network of other healthcare practitioners.

Saint Francis was located near downtown Pittsburgh, so many of the alcoholics and addicts we admitted came from inner-city households. And this experience would provide my introduction to working with such a population. Again, I had been born and raised in rural America. So my exposure to the struggles of people growing up in inner-city environments had been limited. But while there remain many similarities in the substance-use and mental health concerns found among people living in both rural and urban settings, there can also be some very real differences.

At Saint Francis, the inner-city clients we served typically came from crime-ridden neighborhoods fraught with poverty, mental illness, substance dependence, abuse, and violence. Again, although these concerns are sometimes present for clients living in more rural settings, they seemed particularly common for those substance-using persons hailing from Pittsburgh's inner city. And as might be expected, living in such conditions often yielded individuals having multiple diagnoses. Clinicians typically refer to the presence of such coexisting problems as comorbid conditions; in our case, wherein both mental health *and* substance-use diagnoses existed simultaneously. So given my background in psychology, as well as my more recent experience in the field of addictions, working at Saint Francis would give me the opportunity to enhance my expertise working with these "dually diagnosed" clients.

Most of us can assume that for a child to grow up and become a healthy, socially well-adjusted adult, he or she needs to come from a reasonably stable, nurturing, and caring household. Certainly, as mentioned previously, children need a viable social and cultural environment as well. But psychologists have long known that the most important factor in any child's development is the quality of parenting and the stability of the family system in which the child is raised. Children born of parents who themselves struggle with intellectual disabilities, mental illness, and substance abuse all too often suffer the consequences.

Children of parents who are not gainfully employed or who cannot provide adequate nourishment, health care, or guidance on healthy lifestyle practices are also at a real disadvantage when it comes to becoming healthy adults. And of course, this is also true for those growing up with parenting figures who cannot or do not adequately protect them from the dangers prevalent in the community at large. Likewise, children who do not receive adequate support for attending school and developing their academic aptitudes, who do not have healthy role models demonstrating the benefits of striving to be productive and to earn a living, and who are not given encouragement to avoid the ravages of substance abuse and criminal behavior are also less likely to flourish in a modern-day society. On the contrary, these children often end up being physically, emotionally, or sexually abused, dropping out of school, and/or getting involved with gangs. They are also vulnerable to misusing alcohol and drugs, getting arrested, being incarcerated, and becoming victims of crime themselves. Finally, such children are increasingly likely to struggle with despair, hopelessness, trauma, unreasonable fears, and all the many other mental health concerns that are all too prevalent in our world today. However unfortunate, the truth is that many of the problems common in our society today, whether in rural or urban settings, are directly related to the disadvantaged and dysfunctional home environments in which children grow up. And many of the clients admitted to Saint Francis would come from such households.

Now I understand how social activists might want to attribute many of the problems outlined above to long-standing societal or cultural problems. Others might attribute these problems to the perceived breakdown of values our society seems to have fostered over the past several decades and to the choices arising therefrom. And I also understand how people can get caught up in blaming the world for such problems. For the longest time, I too blamed society while growing up poor and amid a broken family in my hometown. We'd probably all agree there are many things society could do differently to improve the lives of the less fortunate. And striving to solve these larger social problems in hopes of one day bringing about more global change can be a noble undertaking. But this is not me. As an addictions treatment specialist (and psychologist), my focus has always been on helping people resolve the day-to-day problems of life by working with individuals and family systems directly to alleviate the pain and suffering individuals experience in the here and now. So this would be my role as part of the adult inpatient rehabilitation team at Saint Francis.

Accordingly, I soon learned that treating individuals having dual diagnoses had a good deal in common with treating alcoholics and addicts in general and with treating criminal justice clients having substance-use problems in particular. The starting point would always be screening one's appropriateness for care and stabilizing any acute symptoms or life-threatening conditions. For those who were incarcerated, this had usually been handled by the warden and medical personnel serving the jail and prior to my ever meeting with the inmate. For those I'd see at Saint Francis, this would usually be dealt with by the admissions unit and hospital doctors. This process would reduce the chances of withdrawal-related medical complications while assisting the client with achieving abstinence from alcohol/drugs (detox). In the case of individuals with comorbid concerns, however, this step provided the added benefit of facilitating the identification of any acute psychiatric symptoms and of protecting an individual from tendencies toward harming self or others. It would also help the medical staff with initiating any pharmacological intervention for such symptoms. For all these reasons, while there might be occasions whereupon such efforts might be undertaken on an outpatient basis, hospitalization on the detox unit would frequently represent the option of choice.

Whether or not hospital detox was required, once acute symptoms were stable and there was no longer any immediate threat of harm to self or others, I and the team could complete the assessment process and initiate treatment. As already noted, effective treatment outcomes invariably depend on accurate assessment of the problem(s) one is hoping to treat. And in keeping with my earlier instruction, meaningful assessment always included identifying the client's view of their problem and what, if anything, he/she wanted to change. Again, this is in keeping with the philosophy that the client is in charge of his or her life and that I am only there to help the client get to where he/she wanted to go.

From my training through the CARE Center, I'd also learned that clients can be ambivalent about change or in denial of having a problem, and this might prove true whether the problem was of a substance-use or mental health nature. Consequently, sometimes assessment would necessitate my helping the client resolve this ambivalence by exploring the persisting nature of problems or symptoms attributable to their substance-use or mental health syndrome. On many occasions, resolving the ambivalence would allow the client to finally acknowledge what they may had long been seeking to ignore or avoid. However, when such efforts didn't work, when the client didn't see substance-use or mental health symptoms as problematic or did not want to change, then there would typically be limits to what might be done to promote more lasting recovery. Of course, in some cases, a person might have been court-ordered into treatment, even court-mandated to take psychotropic medications. But such coercion seldom proved to have any lasting results as coercion never could guarantee *willing* participation in longer-term or more meaningful treatment—especially once the individual had been discharged from the program.

Again, in assessing those having comorbid concerns, I'd also learn that it was not uncommon for those in the midst of full-blown alcoholism to appear depressed. Alcohol is, after all, a depressant drug. Likewise, I'd learn that in some instances, paranoia, even hallucinations, might accompany certain types of substance abuse and/or withdrawal therefrom. By contrast, there'd also be times when one having bipolar disorder or schizophrenia would self-medicate with psychoactive substances. So while it might not be unusual for mental health and substance-use symptoms to appear simultaneously, on many occasions, one or the other of these problems might clear up once effective treatment of the primary syndrome had been initiated. In other words, the fact that one originally presented with comorbid symptoms (e.g., alcoholism and depression, amphetamine use and psychosis) did not necessarily mean that dual diagnoses were warranted. Sorting out whether the coexisting symptoms first observed actually represented separate and diagnosable comorbid conditions or simply confounding features of a primary substance-use or mental health concern would be essential to completing effective assessment and directing subsequent treatment as making an accurate diagnosis would prevent me from mistakenly encouraging treatment for an *apparent* problem that might, in fact, not require treatment at all.

Once a client's problems had been effectively identified and he/she expressed a desire for change, then the treatment plan proper could be established. Because different clients have different needs and respond differently to different treatment strategies (as well as different medications), the specific interventions implemented would need to be individualized. This meant treatment options, including the duration of hospitalization, kinds of therapy, types of skill-building exercises, medications, etc., might vary depending on the particular needs of the client and the goals the client and treatment team wished to achieve. Finally, the best way to determine if the treatment was on track, as well as increase the chances a client would follow through with any treatment strategies recommended, was to thoroughly explain the available treatment options and reach a mutual agreement on the implementation of any final plan. Again, all this was in keeping with Duquesne's idea of collaborating with the client.

As previously suggested, in situations where both a substance dependence *and* mental health problem were present, most clinicians would approach treatment by addressing each of the conditions simultaneously. Approaching comorbid concerns jointly would reduce the chances that a flare-up of either problem would undermine effective treatment of the other. A cocaine addict, for example, might relapse into cocaine use if coexisting bipolar symptoms were poorly managed, just as one's bipolar symptoms would more likely flare up if the client relapsed into cocaine use. Similarly, an alcoholic with depression would be more likely to experience increased depressive symptoms if he or she relapsed into alcohol use and vice versa.

I've already noted how one of the more important lessons I learned from treating those with substance dependence problems was the necessity for a client to take responsibility for his or her recovery. This would prove true for individuals with mental health problems as well. While practically all treatment plans include components designed to offer symptom relief, education, skill building, promotion of insight, etc., neither substance-use treatment specialists nor psychologists are equipped with magic wands. We are not able to miraculously make problems disappear. And it is the exception rather than the rule that such problems just go away on their own. *One of the cold hard truths about substance-use recovery, as well as effective mental health therapy, is that it doesn't just happen to you. Effective recovery, like effective therapy, requires the client's active participation. And again, active participation means change.*

In the Alcoholics Anonymous program, it is often said that "if you always do what you always did, you'll always get what you always got." An alcoholic or addict cannot break free from the ravages of addiction if he or she does not change those behaviors that previously led to or sustained the addiction. Hanging out with drinking buddies or friends who use drugs, frequenting bars or crack houses, abusing loved ones, stealing from employers, and blaming the world for your problems, all these kinds of behaviors invariably lead a recovering person to relapse. And the same can be said for tendencies to avoid emotions like guilt, shame, anger, fear, etc. or efforts to ignore other forms of self-defeating behavior. In a similar vein, one's refusal to actively engage in therapy, to talk openly about one's problems, to address inner conflicts, or to take medications needed to help stabilize certain psychiatric symptoms can undermine one's recovery from mental health concerns. And whether we speak of giving up harmful friendships; finding new ways to deal with people, emotions, and the stresses of life; dealing with compulsive behaviors; even choosing to attend therapy or take certain psychotropic medications to manage psychiatric symptoms, these are all decisions that necessarily require change.

Most would agree that humans generally don't like change. Rather, people prefer sticking with that which is easy, familiar, and safe. And avoiding change is especially common when it comes to altering long-standing patterns of behavior (even when they haven't been working). Change usually requires giving up old ways of coping in order to try something different. Change means surrendering that with which we are familiar for the sake of doing something new. And for all these reasons, change, by its very nature, is usually not easy, comfortable, or safe. Moreover, real change is usually scary and takes time, especially when the change means establishing new patterns of behavior that require one to take responsibility for the consequences. What if the new choices don't work out? What if the consequences prove undesirable, even painful? What if the situation gets worse? These questions all represent reasons why people don't generally like to change. Nonetheless, for lasting recovery to be achieved, for therapy to be truly effective, change must occur. And whether one is speaking of a substance-use problem or a mental health concern, when a suffering person fails to pursue change, more often than not, misery persists. *Only through choosing to change can a struggling person hope to rise above existing struggles, achieve lasting recovery, and create a more meaningful life.*

Now in saying that recovery from substance-use problems or mental illness requires change, I am not saying individuals are responsible for having created their problems. I am not "blaming the victim." The research is pretty clear on how genetics may predispose one to chemical dependency, bipolar I disorder, schizophrenia, certain forms of depression, etc. And we all know people are not responsible for their genetic makeup. Likewise, the research is pretty clear about the profound effect of traumatizing life experiences. If we have inherited certain predispositions for alcoholism, addiction, or various mental illnesses, then our vulnerability may be set. Growing up in an impoverished environment or where one or more parent has a substance-use or mental health problem of their own invariably takes its toll on any child. And if one grows up being neglected or abused, if one is sexually assaulted, or if one serves eleven months in a combat zone, escaping the painful consequences of such trauma may not be possible. Clearly, people are not responsible for becoming an alcoholic or addict any more than they are responsible for having mental health concerns. But substance-use problems and mental illness are, nonetheless, conditions people can learn to accept, manage, and recover from. And if recovery is the desired outcome, one must assume responsibility for his or her recovery and the change this requires. Admittedly, the treatment process might be painful and take time. And it might be more difficult where comorbid conditions are present. But even in these instances, helping a client to accept coexisting problems, to take responsibility for managing them, and to make change would always be a crucial component of any treatment plan devised.

As a sidenote, some have asked whether or not it's truly possible for people to change. Does treatment truly work? All I can say is that after some forty-plus years of practicing as a mental health professional, I believe people can change. I've seen people change. I have helped people make change. I have seen treatment work firsthand. I've witnessed people break free from the chains of addiction and go on to create a life of recovery spanning many years. I've seen former alcoholics and addicts restore their health, become productive workers, establish lasting relationships, and create a life of meaning that may never have existed before. I've seen individuals so troubled by the voices in their heads; so trapped by fear, anxiety, and worry; and so caught in their loneliness and despair that only the promise of death seemed to offer any hope of peace. And I've seen such people rise above their suffering to find hope, love, and a life of meaning. I've seen people come to recognize how their future depends just as much on the choices they make in response to their problems as on the problems themselves. When people make different choices regarding the path they choose to walk, those different choices can yield different outcomes.

On the other hand, I've also seen people come to recognize that ignoring or denying a problem, or trying to wish it away, simply does not work. I've seen people come to realize that focusing on the past, blaming their genes, blaming other people or society at large, or dwelling on all the other contributing factors we may not be able to control is unlikely to be productive. Again, focusing on the past or blaming elements beyond our control only results in giving up the power we actually do have for working in the here and now to create that future we might otherwise desire. There really is no magical cure. For recovery to be effective, we cannot give in to the temptation of seeing ourselves as helpless victims of circumstance. Rather, we need to see ourselves as capable of change and capable of making choices that will allow us to actively strive for the new life we seek. Many times, we may need the help of a therapist and/or a Higher Power. But I have seen people change. I've seen recovery and therapy work, even for people having multiple, coexisting problems. And this work would constitute much of what I'd do at Saint Francis. It too would prove both challenging and rewarding.

During this same period, around 1989, I was again contacted by Mike Sprague. He and I had all but lost contact since my leaving Indiana in the early 1980s. But our high school reunion committee was reaching out to the graduating class of 1969 to notify them of our upcoming twentieth reunion. Mike called to let me know, and I agreed to attend. I'd also learn that over time, he and his wife had divorced and that Mike was the father of three girls. He'd also gotten back involved with music—working as a DJ for a local country western dance hall, in addition to serving as the emcee for a live music venue (the Little Nashville Opry) in Nashville (Indiana). Finally, Mike had developed a four-hour weekly radio show which he recorded in his home for distribution to stations in other markets. Renewing our friendship at our high school reunion was great. It never ceases to amaze me how some friendships never seem to die, no matter how life circumstances might get in the way. There were only a few others at the reunion with whom I felt close, and I was poignantly reminded of the social discomfort I'd felt while attending high school. I was also struck by the reading of names of all those who had died since our 1969 graduation. But most of all, I was just pleased to see Mike again. It was a very rewarding experience.

A couple of years later, some four years after my being hired at Saint Francis, Kathy Coleman would be promoted to a position as clinical director over all the substance-use programs at Saint Francis. These programs would include the Detoxification Unit, the Outpatient Drug and Alcohol Treatment Program, the Methadone Treatment Clinic, the Geriatric D&A Rehabilitation Program, the Adolescent D&A Rehabilitation Program, and the Adult Inpatient D&A Rehabilitation Program. For her, it was quite a promotion. By this time, I had started to become aware of some of the limits my current job and credentials placed on the work I could do to help others, and I'd also realized the limits for any income I might ever generate with only my master's degree. I was also growing increasingly tired of living in Pittsburgh. Finally, in recent years, working with a couple of my former professors from Duquesne University had made it possible for me to take a few of their doctoral-level courses (ethics, statistics, and Rorschach assessment) as a nondegree student. All this, along with Dr. Hawthorne's continued encouragement, would result in my getting more serious about returning to school and pursuing doctoral studies. I was pleased with the clinical experience I'd been getting and with being able to help those having coexisting substance-use and mental health concerns. And had Ms. Coleman not been promoted, I might have remained at Saint Francis for years to come. But with the culmination of all these factors, in the winter of 1991, I started exploring doctoral training programs.

I would eventually consider three such programs: those at the University of Pittsburgh, at Indiana University of Indiana, Pennsylvania (in no way affiliated with IU of Bloomington,

Indiana), and at Wright State University in Dayton, Ohio. All three were approved by the American Psychological Association, which would be important for obtaining internship placement later on and for my eventually gaining state licensure. The programs at the University of Pittsburgh and Indiana University of PA also had the added benefit of being within driving distance of Pittsburgh. This proximity to Pittsburgh meant I might be able to continue working at Saint Francis while completing my coursework. Unfortunately, these two programs were both PhD programs and typically required seven to nine years for completion. These programs also admitted only three students per year (thus reducing my odds for being admitted). The program at Wright State University, on the other hand, would require leaving my job (and income) and relocating to Dayton, Ohio. But due to its being a PsyD program, it had the advantage of requiring only four years for completion. It also admitted a larger number of students per year. Each of the programs made good rational sense for differing reasons, but the program at Wright State had the added advantage of *feeling* like the place where I was supposed to be. Since leaving Columbus and making a commitment to pursue a life of spiritual mindfulness, I had long come to understand the rewards that could come from "trusting my spirit."

In the late summer of 1992, after completing the interview and selection process, I was invited to pursue my doctoral studies through the School of Professional Psychology (SOPP) at Wright State University. I would leave Saint Francis that August. My going-away celebration held many mixed emotions. I was excited about pursuing doctoral studies and moving on to the next chapter in my life. And I was more than okay with the idea of getting away from the city of Pittsburgh. Still, I had made many good friends at Saint Francis and was sad to be leaving them. Moreover, giving up my job and stable income to return to school at forty-two years of age was downright scary. Oh well, *nobody* likes change!

One last note about my time in Pittsburgh. Only a month or so before leaving Saint Francis for Wright State, I had traveled to Columbus to visit family. While there, I stopped by Tom Pickett's Music Center to catch up with Tom and renew our friendship. I had been thinking about replacing the Martin guitar I'd given up after leaving Columbus some years earlier, and buying another Martin would have been my preference. Clearly, the handcrafted guitars made by Martin and Gibson had long been considered top-of-the-line for acoustic stringed instruments. Unfortunately, Martin and Gibson were still manufacturing instruments by hand, and since the boom of folk and rock music beginning in the 1960s, both of these companies had struggled to keep up with demand. This resulted in opening a door for new manufacturers of high-quality acoustic guitars, and Taylor Guitars would be one such company.

The Taylor Guitar Company used new technology in their manufacturing process, which allowed them to produce high-quality instruments in a more timely fashion. And given the extended wait required for receiving guitars from Martin and Gibson, Tom had decided to carry a line of Taylor instruments. Tom would persuade me to buy a beautiful Taylor 810 dreadnought model, having rosewood back and sides and a spruce top. This would be my second high-quality acoustic guitar and my first professional-grade instrument since parting with my Martin D-18 in 1977. The purchase of this instrument would also precipitate a return to playing music that would last the remainder of my days. Some months later, I added a Rickenbacker 360, 1964 Vintage Reissue model (similar to the one mentioned earlier and owned by Don Smith's father) and a Fender amplifier. Now I could play acoustic or electric guitar music. In just a matter of weeks, I was playing tunes from my "glory days."

"The real cycle you're working on
Is the cycle called yourself".

—R. Pirsig

From <u>Zen and the Art of Motorcycle Maintenance</u>, Pirsig, Robert (1974), a Bantam Book/published by arrangement with William Morrow and Company Inc., New York, New York, 10016

PROFESSIONAL TRAINING

The move from Pittsburgh to Dayton, Ohio, would put me some four hours closer to Columbus. Consequently, attending Wright State University meant I could visit family much more often. On one of my first trips home following the move, I'd discover that Dave's recovery from alcoholism had greatly changed his life. He was working steady, paying his bills, and regularly attending church. He was being a responsible husband and father, earning a reputation for being a skilled auto mechanic, and gaining the trust of all those who knew him well. The change was quite evident. There is another saying in AA that goes, "If you want to know when an alcoholic is lying, you simply watch for his or her lips to move." Dave was no longer given to lying at every turn, no longer given to exaggerating every little thing regardless how trivial, no longer working to impress others in order to compensate for his feelings of shame, guilt, and inadequacy. He was trying (again, as AA says) "to live life on life's terms," being honest, "walking his talk," and showing more love and compassion to others. And all these changes reverberated throughout his marriage, his relationship with his children, and his relationship with our mother and stepfather as well. Gradually, even our own relationship would improve, and we'd grow closer than we'd been in years.

A short time later, Dave and I started getting together every few months to play music. About a year or so after that, we'd even decide to take a weekend jaunt to Nashville, Tennessee. There we attended the Grand Ole Opry, checked out the famous Tootsie's Orchid Lounge, visited Gruhn's Guitars, and heard more really good guitar pickers than one might ever imagine. I remember well how intrigued we both were by the number of really talented musicians still sleeping in their cars and scrounging for food while awaiting to be discovered. Clearly, making a living as a professional musician was a competitive business, and we both needed to keep our day jobs, lest we too end up struggling to survive. When I remarried some years later, Dave would also serve as my best man. And he and his wife regularly visited after I graduated from Wright State and my wife and I relocated to southeastern Kentucky.

    The School of Professional Psychology (SOPP) at Wright State University was actually one of the first such programs established in America. Schools of professional psychology (also called PsyD programs) differ somewhat from the doctor of philosophy (PhD) programs in psychology offered by many schools. The former, much like MD programs for medical students, focus on developing psychology clinicians. Whereas the latter often place a greater emphasis on developing psychology researchers and teachers.

    The psychology training offered through the SOPP consisted of three years of full-time coursework, accompanied by two years of half-time, supervised practicum placement (intended to develop one's clinical skills). Oral exams and a dissertation were to be completed in conjunction with the coursework and the practicums and by the end of the third year. This would be followed by a one-year, full-time supervised internship intended to further refine one's professional training and prepare the student for independent practice. The internship placement was contingent upon successful completion of all coursework, the oral exams, and the dissertation. Graduation then followed successful completion of the internship.

Again, in order to finance my professional training, it would be necessary to supplement student loans with part-time employment. Fortunately, because I already held both a master's degree in psychology and my drug/alcohol certification, I was able to hire on as a psychological practitioner with John P. Laye and Associates in neighboring Yellow Springs, Ohio. Dr. Laye was a respected local psychologist and astute businessman who had created a small empire consisting of some six or seven psychologists, spread out over three offices in and around the Dayton area. He agreed to hire me for twenty hours per week while I attended Wright State and (truthfully) paid me far more than any of my peers earned through their work-study positions with the university. Still, while he was quite generous with the salary, I'm sure he made money from billing my services to third-party payers. As noted above, he was a very good businessman.

My coursework at Wright State was the standard fare for doctoral programs in clinical psychology: developmental psychology, theories of personality, research design, statistics, psychopathology, human physiology, individual psychotherapy, group psychotherapy, intellectual assessment, personality assessment, Rorschach or projective assessment, geriatric psychology, forensic psychology, etc. Several of the courses covered the same content as those in my bachelor's and master's programs, but all were of a more advanced nature.

My two practicum placements consisted of working twenty hours per week in each of the Dayton Mental Health Center (an Ohio State psychiatric hospital) and the Dayton Veterans Administration Medical Center. My dissertation was titled "MMPI-2: Normative Data for Adult Inpatient Chemically Dependent Populations." Upon finishing my coursework, passing my oral exams, and defending my dissertation, I completed my one-year internship through the Veterans Administration Medical Center of Lexington, Kentucky, in the fall of 1996. I graduated SOPP immediately thereafter.

My training at the state hospital in Dayton would be meaningful in many ways. While working at Saint Francis, I had already been introduced to clients having such disturbing problems as delusional thinking, paranoia, hallucinations, and the like. And this had given me a fair idea how these phenomena differed from people's everyday life experiences. On the other hand, my training through the Dayton Mental Health Center would give me a greater appreciation for the similarities of these psychiatric symptoms to the so-called normal perceptions, beliefs, and behavior we all share.

For example, most of us have probably had the experience of seeing something out of the corner of our eye, only to discover that nothing was really there. Likewise, at one time or another, most of us have probably thought we heard someone calling out our name, only to discover no one was truly present. We usually just dismiss these experiences without giving them much thought or attention. And seldom are such perceptions considered signs of psychosis. But for one actually experiencing hallucinations, the false visions or voices are all too often perceived as being real. True, at one level, an individual may wonder about and even be confused by seeing or hearing things others cannot. And at times, these experiences may prove disconcerting (even terrifying). But try as they might, those experiencing these problems usually have trouble rejecting their *perceived* reality.

In a similar fashion, while there is a clear difference between the delusional thinking of paranoia and what we generally consider reasonable cautiousness or suspiciousness, both involve a certain degree of social distrust. Most people, for example, would acknowledge there to be people in the world who intentionally take advantage of or harm others. Jails and prisons are full of such individuals. And learning to accurately recognize the warning signs of such a threat is essential to effective social functioning and day-to-day safety. It is commonplace, for example, for parents to warn small children not to get into the car of or accept candy from a stranger. And however much we might wish it not to be true, vulnerable or frail teenagers are probably best served by being warned about the dangers of the internet or of wandering around the streets of a big city or college campus alone after dark (lest they risk being assaulted). We don't consider taking precautions in such situations to be based on unreasonable fears. On the other hand, paranoia seems to be what arises when social distrust becomes so overwhelming, when the ability to read warning cues becomes so impaired, and one's sense of vulnerability becomes so great that the paranoid individual seems never to be able to escape their fears. Here, the scariness and conviction of being in danger becomes so powerful that they oftentimes misread or exaggerate even the most benign actions or situations to represent genuine threats.

Understanding the similarities as well as the distinctions between these kinds of phenomena and our everyday experiences would be crucial to helping me view the troubled soul as a fellow human and not simply as a "crazy" person or someone to be pitied or feared. As the old saying goes, "But for the grace of God, there go I."

My training at Dayton Mental Health Center would also help me realize that while people with psychiatric disturbances sometimes manifest troublesome symptoms and behave bizarrely, their symptoms are not *always* present. More often than not, these symptoms come and go. Yes, the symptoms do tend to recur over time. But in between episodes of acute disturbance, these individuals may experience extended periods of

PROFESSIONAL TRAINING

relative stability. As importantly, prevailing psychiatric symptoms are oftentimes quite treatable (especially given the availability of modern psychotropic medications). Mental illness can be a disabling condition, but it does not have to ruin one's life.

At the Dayton Mental Health Center, I'd also learn that while individuals with chronic mental illness *sometimes* act in violent ways, contrary to what might be portrayed in the movies or on the evening news, this is by no means the norm. The vast majority of people with mental health disturbances *never* become violent without direct provocation. Rather, more often than not, they suffer in silence or turn their suffering on themselves. By contrast, many people in our society who do not struggle with mental illness per se clearly do behave in violent ways. It has long been said that the people whom we need to fear the most in the world are those troubled individuals estranged from others who are *not* getting help rather than those in a hospital or otherwise engaged in treatment.

Another important lesson learned at the Dayton Mental Health Center would be distinguishing between those deemed mentally ill and those identified as criminally insane. *Mental illness* is the term we use when referring to one having problems that significantly impair his or her perception of and interaction with the world at large. And as a teacher of mine once said, "Most people with mental illness never get locked up in a psychiatric hospital. And if they do, it's usually not because of their illness but because they got into somebody's way." In other words, when a person with mental health problems is in a protective home or social environment, when basic needs are met on a regular basis, and the individual is provided understanding and support to prevent symptoms from becoming acute, there is seldom need for hospitalization. Rather, only when symptoms become pronounced and support is unavailable, or when one with mental illness becomes homeless or otherwise unable to function in socially acceptable ways (e.g., becomes a threat to self or others), is hospitalization typically needed. And even then, such individuals may not be considered "criminally insane."

Insanity or being found "criminally insane," on the other hand, is a *legal* term used to describe one having significant mental health problems whose symptoms are deemed responsible for behavior that violates a socially defined criminal statute. As we all know, it is not unusual for laws to change from time to time, much as society changes. Behavior once deemed criminal might not be criminal at a later date or in a different jurisdiction (e.g., certain sexual acts, certain substance use, etc.). The opposite is also true. Certain forms of disciplining children with physical contact may once have been considered acceptable in many communities, even though such discipline might be against the law today. Accordingly, one with mental illness may never be deemed criminally insane if their behavior, however troubling, is *not* associated with their violating a criminal statute. Thus, the vast majority of psychiatric patients are never adjudicated criminally insane. But when one with mental illness commits a serious crime (e.g., homicide, manslaughter, etc.) and the mental illness is believed responsible for his or her actions and/or capacity for being fairly adjudicated, then grounds for a finding of criminal insanity may be present. And it is in these instances that involuntary hospitalization for "reasons of insanity" may be court-ordered.

Finally, and perhaps most importantly, my training at the Dayton Mental Health Center taught me how to *feel comfortable* working with individuals having chronic psychiatric problems like schizophrenia, schizoaffective disorder, bipolar I disorder, and the like. One might assume this to be a given for one choosing a career in clinical psychology. But to the contrary, it is probably more common, even for aspiring psychologists, to feel a certain degree of discomfort, even fear, around people who are appreciably different than oneself. And this can be especially true for individuals with mental health concerns who, oftentimes, behave bizarrely, manifest unusual experiences, or act in troubling ways. Human beings, by their very nature, can be slow to adapt to differences, especially extreme differences. But working in this hospital setting taught me how people with chronic mental illness are, in fact, more similar to "normal" people than not and how they need the same love, understanding, and respect as do we all.

My practicum placement at the Veteran's Administration Medical Center (VAMC) would also be constructive in many ways. In particular, this training gave me a better understanding of brain development and cognitive processes and how each of these can become impaired through a variety of causes (both natural and tragic). It helped advance my skills working with individuals suffering brain trauma, strokes, dementias, multiple sclerosis, and various other neurological disorders. And this training also helped me understand how conditions other than those directly related to brain function (e.g., depression, substance use, infections, etc.) can sometimes mask themselves as organic brain impairments.

My VA training would also introduce and train me to utilize a wide variety of neuropsychological tests commonly used to assess brain/behavior relationships. As a whole, this training would provide the foundation for those neuropsychology and geropsychology rotations I would later complete during my internship at the VAMC in Lexington, Kentucky. And it would lay the groundwork for much of the work I'd do through the Baptist Regional Medical Center Rehabilitation Unit following my internship and for work I would do later on in private practice.

Obviously, all the formal training received while attending SOPP would be important to my future career as a psychologist. But in certain ways, I would not find my time spent at Wright State to be as meaningful as that spent working on my master's degree through Duquesne. At Wright State, I would advance my scientific understanding of those things I'd been introduced to earlier in my education: psychological theory and processes, statistical analysis, research design, diagnostic categories, and mental health practices in general. At Wright State, I'd also gain important practical experience, develop my clinical skills, and learn how a psychologist's work might interface with other health-care systems and professions. And all this learning would be important. But at Duquesne, I'd been able to nurture those philosophical/existential, dare I say spiritual, ideals that would forever guide my personal life and clinical practice. Both types of learning, those acquired at Wright State and at Duquesne, would be critical to my becoming a professional psychologist. But for me, as suggested previously, the science component of my training would always be far less important than understanding what it meant to be distinctively human. Coming to accept myself as being human had helped me make peace with the fact that regardless how much knowledge, education, training, and experience I received, there would always be limits to that which I might be able to know or understand. And knowing such limits would forever help me to remain humble, remain open to the experiences and struggles I myself might encounter, and be patient and empathic with all those I would one day attempt to help.

Finally, I can't move on from talking about my experience at Wright State without also mentioning my mentor and dissertation chair, Dr. James Webb. Not all my professors would prove equally important for me. As is probably true for most educational or training programs, I'd learn more from some of my instructors than others. Some would be especially astute teachers. On the other hand, some seemed to have personal biases or agendas that (from time to time) would distract from their instruction. One or two may have even had unresolved personal issues that contaminated their teaching. I know some of my peers believed this to be true. But Dr. Webb seemed free of such troubles and would turn out to be exactly what I needed.

Dr. Webb had been one of the founding fathers of the School of Professional Psychology at Wright State and had been with the program for many years. He was also a well-published author, researcher, and respected professor who had been teaching long before his tenure at Wright State. At the time I attended the school, Dr. Webb specialized in the areas of psychological assessment (intellectual, personality, etc.) and in working with "gifted" youth. Some years earlier, he had coauthored a textbook on administering and interpreting the original Minnesota Multiphasic Personality Inventory (MMPI). This test was designed to assess those pervasive and persisting patterns of attitudes and behaviors (personality) that tend to characterize one's decision-making across the various situations and the challenges of their lives. All of us have personality traits and tendencies that characterize our typical functioning. Some of us are more outgoing or extroverted and tend to enjoy being with others and seeking gratification from outside ourselves. Others may prefer to keep to themselves or to be more introverted and less social, while seeking gratification from more solitary activities. Likewise, some of us are more trusting, even gullible, while others maybe be less trusting, even cynical. Some of us are more emotionally expressive, while others keep their emotions under wraps (as they say). But we all have some combination of personality traits. The more flexible these patterns are, the better one's adjustment to life usually is. The more rigid or extreme these patterns are, the more one seems to struggle in dealing with life. The MMPI (and subsequent versions) represent broadband tests of personality and psychopathology that have long been considered the benchmark for assessing these traits (especially in forensic or legal settings). And Dr. Webb was considered an expert on the test.

Dr. Webb had also authored multiple books (in addition to founding a nationally recognized assessment and treatment program) on helping "gifted" children. By working with Dr. Webb, I'd learn that so-called gifted children are those who, because of their superior intellectual abilities, oftentimes struggle with adjusting to and benefitting from more conventional learning environments typically geared toward teaching the broader spectrum of *average* students. Gifted students, for example, frequently have problems fitting in with traditional public school settings because their superior intellect results in their learning more quickly than average students. Learning more quickly often leads gifted students to become easily bored and to lose interest with standard classroom instruction. This, in turn, leads to problems paying attention and to their behaving in ways that are often seen as distracting to others. Such behavior can include daydreaming or engaging in attention-seeking or disruptive behavior. Unfortunately, this behavior oftentimes results in their being erroneously diagnosed with attention-deficit/hyperactivity disorder (ADHD).

Misdiagnosing individuals with inattention problems or acting-out behavior is probably far more common than one might think. Of late, it has become almost in vogue to identify such persons as having ADHD, even though, in many cases, the problems with inattention and/or acting-out behavior may be the result of any number of independently existing conditions. Children growing up in alcohol-ridden or violence-prone families, for example, or who are being abused commonly exhibit problems with inattention or disruptive behavior. Likewise, such problems can arise for adults suffering with depression, substance use, relationship problems, and even sleep deprivation associated with spending long hours at work. And in most of these latter instances, the problems with inattention or behavior resolve themselves with effective treatment of the coexisting condition.

As a clinical psychologist, I can't begin to count the number of times I have had students struggling to achieve in college referred to me for assessment of possible ADHD when, on many occasions, the real problem was too much partying, chronic marijuana use, depression, or simply an unwillingness to admit they lacked the aptitude necessary for achieving at the college level. Likewise, I've had multiple cases wherein over-the-road truckers, factory workers, oil rig workers, etc., individuals working sixty- and seventy-hour workweeks in hopes of making more money, come to me for such an evaluation when working these kinds of hours almost always lead to physical exhaustion and impaired work performance over time. Truth be told, the human body and mind just can't work such schedules for any extended period without eventually breaking down. Unfortunately, misdiagnosing these problems as ADHD (particularly when doing so results in an individual being placed on addictive, amphetamine-type medication) does nothing to address the underlying cause. In fact, oftentimes, such a diagnosis only exacerbates or contributes to other problems down the road (e.g., hypertension, heart disease, suicide, substance dependence, etc.).

ADHD is a very real condition, and it can create lasting adjustment problems for those suffering from it. This is especially true for those young children trying to learn in a school setting or develop effective social skills and fit in with peers or those adults seeking to maintain employment. But *misdiagnosing* problems with inattention and behavior as ADHD is a real problem as well. And bringing us back to the topic at hand, all too often, misdiagnosing a "gifted" child as having ADHD only results in their being placed on medication that is intended to bring their behavior more in compliance with the average student. Regrettably, such an intervention only stifles a gifted child's learning, thereby preventing the realization of his or her full potential or achieving at the higher level of which they are actually capable. Dr. Webb's work with gifted children was considered groundbreaking.

Fortunately for me, Dr. Webb and I clicked from the very onset. Whereas many of my peers were impressed by his overall knowledge of the principles, theories, and practices pertaining to psychology, I was just as impressed by his caring demeanor and professional comportment. Dr. Webb, on the other hand, seemed to respect that I was somewhat older and had more life and clinical experience under my belt than many of my peers. He also seemed to appreciate that I was experienced with using the newest version of the MMPI, the MMPI-2. I had administered, scored, and interpreted over 1,200 of this revised edition while working on the chemical dependency unit at Saint Francis Medical Center and prior to enrolling at Wright State. And given my experience with the MMPI-2, and his history of having previously authored a book on the test's predecessor, he agreed to serve as my dissertation chair. Again, my dissertation was titled "MMPI-2: Normative Data for Adult Inpatient Chemically Dependent Populations." And shortly before leaving Wright State for my internship training, and with Dr. Webb's encouragement and guidance, I would be invited to present the findings from this dissertation at the American Psychological Association's Annual Convention in New York City. Dr. Webb attended my presentation, and this experience proved a wonderful opportunity to share my dissertation findings with other budding psychologists.

PROFESSIONAL TRAINING

Presenting at the APA annual convention also gave me a wonderful excuse to visit the Big Apple. In addition to presenting findings from my dissertation, my guest and I did all the things tourists typically do in New York: took in a play on Broadway, went to the top of the Empire State Building, visited Central Park, Strawberry Fields, and the Dakota Apartments, and ate at the Tavern on the Green. Finally, I was also able to visit Rudy's Music Shop on Forty-Eighth Street to check out his selection of vintage guitars. All in all, it was quite an experience.

While I had valued the supervision previously received from Dr. Hawthorne (at Saint Francis), Dr. Webb would be the first of two *mentors* to prove instrumental in advancing my development as a professional psychologist. He would help me through his teaching of psychological knowledge and skills and his overall guidance of my development as a clinician. But he also helped me by living values I could aspire to, and that would help sustain me throughout the remainder of my days. We would remain friends long after I graduated from Wright State.

During the final year of my coursework, while I was completing my dissertation, I also began the process of applying for internship placement. As already suggested, the internship component for my doctoral training would entail twelve months of full-time, supervised clinical experience designed to further bolster application of the knowledge and skills learned during my classroom instruction and practicum placements. To increase the odds of my landing a desirable internship once my coursework came to an end, I applied to several different prospective settings, each being attractive for various reasons. Some were located closer to the Dayton, Ohio, area, thus minimizing some of those life disruptions commonly associated with moving to a completely new city. Others were located in places I might want to live upon completion of the internship (e.g., the states of Indiana, Kentucky, Tennessee), thus leaving me closer to family.

Most would be at VA Medical Centers as these internships typically offered advanced training in those areas of primary interest for me (neuropsychology and geropsychology).

During my internship interviews at the VAMC of Lexington, Kentucky, I would meet Dr. Thomas Shurling. He was the assistant director of the psychology department and head of the internship program, and as had been true with Dr. Webb, Dr. Shurling and I connected immediately. He too was a well-schooled psychologist and a caring person. But he also oversaw the geropsychology department at the VA. The connection between geropsychology (the study and treatment of aging adults) and neuropsychology (the study and treatment of individuals with brain/behavior disorders) is natural, inasmuch as many of the conditions affecting aging adults (e.g., strokes, dementias, Parkinson's, etc.) also have a neuropsychological component. Because I was interested in each of these areas, and Dr. Shurling was in charge of internship placements, he could get me appointed to both the geropsychology rotation and the neuropsychology rotation. The VA in Lexington was where I would choose to complete my doctoral training, and Dr. Shurling would become my second professional mentor.

To this day, I hold a special place in my heart for Lexington, Kentucky. It was a little larger than Columbus, Indiana, but not as large as Indianapolis or Pittsburgh. It was surrounded by the lush green pastures of horse farms (bordered with white, wooden slat fences) that serve as Lexington's primary industry. Due to the relative absence of factories, there was essentially no pollution. There was also practically no crime. Finally, Lexington was home to the University of Kentucky (UK). While the long-standing basketball rivalry between IU and UK meant I would never become a Wildcat fan, the University of Kentucky did bring a certain youthfulness and energy to the city that other communities sometimes lack. For many reasons,

PROFESSIONAL TRAINING

Lexington would be the perfect place to complete my internship. It was also where I'd discover the Firehouse Pickers and learned to play bluegrass music, where I'd meet new friends that would be treasured for many years to come, and where I'd meet the love of my life, Pamela Mortellaro.

My internship was a one-year program consisting of two thousand hours of full-time, paid employment broken down into three, four-month rotations. In my case, I would complete one rotation each in geropsychology, neuropsychology, and vocational psychology. The geropsychology rotation focused upon my gaining knowledge and experience with assessing and treating aging adults having a host of psychological concerns not common to younger people. Aging persons can and do experience the mental health problems found in younger age groups as well (e.g., depression, anxiety, substance use, bipolar disorder, schizophrenia, etc.). But older persons also experience those physical problems arising with the more general decline in health occurring with the aging process: problems such as hypertension, heart disease, diabetes, arthritis, glaucoma, and so on. And each of these conditions can contribute to or exacerbate mental health concerns. Moreover, in addition to the impact of physical ailments on mental health, aging adults also struggle with psychosocial stressors that are less common for younger clients. For example, as we age, we increasingly experience the loss of family, friends, and other loved ones to death. And we also experience the loneliness and social isolation that accompanies these losses. Eventually, older adults encounter an end to employability, a loss of the capacity for generating income, and (all too often) loss of financial independence. With time, aging adults also experience a gradual decline of muscle tone and strength, loss of physical mobility, an increase in fall risk, and a general decline in personal autonomy. Lastly, all these concerns may be accompanied by problems with cognition arising due to head trauma (from falls), strokes, dementias, etc.

I understand why some clinicians dislike working with aging people. At some level, each of us probably knows that we too could get old someday and that if we live long enough, we too may experience the death of our parents, our siblings, and our friends. We probably also understand that we too may become vulnerable to the issues of failing health that emerge with late-onset medical conditions, to the loss of independence that comes with declining visual acuity, hearing loss, arthritis, and related problems with ambulation and driving an auto safely. At some level, we may even know that we too might experience the cognitive problems accompanying such concerns as Parkinson's, cerebral vascular accidents (strokes), Alzheimer's, and the like.

There is an old tale of a woman living with her ten-year-old daughter. As the woman's own mother becomes increasingly feeble, the woman brings her into their home to provide for the grandmother's care. Finally, one day, the woman tells her daughter to go the local store and buy a wooden bowl for the grandmother. When the girl asks why, the woman explains that the grandmother keeps dropping all the dishes and breaking them. The girl objects, saying the wooden bowl would only embarrass and humiliate her grandmother. But the mother insists. When the girl returns from the store, she has two bowls. When the mother asks the girl why she bought two bowls, the girl says, "I just figured someday you'd get old too." All too often, because of all the losses aging client's experience, clinicians view their situations to be hopeless and the prospects for working with them discouraging. I, on the other hand, would grow to believe that only through coming face-to-face with the aging process can we learn to look beyond our physical bodies, beyond our own factical existence, to find a sense of identity that transcends

PROFESSIONAL TRAINING

our individual selves and makes this human experience truly meaningful.

As noted above, my supervisor for the geropsychology rotation was Dr. Shurling. And because of the heavy emphasis this rotation offered on assessing and treating cognitive problems, Dr. Shurling agreed that my second rotation at the VAMC, the one I was most interested in, would be in neuropsychology. Accordingly, Dr. Shurling helped me set this rotation up as well. It included stints at the Sanders-Brown Alzheimer's Clinic, the University of Kentucky Medical Center brain autopsy lab, and rounds on the VA Neurology and General Medical units.

Like most professionals, attorneys, medical doctors, and the like, psychologists usually develop certain areas of expertise, based upon personal interest or populations with whom they either prefer to work or with whom they seem to have greater success. For example, as noted earlier, I've always loved working with alcoholics and addicts. And as just mentioned, I also enjoy working with geriatric populations. I've just always identified with their values, their work ethic, and the sacrifices they have often been willing to make for family, God, and country. But a third group I have always liked to work with is those having organic brain impairments.

As with geriatric populations, many clinicians find it uncomfortable to work with the cognitively impaired, whether because of the perceived desperate nature of one so afflicted or out of uncertainty regarding how best to help the impaired individual and/or family to cope. But from my earlier days of working with alcoholics, some of which had developed organic brain syndromes secondary to their alcohol use or fall-related head injuries, to the problems my stepfather would have with strokes, I'd long found brain-behavior relationships intriguing.

With my rotation in neuropsychology, I'd quickly learn that problems of cognition (neurocognitive disorders) can be associated with a variety of causes. Some may be a direct result of head trauma, stroke, oxygen deprivation, dementing diseases, etc. Others can be related to medical problems, as in the case of a urinary tract infection or mineral deficiency. Cognitive impairment can also be the result of substance abuse or medication side effects (e.g., alcohol intoxication or medication used to treat anxiety, pain, etc.). And in some cases, even psychiatric conditions can create cognitive impairment (e.g., major depression). Again, learning to accurately identify the specific cause of the presenting cognitive deficits would be crucial to making an accurate diagnosis and to providing treatment for one struggling with recovery or adjustment.

In a similar fashion, I'd also learn that many types of cognitive impairment can be reversed with appropriate care. Thus, learning to distinguish between reversible and irreversible types of cognitive impairment would also be a crucial part of my training. Wrongly identifying the situation could lead to an individual being *incorrectly* diagnosed as having a progressive disorder that might, in fact, be easily reversed with a simple change of medication or effective treatment of the underlying substance-use, medical, or psychiatric problem.

By way of example, while completing this training rotation, I quickly learned how urinary tract infections, common to aging women, could manifest as confused thinking or disorientation. Unfortunately, family members all too often confuse these symptoms as representing an irreversible neurocognitive disorder such as Alzheimer's. Appropriate medical examination and simple blood work would usually identify the elevated white-blood count and other symptoms signifying the infection. And when treated with antibiotics, the related problems with cognition previously thought to be irreversible typically disappear.

As another example, later in my career, I would meet a forty-five-year-old professional woman who was *misdiagnosed* with a progressive/irreversible neurocognitive disorder at a major hospital in upstate New York. The woman traveled a fair amount for her job and was given to working long hours. As a result, her husband seemingly came to feel neglected and got involved with another man's wife. This left the woman increasingly distressed and, in conjunction with her traveling and working long hours, having problems focusing attention and effectively processing information. Cognitively, she began to falter.

When I met the woman, she clearly had problems with cognition. But there were many other factors that contraindicated the likelihood of her having an irreversible neurocognitive disorder. First, the age of onset seemed off. In general, irreversible neurocognitive disorders not related to head trauma or stroke usually have an onset around age sixty-five or later (not always, but usually). This lady was only forty-five. Second, her cognitive problems seemed to be inconsistent, to wax and wane, and to not fit the profile of any one particular dementing syndrome. Generally speaking, for example, a person with organically based cognitive deficits is often either unaware of or untroubled by any existing problems. Loved ones may be well aware of and troubled by the person's cognitive decline, but the individual him or herself (in varying degrees) oftentimes is not. Individuals with marked clinical depression, on the other hand, in addition to manifesting other symptoms of depression, are often acutely aware of and deeply troubled by any existing memory or cognitive problems. This woman (in addition to appearing sad and having legitimate reasons for being depressed) was quite distressed by her failing cognition.

As I'd learned, the *rule of thumb* is that in the absence of other convincing data to the contrary, you never diagnose an irreversible neurocognitive disorder when depression is clearly present. Rather, you always treat the depression first. This is because, in many instances, what initially looks like a neurocognitive disorder may prove to be a depression-based pseudodementia that disappears once the depression has lifted. So after some two years of working to elevate this woman's mood; stabilizing her sleep, energy, and appetite; and helping to resolve her marital problems, the cognitive impairment abated. Misdiagnosing this lady's problem as having an irreversible neurocognitive disorder would clearly have been tragic.

In addition to helping me learn to identify the causal factors for various neurocognitive disorders and to distinguish between reversible and irreversible dementias, my neuropsychology rotation also helped me learn how functional deficits arising with many cerebral vascular accidents (i.e., strokes) might be partially, if not appreciably, alleviated through prompt treatment and/or the natural healing that occurs with the passage of time. Certainly, this is not true for all stroke-related deficits. But it is more common than one might expect—depending upon the type or location of the stroke, the extent of the tissue damage, and the timeliness of treatment. Damage caused by a cerebral hemorrhage (for example) can be greatly reduced through prompt treatment of the arterial rupture, whereas stroke damage caused by a blood clot can be greatly mitigated via the prompt administration of blood thinners designed to dissolve the clot. In both instances, when treatment is quickly made available, the damage resulting from a stroke is usually less dramatic than when treatment is delayed. And in nearly all cases, the natural healing process may allow stroke victims to experience at least some improvement of deficits within the first six to twelve months from the onset of symptoms. In those cases of very minor stroke activity, often referred to as transient ischemic attacks (TIAs), prevailing cognitive deficits may resolve themselves in a matter of hours or days with minimal or no treatment.

By all this talk about reversing neurocognitive disorders (and their functional deficits), I do not mean to imply that irreversible, progressive neurocognitive disorders don't exist. Clearly, such conditions as Alzheimer's are real, progressive, and irreversible. And while newer medications may arrest the memory decline and slow the progression of the disease, in truth, these diseases have a very poor prognosis. But again, not all types of neurocognitive disorders are irreversible. And it is essential the diagnosis be as accurate as possible. Misdiagnosing a disorder can result in one erroneously believing a situation to be hopeless when, in fact, this may not be the case. And this, in turn, can lead to much unnecessary worry and suffering for both the individual and their loved ones alike. Even on those occasions when a condition proves to be irreversible (as in the case of Alzheimer's), making an accurate diagnosis can help the clinician with effectively advising the individual and family on what to expect as the disease progresses.

Finally, as just suggested, with this rotation, I'd learn skills for effectively intervening or counseling those affected by neurocognitive disorders. Again, in some cases, the treatment for the cognitive impairment may be medically based. In other instances, the treatment may be psychologically based. But for those instances wherein the condition is clearly irreversible, the treatment would usually consist of educating the individual and family on what to expect over the months and years to come and how to best proceed in order to preserve the client's quality of life while planning for the future. This can include helping the family secure the appropriate neurological care (if this has not already been done), instructing the family so as to establish effective caregiving strategies, and even helping loved ones with choosing a lawyer qualified to handle end-of-life matters.

Much like working with aging adults, I understand why many clinicians shy away from working with the cognitively impaired. Working with this population is delicate work, requiring much attention to detail. But it is also immensely rewarding work when you get it right. And for me, this is work that also reaffirms the importance of having a firm spiritual foundation.

My third rotation at the VA in Lexington focused on assessing vocational needs and facilitating meaningful job placement for the un- or underemployed. This latter rotation was selected by me simply to round out my overall doctoral training and because the actual work expectations seemed a little lighter than those of other options. I knew I'd be winding down my training and spending an increased amount of time seeking postgraduate employment in the months immediately prior to my upcoming graduation. So there was no sense adding additional stress to what was already figured to be difficult time. Nevertheless, this rotation would allow me to gain experience working with test instruments used in assessing vocational interests and abilities, to learn about community resources for job training and placement, and to learn how to assist others with identifying job and career options that matched their interests and for which they were truly suited. This latter objective might seem self-evident. But over the years, I'd witness many counselors trying to match people to jobs or careers they thought would be good even though the client lacked the requisite training, skills, aptitude, or interest necessary for realizing vocational success in those jobs/careers. When a person either lacks the ability or aptitude required for a given job or has little interest in doing the work, employment success is seldom achieved. Again, as I learned at Duquesne, the starting point for any effective intervention is accurately identifying what the person views as important for giving life meaning and working with who the person is as an individual so they might reach this goal.

Before concluding my recollections on time spent in Lexington for my internship, I need to share a few other

PROFESSIONAL TRAINING

important happenings. First, along with my renewed interest in playing guitar, I had begun frequenting local music stores to check out the latest gear and talk with other musicians. During one such visit, I was told of a group of musicians who met regularly at an inner-city firehouse to play bluegrass music. Some of the pickers were quite talented. Others, like myself, were clearly amateurs. For many, Kentucky (and southeastern Kentucky, in particular) is considered the mecca of bluegrass music. Bluegrass is that form of music most generally associated with the Appalachian Mountains and with such instruments as acoustic guitars, banjos, fiddles, mandolins, upright basses, resonator (or Dobro) guitars, etc. And southeastern Kentucky is the hailing place of such bluegrass greats as Bill Monroe, the Osborne Brothers, Ricky Skaggs, Patty Loveless, and many more. Apart from their musicianship and vocal abilities, what oftentimes makes musical artists truly great (regardless of the genre) is their songwriting skills. And whether or not you enjoy the twang of hillbilly/mountain music, many agree that bluegrass songs like "Blue Moon of Kentucky," "Rocky Top," "Foggy Mountain Breakdown," and others may well live on forever. Being a lover of music and living in the heart of Bluegrass Country, it only made sense that I check out these players and take advantage of the opportunity to learn some of their music.

One of the guys working at the firehouse was a well-rounded musician named Mike Carr. Mike was especially talented at playing banjo, fiddle, and guitar. And he was also well-known in the area for his songwriting skills along with another guitar player who specialized in Travis picking (a particular style of fingerpicking introduced by Merle Travis some years earlier and made even more famous by Chet Atkins). Mike Carr and Mike Hammond made up a duo called *the Moron Brothers*. And this duo represented the core of the "Firehouse Pickers."

As is common for firemen, Mike Carr worked shifts of twenty-four hours on duty and forty-eight hours off. And to pass time between calls, Mike would play music and write songs. Eventually, Mike Hammond and other musicians began showing up to join him, and the Firehouse Pickers were born. There were probably twenty or more pickers in all. But apart from Mike Carr and his sidekick Mike Hammond, it was kind of an open format. No one ever knew for sure just who else might show up. From the first time I sat in with these players, I was hooked. No alcohol, no arguing, no ego struggles, none of the things that all too often plague music groups, just good clean musical fun. Gradually, I learned some of the tunes and began playing along with them. We'd play two or three nights a week. And over the course of my internship year, I too became a Firehouse Picker. Occasionally, we'd play at a local nursing home. And in the summer of 1996, we played at a couple of bluegrass festivals in the Lexington and surrounding area. Playing music with this group would leave me with some of my fondest memories of my time spent in Lexington. And to this day, I remain in touch with some of the players and consider them among my dearest friends.

The other thing I wanted to mention about my time in Lexington was that of meeting my wife of twenty-seven plus years. In the spring of each year, internship sites such as the VA would interview intern applicants for positions in the upcoming class. This was what I had gone through the year prior to undertaking my own internship placement. And current interns, such as myself, would often participate in the interviewing of these prospective candidates. This was where I would meet Pamela Mortellaro, my future wife.

I actually don't remember much about Pam from the time of the interviews as she was one of several such candidates I had met. But later, I'd be informed she had been chosen to join

PROFESSIONAL TRAINING

the class of 1996–1997. And like the other incoming interns, she was planning on coming to Lexington that summer to scout the area for an apartment. I agreed to serve as her host. From the start, Pam seemed like a nice person, and I was happy to show her around town. She ended up reserving an apartment in the same complex where I had been staying (Stoney Falls Apartments, "Where Success Meets Pleasure"). She then returned to her home in Mobile, Alabama, for the remainder of the summer.

I was forty-five years old when I first met Pam. She was thirty-five years old. But our ages didn't matter all that much as we were just acquaintances, and I wasn't really looking for a serious relationship. It had been close to twenty years since Teresa and I had divorced, and though my family was still intent on my remarrying, I had pretty much accepted the possibility that this might never happen. I had my spirituality, my health, my education, my music, my family, and my friends, and I was looking forward to a career in my chosen profession. I was quite at peace with my life and in no hurry to force anything. Some years earlier, Chris, my therapist, had told me, "If God wants something for you, regardless of how you might resist, it will happen in time." My take on this was that if my Higher Power wanted me to be married, then it would happen when and at such time as God deemed it appropriate. If not, then I'd be okay with this as well. Then Pam came into my life.

Pam was an attractive, bright, and caring woman, who was also pursuing a career as a psychologist. This immediately gave us something in common. But Pam also struck me as being an unselfish person with strong spiritual values and a desire to help others. These qualities, combined with an ability to laugh and an overall love for life, were things I'd grown to look for in others—be they friends or dating partners. I remember once being told that "negative people will bring you down quicker than you can lift them up." I believed there to be some truth in this observation. And over time, I had learned to distance myself more and more from those negative voices that only want to criticize, judge, blame, argue, or fight with others. I'd simply come to realize that life was too full of pain and suffering to invest energy in those who seemingly wanted to remain stuck in such drama. As a result, I tried to surround myself with more positive people, and Pam was one of the positive ones. She could be a friend.

Shortly before completing my internship and doctoral degree, and prior to Pam's return to Lexington in the fall, I'd begin making plans for my future employment. I had grown to feel at home in Lexington and truly valued the new friends I had made. As a result, upon graduation, I hoped to find employment in that area or as close by as possible. Of course, my first choice would have been to stay at the VAMC. Unfortunately, the VA system wasn't hiring new psychologists at the time (it being before the 9/11 terror attacks and ensuing military buildup and Mideast conflicts). So once I graduated from Wright State, I interviewed with a couple of private hospitals within driving distance of Lexington. In September 1996, I hired on as a clinical psychologist for the Baptist Regional Medical Center (BRMC) of Corbin, Kentucky. Pam and I would become reacquainted shortly thereafter upon her return to Lexington.

**So faith, hope, love remain, these three;
But the greatest of these is love.**
—1 Corinthians 13:13

From the Holy Bible (1970). Catholic
Bible Publishers, Wichita, Kansas

WORK AND LOVE

SIGMUND FREUD, LONG CONSIDERED ONE OF THE founding fathers of modern psychology, was well-known for his belief that work and love are two of the more important elements to healthy personality adjustment. Whatever else one might think as regards the pros and cons of his theory of psychosexual development and practice of psychoanalysis, the concepts of work and love were crucial to his thinking and writing on the human condition. This principle has been instrumental in giving my own life meaning as well.

For me, work means any kind of practical endeavor that allows me to give back to the world, the society, the culture, or the family into which I was born. Giving back is that which allows me to connect with life. Work helps me to exist harmoniously with all that of which I am a part, all that from which I came, and all that to which I might one day return. In a sense, work is what allows me to feel a part of that which some might call God. The alternative suggests taking from life without regard for that which gives it sustenance, to live as though life owes me something, as if I am in some way entitled. The longer I live, the more I come to believe there is very little in this world to which I am entitled: not peace or happiness, not the respect or love of others, not social justice, and certainly not material possessions, fame, or wealth. Living life with an attitude of entitlement always leaves me looking outside myself for the source of my serenity and peace. And this invariably results in my feeling unhappy, powerless, bitter, resentful, and all too often angry. More often than not, living with a sense of entitlement has also left me wanting to blame something or someone or God, when I didn't get that which I wanted or felt I deserved. Over time, I've come to believe that real joy, real peace, is to be found in accepting who I am, in working diligently to *earn* that which I desire, and in relying upon God to bring me anything else I truly need.

When speaking of love, I'm referring to the act of *caring* about anything and everyone encountered. It might be equivalent to the love Jesus spoke of so often. It may also be found in that which the Buddha refers to as Enlightenment or what Martin Heidegger meant in *Being and Time* when suggesting "care" as a primordial existential of the human condition. It's not what people mean by romantic love or brotherly love or compassion. And it's clearly not the same as feeling sympathy for those less fortunate. All these may be expressions of love, but for me, love means something far more. Love means making a conscious and mindful choice to *be* loving or caring toward all that with which I come into contact through my worldly experience, even the least little thing.

For example, on any given day, I can encounter people from all walks of life, many of whom look or behave very differently from me. They may also hold values and beliefs quite different from my own. And on some occasions, I might even experience wildlife of various species, trees, rivers, deserts, even natural calamities like thunderstorms, hurricanes, floods, and so on. And in each of these instances, I may be confronted by "decision points" or opportunities calling me to choose how I will respond. In my professional life, I might be called to help a client who's gravely assaulted another, committed incest, abandoned his or her spouse or child, or is contemplating suicide. In my personal life, I might encounter more mundane things like a child falling down or a neighbor's home being damaged by a storm or a turtle struggling to cross a busy road. Maybe I witness a panhandler alongside the road or see an opportunity to get ahead financially by deceiving another. These and countless other happenings can arise in the course of my daily existence. And each of these provides an opportunity for me to choose how I want to respond, how I want to live my life, and what kind of person I want to be. Nobody forces these situations on me; they arise as the substance of my day-to-day experiences. And it is up to me to decide what to do with these opportunities. I can choose to ignore them, I can choose to respond in a selfish or self-serving manner, I can choose to be judgmental or condemning, or I can choose to be understanding, loving, and caring. Sometimes the choices are easy; sometimes they are not. Sometimes my ego gets in the way, or my intellect rationalizes away the harm I do by taking the easy way out. Sometimes I try to ignore what I see, or I find myself thinking only of my own needs or wants or fears. Maybe I find myself giving in to hedonistic appetites or seeking immediate gratification. I too face temptations. I too struggle to do the *right* thing, the loving and caring thing. I too fall down. But every moment of my life, I am given choices to make.

Over the years, I've gotten better at realizing when I screw up and better at recognizing when I've chosen to do things *my* way instead of the caring way, the way that is in harmony with existence, God's way. And I have also gotten better at forgiving myself when I don't get it right. I've gotten better about picking myself up and dusting myself off and trying again. And I've gotten better at realizing that I am not Jesus of Nazareth. I'm not the Buddha, just Ken: a work in progress like all other human beings—for better or worse. Pam and I still recall the words of a priest from the church we once attended. He would always end the weekly mass by saying, "The mass never ends. It must be lived. So let's go forth to love and serve the Lord." This is my goal, even when I don't get it right.

But while trying to put both work and love into my *daily* life has not always proven easy, striving to do so has made my life rewarding in ways it might otherwise never have been. Once I began living in accordance with this perspective, I would no longer be at the mercy of those around me, no longer be a victim of fate, and no longer be dependent on the "good will" of others for my inner peace. I, in collaboration with my God, would become the author of my life. And experiencing life from this perspective would also give me a vision for helping others that I might otherwise never have known.

Corbin, Kentucky, would be a small community of about five thousand people located some seventy miles south of Lexington, in southeastern Kentucky. It was situated in the foothills of the Appalachian Mountains, and like many rural communities near or around these mountains, it was fraught with poverty, unemployment, substance use, incest, and all manner of violence. In some ways, I would always be struck by how similar the problems of this region were to those I'd encountered with inner-city Pittsburgh—not exactly the same, but similar.

The region had long been known for its struggles. I read once that much of the Appalachians had been settled hundreds of years earlier by predominantly indentured servants coming over from Europe. Many of these individuals were reported to have had limited intellect, poor education, few employable skills, mental illness, and/or histories of criminal behavior. And such problems commonly left these individuals struggling with effectively adapting to life in their native countries. More often than not, these individuals would wind up destitute, homeless, or in jails.

As the call went out for people to help populate the colonies of the "New World," many community leaders saw this as a way to rid themselves of a perceived drain on their societies. At the same time, many of these struggling souls viewed it as an opportunity to start a new life. Thus, in exchange for committing themselves to seven years of servitude (give or take), these individuals would be relocated to America where they'd be provided food, shelter, etc. until such time as they had satisfied their debt and earned their freedom. Unfortunately, the personal concerns that had made it difficult for them to fit in with European society didn't just vanish once they were in America. These individuals remained troubled by the same problems that once made life difficult in their countries of origin. And as a result, once free, they would have similar struggles adjusting to their new life in the colonies. This would lead many of those indentured servants who had earned their freedom to settle in the remote areas of the Appalachian Mountains. Here, life would be hard, but it was a place where most other colonists did not want to settle and where those who did might be left alone.

In some respects, after several generations, not much has changed for this region. Even President Johnson's valiant attempt at spending countless US tax dollars in a 1960s social program designed to bolster infrastructure, education, employable skills, income levels, and the overall standard of living would yield only marginal benefits. To this day, the intellectual functioning generally remains one standard deviation below the national average, education is substandard, and substance abuse is widespread. Poverty is ever-present, employment opportunities remain limited, poor sanitation and pollution all too often contaminate the water table and environment, and welfare and disability serves as a primary source of income for an estimated 20 percent of its population. Children growing up in this region are frequently raised by parents struggling with their own mental health or substance-use problems and who have trouble modeling effective coping or problem-solving skills or instilling in their children any aspiration of hope for a brighter future. The result of all this is that too many children are raised in poverty, lacking adequate food and nutrition, receiving poor health care, and struggling to develop effective social, academic, and employment skills. Children from this region are also vulnerable to becoming frequent victims of physical and/or sexual abuse. Again, the situation is reminiscent of problems with inner-city Pittsburgh.

In those less common instances where a child demonstrates average or above average intellect and/or academic skills, or is lucky enough to have healthy parents who encourage striving for better life circumstances through pursuing meaningful employment or education, the child typically recognizes their best chance for achieving success in life is to leave the region in search of opportunities for advancing their dreams elsewhere. And once they leave, they seldom return. This only serves to further deprive the region of any chance for climbing out of its poverty and despair.

If it seems I've painted an unduly negative picture of life in Appalachia, such is not my intent. I only want to describe some of the tragic conditions under which people living right here in America sometimes exist as these were some of the problems faced by those clients and patients I'd work with at BRMC.

Corbin's only real claim to fame would be that of it being the home of Colonel Harland Sanders's original Kentucky Fried Chicken restaurant. Colonel Sanders hadn't actually lived in the town of Corbin proper. Rather, he lived just outside the city limits in the county of Laurel. The county seat for Laurel County was a similar-sized town named London.

INDIANA BOY

While Corbin quite accurately claimed to be the home of Colonel Sanders's first restaurant (and attached motel), London, Kentucky, laid claim to being home of the annual World Chicken Festival. This shindig was a four-day arts-and-crafts festival celebrating the county's favorite son, Harland Sanders. And it was complete with a carnival, nightly music, assorted vendor booths, the world's largest chicken frying pan, and a Colonel Sanders's look-alike contest. The London newspaper boasted of its attracting one hundred thousand attendees, although this number might have been somewhat exaggerated. London was located about sixty miles south of Lexington (and ten miles north of Corbin) along I-75. And this was where I would rent a townhouse and live while working at BRMC.

During the same time as I joined the staff of BRMC, Pam began her internship at the VAMC in Lexington. As I was still traveling back and forth to Lexington on a weekly basis to see friends and play music with the Firehouse Pickers, stopping by Pam's apartment to visit seemed a convenient way of remaining in touch and helping her adjust to life in Kentucky. I'd show her around Lexington, introduce her to some of the better restaurants, take her to an occasional concert at one of the local venues, or invite her to accompany me to local arts-and-crafts festivals (including the famed World Chicken Festival mentioned above). On one such occasion, I asked her to go with me to see the Firehouse Pickers. And I remember well how she was immediately taken by the experience. To this day, there is some disagreement on exactly when we began dating as I apparently thought we were dating long before she did. Nevertheless, we started dating sometime that fall.

The position I had hired into at BRMC would actually be a pretty good gig for an as-yet unlicensed but doctoral-trained clinical psychologist. Having my state certification as a drug and alcohol treatment specialist may also have helped me negotiate a more favorable contract. And I suspect scoring this job was also made possible by the fact that the hospital was located in a very remote area of southeastern Kentucky where few other professional psychologists were willing to move. Moreover, the hospital seemed in need of attracting someone with my credentials to anchor their newly established outpatient mental health department. In any event, my salary would be almost double that which many entry-level psychologist made at the time, and I was also able to negotiate an executive benefits package that included top-tier health care, retirement benefits, a life insurance policy, and more paid time off than was usual. Finally, the contract also covered payment for a licensed psychologist of my choice to help me complete requirements for my postdoctoral supervision. By the end of the first year, meeting this requirement would render me eligible for state licensure. Dr. Shurling (from the VA in Lexington) would be my supervisor of choice.

My duties at the hospital were split between working as an outpatient psychology clinician, a psychologist/addictions specialist on the adult inpatient addictions unit, and as psychologist for the inpatient physical rehabilitation unit. Working in the outpatient department was useful in that it allowed me to further my experience with traditional mental health assessment and therapy. Working on the addictions unit allowed me to maintain my skills working with alcoholics and addicts. But it was my role on the rehabilitation unit that was especially rewarding as this assignment allowed me to further advance my skills and expertise working with both aging adults and persons having all sorts of organic brain impairments. For a while, the job would truly represent the best of all worlds.

About a month or so after going to work at BRMC, around November of 1996, I received word that my brother Kevin had been diagnosed with a fast-growing brain tumor. His prognosis was considered poor. As noted above, Kevin and I hadn't been especially close since he left Columbus for Ball State University in the fall of 1967 (and the military shortly thereafter). Upon returning from the Army in 1969, he married and returned to Muncie, Indiana, and Ball State University to complete his degree in art education. Again, he would remain living in that area (actually, in the neighboring community of Anderson, Indiana) for the remainder of his life. Over the years, I'd heard reports of his becoming a bit of an adventure hound. It seems he raced motocross bikes for a few years, until mounting injuries led him to give that up. Later still, he had gotten into flying hot air balloons competitively. Prior to his onset of medical problems, he had participated in several National Championship Hot Air Ballooning competitions. In fact, he was away from home at a flying competition the weekend he became incapacitated with headache, nausea, and the rest. Upon returning home, he underwent a brain scan and was promptly diagnosed with cancer.

After learning of Kevin's diagnosis, I'd travel from Kentucky to be with family in Columbus. I remember driving up the interstate from London with tears flowing down my face and, at one point, needing to pull off the road and stop, lest I wreck my car. This crying made little sense to me as I was a trained psychologist with advanced education regarding loss and grief and figured I shouldn't be affected in such a manner. Yet there I was sobbing like a child. The lesson would be yet another reminder of the fact that, whether I was a psychologist or not, I would always be a human first, with all the vulnerabilities inherent therein.

A few months later, in the spring of 1997, Kevin and I would be talking on the phone. I can still recall his telling me that the saddest part of dying was knowing he'd never get to see his daughters grow up, graduate high school, get married, have kids, and the like. Realizing there was little I could do to change any of this, I suggested he might want to seek the support of his Higher Power. I'll never forget his responding, "What if I don't have one?" This response struck me as simply tragic. Again, it emphasized how fragile we are as humans. It also reminded me of the importance of never putting off the pursuit of God as we never know when tragedy might come. Pam and I would attend Kevin's funeral only a short time later.

Pam and I had dated throughout this period, became engaged, and would ultimately marry in July 1997. I mentioned above that, among other desirable qualities, Pam was essentially unselfish. Probably no one wants to think of themselves as being selfish, but the tendency is probably much more common than we like to admit. At one time or another, each of us has probably struggled with being selfish, with managing fears of not getting our needs or wants met, fears of not being treated fairly by others or being taken advantage of. I know I have. But selfishness can be deadly to lasting relationships, especially intimate ones. Why would I say this? Because any lasting relationship necessarily requires a certain degree of trust. And it can be genuinely difficult, maybe impossible, to trust another who is always putting their own wants and needs first.

Given this, one of the greatest gifts I'd ever receive from Pam would be that of learning to be unselfish. For me, learning to be unselfish (or less selfish, if you will) would teach me the value of letting those things that matter to Pam also matter to me. And this, in turn, would help me realize how caring about that which matters to another is *fundamental* to any mutually, loving relationship as being less selfish helps me appreciate the wisdom inherent in giving up some of those things I want or believe I need in the immediate present in exchange for those rewards that might come by sharing my life with another over the long haul. I've since come to believe that when mutual sharing is present, selfishness cannot exist. But where selfishness reigns, trust falters, and love dies.

Another of Pam's virtues that I valued would be her strong commitment to spirituality. As a youth, she had been raised in the Catholic church and attended Mass regularly. And shortly after we began dating, I'd start attending church with her. I didn't consider myself a Catholic at that time, and after some twenty-five years of attending Mass regularly, I still don't consider myself a Catholic. If I had to ascribe to any one specific spiritual path or other, it would probably be that of Taoism. But when it comes to matters of spirituality, I really don't like planting myself in any one spot. This is due to a couple of reasons. First, as mentioned above, though I've devoted a fair amount of time to studying the scriptural texts of several of the world's great religions, I've also come to believe that getting stuck on any one of these texts (be it the Bible, the Koran, the *Tao Te Ching*, or whatever) puts one at risk of never moving beyond such scriptures to reach the true spiritual destination one seeks. Again, Alan Watts likened scriptures to a finger pointing at the moon; if the person keeps staring at the tip of the finger instead of looking to where it points, then one may never see the moon. I've always wanted to see the moon. The other reason I don't like hanging my hat on any one doctrine is that holding to one particular doctrine at the exclusion of all others seems to imply a conviction that those believing in alternate or competing doctrines are necessarily wrong. In my earlier Baptist teaching, if you weren't one of us, a Baptist, then you could never hope to enter the gates of heaven (or, more poignantly, were condemned to hell). Such dogma may have been more the misguided beliefs of my particular Baptist ministers than of the Baptist church proper, but in any event, it seemed uncaring, judgmental, and inconsistent with the doctrine of love, acceptance, and forgiveness that I find more meaningful and uplifting.

WORK AND LOVE

Having said all this, while I don't consider myself a Catholic per se, I have never heard anything in a Catholic Mass that I experienced as being out of step with my own spiritual values. I am quite comfortable attending the Catholic church and have had many spirited and meaningful discussions with Catholic priests and parishioners alike. And through all these discussions, and those I've had with leaders of other faiths, I've actually come to believe that, regardless of their doctrine, truly spiritual people tend to have more in common with one another than they have differences. As for Pam and I, whatever our own personal differences, the fact that we both share a strong commitment to spirituality has always been an important factor in our love and marriage.

Again, in the summer of 1997, Pam and I would marry. Pam clearly wanted to be married in a Catholic church and by a Catholic priest. But inasmuch as I had never received formal annulment of my first marriage, and the fact that an annulment of any marriage through the Catholic church tends to be a rather lengthy process, a Catholic ceremony would have to wait until later. Accordingly, our wedding would be presided over by the Christian chaplain with whom I worked at BRMC. We would be married at the Cumberland Inn in Williamsburg, Kentucky.

Williamsburg is a town located some ten miles due south of Corbin (down I-75). And its population is even smaller than that of Corbin's, if you can imagine that. Williamsburg is probably most known for being home to Cumberland College. This college is a small, private, Baptist college having a somewhat prestigious pedigree. I've always suspected Cumberland Inn was built by one of the benefactors of the college in order to serve as a nearby residential facility for housing parents and other dignitaries visiting the college. Former president Jimmy Carter is even reported to have stayed there on one occasion while visiting the college. That was pretty impressive for such a small institution. The inn itself would consist of two structures, the original building and an annex building. The original/main building was a large, two-story, red brick building with great white pillars gracing its entrance and a beautiful domed roof. The annex building, of later construction, provided additional sleeping quarters and an indoor pool area.

Pam and I married in the lobby of the main building. Its splendor is difficult to recreate with words. The floors consisted of white, mirrorlike tiles, and at each end of the lobby was a large fireplace. A beautiful wooden, double staircase led up to the balcony overseeing the lobby, which was decorated with cherub statuettes, red velvet carpet, and velvet-covered chairs. Topping it all off was the most beautiful, hand-painted, angel-adorned dome spanning some twenty-five feet directly above the lobby. The main building also featured hotel-style rooms and some four or five hotel suites, each with its own fireplace. Finally, the inn also had a large conference/reception room and a first-class dining facility. I hope I have done justice in describing this venue. For us, it would be an ideal place to wed. Apart from its beauty and opulence, its location was within reasonable driving distance for both our families, and its proximity to the interstate made it convenient for all the other guests to reach. Moreover, its size and amenities were able to accommodate all those invited to attend the ceremony and reception.

Pam's sister Ann would serve as her matron of honor, and my brother Dave was my best man. Pam's other sister Tina was a bridesmaid, while my brother Kevin (who had died in May of 1997) was to have been my groomsman. We invited some eighty to ninety guests, and the music for the wedding ceremony proper was provided by Mike Sprague (who, as I noted earlier, had experience working as a disc jockey). We were able to reserve the entire main building and much of the annex, so out-of-town guests would all have their own private rooms on-site. The suites were ideal for Pam, our parents, the matron of honor, and the best man. Any other guests of the inn would be located in the annex so as not to intrude on our wedding. The balcony would prove a perfect location for the rehearsal dinner, and the conference room provided ample space for the reception. The dining room staff handled all the catering, and music for the reception was provided by (who else) the Firehouse Pickers. The overall grandeur of the facility also proved perfect for the wedding photography. And as an added bonus, the inn was close enough to the highway to allow for a quick getaway when heading out for our honeymoon.

Pam and I would honeymoon in Nashville, Tennessee. Much as is true today, at that time, Nashville was the center of the country music industry. It was also home to the Grand Ole Opry, the Ryman Auditorium, the Country Music Hall of Fame, the Wildhorse Saloon, and other "touristy" sites. And the late 1990s would be the era of such noted country artists as George Strait, Alan Jackson, Reba McEntire, Vince Gill, Garth Brooks, Randy Travis, Clint Black, the group Alabama, and a host of other big-name performers. Given that Pam and I were both music lovers and fans of country music, Nashville seemed a perfect location to spend our first week together as husband and wife.

We stayed at what was then the Opryland Hotel. Sometime later, this hotel would become part of the larger Gaylord properties, but to this day, it remains one of the most lavish hotels in all of North America (maybe the world). It boasts several hundred sleeping rooms and suites, all in an indoor, climate-controlled environment. Many of the rooms and suites have balconies overlooking lush gardens that include waterfalls, decorative fountains, and elevated walkways. The complex also boasts expansive lobbies with ornate staircases, passageways with floor-to-ceiling murals, an assortment of conference rooms, and an indoor river meandering through a vast convention area. Amid all this luxury, one can also find assorted coffee shops, sports bars, restaurants, clothing boutiques, a health spa, and live music venues. While many might prefer to honeymoon in Hawaii or on some other tropical island, for this small-town boy from Indiana and a girl from south Alabama, it was quite the ticket.

Pam and I would have a third-floor room with a balcony overlooking a waterfall in the Cascade Gardens. We obtained tickets to an outdoor *Shenandoah* Concert, attended the *Grand Ole Opry*, and went to a *Hot Rize* bluegrass show at the *Ryman Auditorium*—all in addition to taking in live music at the Opryland theme park and hotel pubs. We took a dinner cruise up the Cumberland River on the *General Lee*, rode river taxis from the hotel properties to downtown Nashville, danced at the *Wildhorse Saloon*, and were able to walk from the hotel to the theme park. While this would prove to be the final year for the Opryland theme park (as it closed that winter, only to be replaced by a shopping mall), we have never forgotten our time there. The weather was great for the duration of our stay, and it would be a honeymoon we'd always remember.

Upon returning to Kentucky, Pam continued living in her Lexington apartment while completing her internship and doctoral degree, while I returned to my townhouse in London and working at BRMC. On weekends, we'd commute back and forth to be with each other. Pam would then join me in London that fall.

Pam's plan had always been to return to Mobile, Alabama, and live near family upon completing her VA training. But we'd made good friends while living in Lexington, and as I was already gainfully employed and making good money at BRMC, we initially decided to set up house in southeastern Kentucky.

WORK AND LOVE

The fact of my parents being older than Pam's also entered into the picture as we had concerns mine might experience failing health and be in need of our support sooner on than her parents. Traveling from Kentucky to Indiana would prove much easier than making trips from Alabama to Indiana. So by staying in Kentucky, I could be more readily available in case of emergencies. It would remain a part of our long-range plans to relocate to Mobile after my parents' deaths.

For Pam, moving into what was now our townhouse in the London/Corbin area must have seemed like moving to the middle of nowhere. It was probably the most rural and, thus, isolated location wherein either of us had ever lived. After a few months, Pam signed on to a psychologist's position with the community mental health center also in Corbin. As we might have anticipated, this job would eventually become quite stressful for Pam because the pay was considerably less than what I was making, and the center was woefully understaffed relative to the number of clients each clinician was expected to serve. Still, for the time being, working at this center helped to pay our bills and provide Pam an opportunity to gain her postdoctoral supervised experience so she too might qualify for state licensure the following year. Again, once licensed, Pam would be eligible to practice independently.

While our townhouse in London wasn't fancy, it served our needs well. It was a two-bedroom, two-story unit, built amid a row of townhouses just off the main drag of town. It was clean and of reasonably new construction, and we would live there the first couple of years of our marriage. Because of the rural nature of the setting, we continued traveling back and forth to Lexington in order to dine at better restaurants, attend concerts, visit friends, and play music with the Firehouse gang. In late summer of 1998, I would again perform live with the

Firehouse Pickers, this time at the Red Mule Bluegrass Festival in Berea, Kentucky. By then, Pam had also joined the group.

As already noted, London was kind of in the middle of nowhere. But eventually, we'd find other recreation in and around the hills of southeastern Kentucky, attending various fall festivals, state parks, high school sporting events, and so on. One venue we especially enjoyed was Renfro Valley, located some fifteen minutes north of London along I-75. Renfro Valley was established as a live music venue decades earlier and had prevailed over the years despite the many economic hardships of the region. It might best be thought of as a smaller version of Branson, Missouri. In addition to a small motel, an RV campground, assorted restaurants, and novelty shops, Renfro Valley was home to a weekly barn dance featuring a house band made up of predominantly local musicians. I'd learn sometime later that my great uncle, Rex Starkey (who had fancied himself a singing cowboy), performed as a regular at this venue in the late 1940s and early 1950s. Who knew?

Renfro Valley was also home to a larger, more recently built venue wherein first- and second-tier country and bluegrass music artists would perform at various times throughout the year. Again, as Pam and I were both into this style of music during our time in southern Kentucky, we'd attend many a concert at Renfro Valley, including performances by Ricky Van Shelton, Brad Paisley, Steve Wariner, Patty Loveless, and even the Moron Brothers, among others. On occasion, my brother Dave and his wife would come down from Columbus and join us. At yet other times, friends we'd made while playing with the Firehouse Pickers would come down from Lexington. Again, Pam and I would share memories of our outings to Renfro Valley for years to come.

Earlier, I noted how relocating to a new area would inevitably lead to my checking out the local music stores. One such store that became a regular spot for Pam and I was Gibson's Music in Corbin. Historically, music stores have been owned and operated by sole proprietors who themselves have a love for music and a desire for sharing their passion with others. Tom Pickett's Music Center in Columbus was a perfect example of such a store. Over the years, many of these smaller stores have died out or been replaced by corporate-owned "big box stores." Because of their extensive financial backing, corporate stores often carry a much larger inventory of instruments and accessories than the smaller mom-and-pop stores ever could. Moreover, because of their sales volume, the bigger stores can usually sell their merchandise at a larger discount than do smaller stores. But what often works against these larger stores is the fact that they tend to be run by managers whose primary job is to focus more on generating income and making a profit than on serving their communities. Thus, the bigger stores frequently lack familiarity with their clientele and fail to develop personal relationships with their customers. Smaller stores understand that knowing and working with their customers represents their only hope for surviving in today's market. And this was true for the owners of Gibson's Music.

This store had been established by one Betty Gibson, who was a local resident with a love for playing piano. Over time, she began giving piano lessons to others out of her home. And this eventually led to her opening a small store through which she could also sell the occasional piano. As the years passed and her reputation grew, Betty expanded her store to include everything from upright pianos to electric keyboards and even baby grand pianos. By the time Pam and I had moved to the London/Corbin area, Betty was not only selling keyboards and pianos but Gibson, Fender, Martin, Taylor, and other high-end guitars as well. Her inventory also included bass guitars, banjos, mandolins, violins, amplifiers, percussion of all sorts (drum sets, cymbals, tambourines, etc.), brass instruments, PA systems, and a complete range of accessories (guitar strings, picks, straps, instrument cords, drumsticks, etc.). For a store located in such a small, rural community, Gibson's Music had become quite an elaborate operation.

The success of her store would also result in Betty becoming a bit of a business legend in little Corbin, Kentucky. She was a strong, independent woman who had created a local landmark all on her own. And people came from towns and counties miles away to purchase instruments and sound equipment from Gibson's Music. Betty also helped establish the Southeastern Kentucky Fine Arts Guild, regularly sponsoring renowned musicians (violinists, pianists, and others—including guitarist Tommy Emmanuel) to come to the local area and help promote awareness of music and other fine arts. Finally, Betty and Gibson's Music would also join with our private practice (Professional Psychology Services) to cosponsor "Music for Mental Health." This endeavor was a program whereby we jointly donated musical instruments to local mental health agencies and school programs as a way of giving back to the community. Her store celebrated its fiftieth anniversary in 2019.

Apart from her reputation as a businesswoman, Betty Gibson (who eventually became Betty Comer upon marrying Gene Comer) was a wonderfully kind and caring woman. And Pam and I would end up spending many a Saturday afternoon at Gibson's Music visiting with Betty and her husband and (occasionally) helping out on the sales floor when customer traffic got heavy. In addition to purchasing an assortment of instruments from Gibson's Music over the years, at varying times, both Pam and I both took music lessons from the teachers Betty had on hand (Pam on piano, and I on guitar). On three separate occasions, the Comers even arranged for Pam and me to accompany them to the summer NAMM (National Association of Music

Merchandisers) convention. NAMM is a biannual gathering of all the major musical instrument manufacturers organized for the purpose of marketing their latest products to music store owner/operators. In addition to collecting assorted T-shirts, guitar strings, and other complimentary gifts, going to NAMM allowed Pam and me to attend some of the private concerts the manufacturers would hold as promotional events. These were great times creating even greater memories. I am convinced that acquaintances are a dime a dozen, but real friends are more difficult to come by. A person may be lucky to discover even a handful of real friends over the course of a lifetime. Betty and Gene became real friends.

Finally, visiting Gibson's Music also introduced me to one Gary Baxter. Gary was a guitar picker and music teacher who would be invaluable to my ongoing development as an amateur musician. In addition to being a very good guitar player, Gary was also a former schoolteacher who seemingly had become disenchanted with working in public school systems. As a result, he chose to pursue his dream and make a living playing music. Gary was clearly an excellent guitar player. And he impressed me both by his ability to play a wide variety of musical styles and his knack for sight-reading music (as mentioned earlier, a skill I'd never be able to master). But what struck me most about Gary, apart from his caring demeanor and integrity as a person, was his ability to teach guitar in accordance with the needs and skill level of the student. Some teachers have an entire, preplanned method of instruction for students wishing to learn an instrument. They see themselves as the expert in charge. And for some students, this may be exactly what is needed. But Gary seemed to understand that, much like a good psychologist or therapist, teaching music is a collaborative process, not a process where a so-called expert is always in charge but one where the teacher and student work together to achieve the desired outcome.

In keeping with this approach, Gary would have me play music I was already familiar with so he could get an idea of my existing skill level. Then he'd ask me what I wanted to learn or needed help with. Near the end of the session, he'd also check in with me to see if I was satisfied with what I was learning. And as needed, we would alter the direction of the instruction. This collaborative approach to teaching guitar was much like the approach to therapy emphasized by Duquesne's psychology training. It would allow me to have input on the teaching process to enhance the likelihood of my realizing those goals that were meaningful for me. Under Gary's instruction, my guitar playing would progress in a fashion that had never been true with any other teacher. Gary knew guitar, but as importantly, he also knew people.

By December 1997, the vice president and clinical director who had recruited me to BRMC would be accused of sexual harassment by a subordinate. While the allegations would go unverified, concerns of BRMC administrators that a lawsuit might ensue resulted in his being released from the hospital a short time later. The next clinical director promptly began questioning the reason for my generally lucrative contract. Fortunately for me, before she could make any changes to my salary or benefits, she too would be terminated. The next clinical director would succeed in freezing my salary and benefits package, but not until after I'd successfully passed my state licensure exam and became a fully licensed psychologist. This director would last only a year before recognizing the administration's apparent instability and leaving for a similar position at a hospital in a neighboring state. By this point, I was beginning to think the chaos would never end. Moreover, the repeated turnover of supervisors had made my work increasingly difficult as each incoming department head seemed to have his or her own agenda and ideas about how things should be run. Dealing with all these changes, in addition to my having to reeducate each on my skills, areas of training, expertise, and the limits thereto, left me increasingly frustrated.

Three years into my time at BRMC, I'd finally become sufficiently concerned about the hospital's administrative workings to question the viability of staying there long term. As a result, with the help of Dr. Shurling, I'd begin exploring other employment options. This included the possibility of opening a private psychology practice. Initially, I would only establish a part-time clinic completing evaluations for the Kentucky Department for Disability Determination Services. But by the end of 1999, Pam had pretty much settled into her job at the community mental health center, and the part-time clinic had proven itself viable. Consequently, I decided to leave the hospital and formally open a full-time private psychology practice in London, Kentucky. In January 2000, Professional Psychology Services, PSC (PPS) would become a reality.

While starting up a private business may seem daunting to some, it really isn't rocket science. Lots of people do it. Still, to establish a viable business that covers the expenses, meets payroll, and can operate with some integrity usually requires a certain vision, a plan for implementing that vision, and a commitment to work with attention to detail. My doctoral training and professional experience, in conjunction with my state license, now meant I had something of value to offer my community. The next step would be to write up the vision and mission statements that would guide the practice. With Pam's input, we decided that providing *quality* psychological assessment and therapy services in an *ethical and professional* manner would be the focus of our private office. Next we secured a post office box and bank account and undertook the task of creating a budget. Lastly, after obtaining guidelines from the secretary of state office for the Commonwealth of Kentucky, we drew up incorporation papers.

It took a little while to locate office space, but eventually we rented a two-story building one block off Main Street in London. The building had previously served as home to a family-owned real estate business. Still, it met our needs perfectly. It had two offices ideal for providing clinical services, a small waiting area, two restrooms, a common area for fax machine, copier, file cabinets, etc., and an additional larger area that could be used for testing purposes and/or storage. Next, we had the office sign prepared, stationery and marketing brochures made up, and purchased the necessary furniture and psychological testing materials. By early 2000, I was able to begin seeing clients through PPS. A month or so later, we had our official grand opening, complete with the mayor of London (KY) presiding over the ribbon-cutting ceremony. Members of the London Chamber of Commerce, as well as other professionals from the community and a reporter/photographer (who had stopped by to prepare an article for the local newspaper), were also in attendance. My mother and Pop made it down from Indiana, along with my brother Dave and his wife. Finally, my mentor Dr. Shurling and his wife, coworkers from the mental health center where Pam worked, and those with whom I had worked during my time at BRMC brought flowers and office plants. This office would serve as my first venture into the world of private practice, and it would eventually prove lucrative enough to generate a comfortable income for both Pam and myself. Two years later, after losing the lease on this space, we'd relocate to a different office in another area of town.

From the onset, a regular source of income for our private offices (both in London and, later on, in Mobile) would be evaluations of claimants applying for benefits through both the

Department for Disability Determination Services (DDS) and the Department for Vocational Rehabilitation Services (DRS). This type of work tends to be more forensic than clinical in nature, insofar as *clinical* assessments are designed to facilitate an individual's *treatment*, while *forensic* assessments are intended to provide data to be used within a *legal context*. In the case of assessments completed for DDS, as well as those for DRS, the psychologist is contracted by a third party to document existing concerns so as to assist with their making a more accurate decision regarding a claimant's application for benefits. Accordingly, for these assessments, the actual client is the agency/judge who is seeking reliable diagnostic evidence to be used in rendering an appropriate legal determination.

To explain further, disability evaluations are assessments of those individuals applying for government benefits to be awarded in keeping with the Americans with Disabilities Act originally passed around 1990. These benefits can come in two forms: an insurance card to assist the claimant with obtaining medical treatment and monthly income to help with paying for food, clothing, shelter, and other necessities of life. Persons eligible for these benefits may include those having disabling health conditions that *significantly* limit achievement in school (children and/or adolescents) or in the workplace (adults). Where alleged disabling conditions are medical in nature (e.g., back pain, blindness, heart disease, COPD, etc.), medical doctors are assigned to gather the evidence of record. Where the alleged disabilities are of a learning, substance-use, or psychological nature (e.g., ADHD, intellectual disability, depression, alcoholism, anxiety, dementia, etc.), licensed psychologists are so contracted.

Our society has long recognized there to be some people who, for any number of reasons, are unable to fend for themselves. In such cases, the humane thing is to provide these individuals with the basic resources whereby they can still meet their day-to-day needs. And this is the intent of the Americans with Disabilities Act (a similar statute exists to assist individuals having certain disabling conditions with getting retrained, when feasible, so they might again become productive, taxpaying workers). But deciding how to best help individuals in need is not always an easy task.

At one time or another, many of us may have fantasized about a utopian society wherein everyone's basic needs are met without reservation. Still, most would agree that the goods and resources necessary for meeting these needs have to come from somewhere. Ultimately, this means someone has to work to produce them. And when it comes to redistributing resources to disabled individuals, it also means someone has to decide from whom the resources will be taken and to whom those resources will be given. Obviously, deciding how to award these social benefits can get complicated.

Due to the disability program being funded by taxpayer dollars, the program falls under the control of politicians. And unfortunately, as we all know, politicians seldom agree on whom and under what conditions taxpayer dollars should or should not be spent. This is where the Department of Disability Determination Services (as well as the Department for Vocational Rehabilitation Services) comes in. DDS (along with a federal hearing judge) is the governmental agency responsible for making decisions regarding an individual's requests for disability benefits.

Now psychologists by their nature (if not their training) are usually aware of the intrinsic health benefits associated with being able to meet one's basic needs. Having the necessary resources to access food, shelter, and the like obviously alleviates much personal distress and suffering. But most psychologists also recognize the very real mental health benefits associated with being productive and providing for oneself. Working (when feasible) bolsters one's self-esteem, one's self-confidence, and one's sense of worth. Working also provides financial resources that help a person feel more in control of their daily existence. Working can help establish the social network commonly needed for one to feel connected with others and less isolated from the world at large. And finally, working helps give personal meaning to one's daily life. All these are psychological benefits of working.

Still, there is a reason that work is called work and not play. Work, by its very nature, requires one to give something of themselves in exchange for something else. Thus, work usually requires sacrifice. And this sacrifice can be unpleasant, fatiguing, and at times, even arduous. Moreover, even when one loves the work they do, there are usually occasions whereupon one would just rather not "show up." Play, on the other hand, usually requires minimal if any sacrifice. Oftentimes, we seek out opportunities to engage in play, and we seldom complain about it. Play is fun.

Given that individuals for any number of reasons may not *like* to work, when it comes to awarding disability benefits, DDS must decide between those truly qualifying for the benefits and those seeking disability benefits who actually could but *prefer* not to work. Similarly, to reduce instances of social security fraud, DDS is tasked with distinguishing between applicants who are or are not being honest about the disabling conditions being alleged. Considering these secondary gain issues when awarding benefits helps assure that tax dollars are being justly spent and that adequate funds are available for meeting the needs of those who truly require such assistance.

Clearly, making decisions to award social security disability benefits can be difficult. So what guides DDS in making these decisions? To assist with rendering appropriate decisions, the law governing issuance of disability benefits requires both a qualifying medical, psychological, and/or intellectual/cognitive diagnosis (as rendered by a duly-licensed professional) *and* a determination of clear functional impairment. Only when each of these conditions are present can disability benefits be awarded. And this is where a psychologist's expertise comes in.

As a psychologist, my role would be to accurately assess for symptoms of any diagnosable mental health, substance-use, or cognitive disorder the individual might have; identify the functional limitations associated therewith; and establish a prognosis for the individual's recovery (in the coming twelve months) with available treatment. As a psychologist, I would also be asked to sort through and report any apparent under- or overreporting of symptoms (dissimulation) associated with secondary gain issues. It would not be my role to draw conclusions regarding the claimant's appropriateness for benefits, any more than it would be my role to assess the claimant's motives or question the wisdom of the judge's legal finding regarding a claimant's eligibility. Rather, for these types of evaluations, I would be expected to remain a fair and nonjudgmental gatherer of evidence to help guide the judge's decision. This same rule of thumb would apply when completing evaluations of applicants for vocational rehabilitation benefits. While this work would not always prove easy, it would nonetheless remain important as, oftentimes, real lives hang in the balance. It's no exaggeration to say that conducting these kinds of assessments would represent a meaningful portion of the income generated through our private practice offices for decades to come.

A few months or so after opening PPS, Pam would be exploring the London countryside and come upon what would eventually be our first house. It was listed as being a 1,750-square-foot, three-bedroom ranch, located in Reed Valley Estates just outside the London City limits. There were probably twenty or so homes grouped together in this subdivision, each of newer construction and built on 1 1/2-acre plots. Behind the house was a sloping hill that ultimately bottomed out and rose again to create a ravine through which rainwater would drain from the surrounding countryside into a large pond located on the adjacent property. Mowing this hill would prove quite an adventure as, on more than one occasion, the riding mower I owned would pick up speed on the way down and run away, with me holding on for dear life. Then it'd bottom out in the ravine and slowly climb the opposite side. I eventually learned to mow side to side so as to reduce this problem, only to encounter other problems with balancing the mower so it wouldn't roll over on the steep slope. Overall, the mowing would be challenging. But Pam and I would grow to love the privacy this hill and the expansive piece of property provided. We also grew to have a greater appreciation for the principle of drainage as we spent the best part of five years figuring out how to reinforce the ravine such that we might eliminate erosion and establish grass in the ditch, while still accounting for the flow of water moving through it.

While the house was listed as being 1,750 square feet, it also had a 1,000-square-foot finished, walk-out basement that increased the overall living space greatly. At long last, I'd have a designated area in which to set up my guitars and other equipment and where I could devote real time to playing music. A few years later, I'd also utilize this space to set up my first in-home recording studio. As for the house itself, it was only about five years old when we purchased it and probably larger than the two of us needed. But we both appreciated having a home to call our own and the chance to create memories as first-time homeowners.

As time passed, Pam and I grew increasingly comfortable living in rural southeastern Kentucky. We'd discover we were close enough to both Knoxville and Gatlinburg, Tennessee, to add these locations to our list of weekend getaway sites (in addition to Lexington). We'd also spend the occasional weekend in Cincinnati, Ohio, as well. And such recreation options helped alleviate the sense of isolation initially felt by living in this remote region of the state. Then to satisfy Pam's desire to be close to her family, once or twice a year, we'd arrange for her to take trips to Mobile. Finally, we also traveled to Indiana to visit my family two or three times a year, and Dave and his wife would visit us in Kentucky as often as possible.

I mentioned above that my stepfather (Pop) had experienced his first stroke while I was attending classes at Wright State in 1994. He was in his late sixties at the time, and the stroke had left him somewhat drained of his zeal for living. Immediately after the stroke proper, he experienced moderate to severe dysphasia (word-finding problems) with some apparent memory loss. But as can be true for some stroke survivors, these issues gradually improved with time. Still, in combination with his advancing age and other health concerns, Pop slowly retreated from the world. I don't think he was clinically depressed, just tired of struggling with life. He'd given up driving, was having problems getting around, and was pretty much unable to take care of the household repairs that had once made up such a big part of his daily routine after retiring. My mom tried her best to keep him engaged, but her own limited coping skills and the decline in Pop's overall functioning all left her at a bit of a disadvantage. She continued to be loving and nurturing and gradually learned to handle the household finances and to farm out household maintenance problems. And she would be successful at establishing a stable homelife for the two of them in their later years. But Pop would never be quite the same. In August of 2000, Pop had another stroke. He died a few days later.

WORK AND LOVE

You never know what you are going to get with a stepparent. In many ways, we kids got real lucky with Pop. He may not have been given to sharing feelings openly. And he was equally reluctant to offer praise. But as indicated above, he agreed to help raise my siblings and me at a time when he truly wasn't obligated to do so. As already stated, Mom's marrying Pop also meant we had regular food, regular heat, and a far nicer place to live than had been true at any other time in our lives. More importantly, Pop's steady demeanor gave each of us a sense of emotional stability and security that had not been present since our parents divorced, and certainly not while Mom was trying to raise us on her own. Finally, I have always believed Pop's willingness to work and assume responsibility for our family helped instill these values in me. Pop would remain a steady source of support long after my biological father died. And eventually, I'd come to see him as one of the most important role models in my life. I grew to love him deeply. I still do.

The end of 1999 brought the now infamous "New Millennium" scare. For those who have never heard of this or who may be too young to recall the event, it turned out to be a real farce. I guess I'd always been slow at adapting to those newer technologies that are now commonplace. So at the time of the century change, I was not particularly concerned. Unfortunately, a lot of people in America and around the world were. Many feared that due to the way computers were programmed to operate and our ever-growing reliance upon them, mankind was facing a worldwide collapse that would throw civilization into chaos at 12:01 a.m. on January 1, 2000. Pam and I had never been given to partying, so we decided to celebrate December 31, 1999, quietly by renting a suite at the Cumberland Inn (the place where we had married) in Williamsburg, Kentucky. New Year's Eve would come and go, and all the anxiety people felt would be for naught. Nothing changed; the world didn't end. Little would ever be heard of the matter again.

This would not be true for September 11, 2001. Many of today's younger generation may not fully appreciate the events that transpired that day. Some might never have heard of them or know of them only through secondhand accounts or television footage viewed later on. But much as has been true with reports of other tragedies the world has known, secondhand accounts of the events of 9/11 could never fully convey the magnitude of the suffering caused or the trauma experienced. For all those whose lives were both directly and indirectly affected by the events, as well as for the psyche of the American people in general, things would never be quite the same. On this day, terrorism arrived at our nation's doorstep. And in some regard, it would never leave.

I remember clearly where I was when I first heard the news—much as I remember where I was when I first learned of President Kennedy's assassination in 1964. I was working out of the private office in London, Kentucky, and had just finished with my initial appointment of the day. I was heading to the post office to pick up the office mail when the news reports came on my car radio. On that day, the most memorable terrorist attack ever to occur on American soil was carried out. Not since the bombing of Pearl Harbor at the onset of WWII had America experienced anything similar. Thousands of American citizens would lose their lives when Middle East terrorists highjacked passenger airliners and crashed them into the World Trade Center towers of New York City and the Pentagon near Washington, DC. Passengers thwarted yet another such plane from successfully crashing into its target (the White House), although all the occupants were killed when the plane was forced down into a field in Pennsylvania.

As for the planes striking the Twin Towers, not only would all the occupants of those planes be killed, but also the resulting explosions killed some three thousand workers inside the buildings and hundreds more in the buildings surrounding Ground Zero. Over time, countless police officers, firemen, and other first-responders aiding those injured in the explosions would also die from related health concerns. And family members would grieve the loss of countless loved ones, with the remains of some never being found or identified. Finally, for years to come, tens of thousands more would suffer from trauma, respiratory problems, and other concerns related to the explosions proper.

Communities all across America struggled to make sense of the events and of the hatred behind them. And many of us also struggle with discerning how to avoid judging all people of Muslim beliefs negatively while still acknowledging that those who attacked our nation had proclaimed their actions to be true acts of Muslim faith. Finally, Americans would struggle for years with knowing the attacks were ultimately responsible for the US launching a Middle East war that would cost hundreds more American lives and affect countless more American families for decades to come. To this day, it can be difficult to fully appreciate the sacrifices made by those soldiers (and their loved ones), while volunteering in service of their country with hopes of reducing the chances for such an occurrence ever happening again.

While Pam and I held little concern for any terrorist attack happening in rural southeastern Kentucky, we would have our own related stress. I had previously worked with several colleagues from the Middle East while employed at BRMC. And both Pam and I had international friends from the region who were living in the London area. As psychologists, we also understood the anxiety that existed throughout America in general and within the American Muslim community in particular. Still, we both knew there were clear limitations to anything we might do in our community to try and fix things. In many respects, I guess we simply felt helpless.

In the midst of all this turmoil, Pam and I decided we needed something a little more positive to focus on. Everything just seemed so dark, so hopeless. As a result, and strange as it might seem, we started talking about the idea of having a child. Even as I write, I understand how odd this might seem, given all the upheaval surrounding the 9/11 attacks. But sometimes a worldwide tragedy encourages one to begin thinking about what's most important in life. And for years, everyone else had been saying we should have kids. While we didn't want to have children simply because others thought it was the thing to do, we both knew our time for having a child could soon be running out. And the attack had clearly reminded us of the fragility of life. Consequently, at least considering parenthood seemed appropriate. Still, the decision to become parents would not be easy.

As noted above, my first marriage had ended in divorce. But while I had grown increasingly confident in my ability to be a decent husband, I still wasn't convinced I had the maturity to be a good parent. Moreover, I was acutely aware of the personal struggles my own parents experienced and the scars it produced for me and my siblings. The thought I might one day wind up putting a child of my own through the pain and suffering I had experienced was scary. Then there was the fact of Pam being in her middle thirties and having some misgivings of her own. In any event, after much contemplation and prayer, and consulting with a reproductive clinic, we ended up not really making a choice one way or the other. Instead, we decided to turn it over to God. This may sound silly to some, but we really had settled into our life together and were comfortable with who we were, both as individuals and as a couple. We had learned to live in the present and to have faith that if our Higher Power wanted us to become parents, then it would happen; if not, then we would accept the alternative. As the years passed, we never would become parents (not of children, anyway). Still, as a result of learning to live one day at a time and in God's grace, I don't think either of us hold any lasting regrets.

These mist-covered mountains,
Are a home now for me.
But my home is the low lands,
And always will be,
Someday you'll return to,
Your valleys and your farms.
And you'll no longer burn
To be brothers in arms.

—Mark Knopfler

From "Brothers in Arms," words and music by Mark Knopfler.
Copyright: 1985 by Chariscourt Limited.

PROFESSIONAL PSYCHOLOGY SERVICES—MOBILE

IN 2002, THE STRESS OF WORKING AT the community mental health center had become such that Pam decided to quit her job and join me at Professional Psychology Services, PSC. Now some people might think working with their spouse would be neat. And for the most part, I think both Pam and I have enjoyed this experience. But in reality, working together is probably not a good idea for most couples. Spending the entire workday with a person and then going home to see the same face during your "downtime" has its own kind of stress. Work conflicts can quickly become home conflicts if one is not careful, and vice versa. Luckily, the respect and love we strive to show each other, and our commitment to God and family first, have made working together a viable option for us. Still, I probably wouldn't recommend it for most couples.

Pam's joining PPS had been made possible because of my having recently completed some sixty-plus hours of postdoctoral training in the areas of forensic psychology and neuropsychology. With this advanced training under my belt, I'd now be able to take on more work in these new areas while Pam could assume much of the work I had previously been doing. And expanding our services would also make the practice successful enough to pay both our salaries.

Forensic psychology, as suggested during my discussion of DDS assessments, is that specialty area of psychology dealing with legal systems, court cases, judges, attorneys, and criminal justice clients. Again, for my practice, the forensic work taken on would almost exclusively be forensic assessment (as opposed to forensic counseling—which is usually conducted in jail or prison settings or for individuals on parole/probation). In addition to those assessments already being completed for government agencies (e.g., DDS and DRS), I'd also start performing assessments for judges and attorneys involved with specific legal cases. This work included assessments of criminal responsibility (insanity), competency to stand trial, and competency to be adjudicated (or sentenced), etc. Sometimes, the assessments addressed questions about one's competency for managing personal, legal, and/or financial affairs. And in a few cases, I completed assessments involving child custody disputes associated with angrily contested divorces.

Again, rather than concerning myself with identifying problems or diagnoses for the purpose of facilitating treatment, these assessments usually involved helping a judge and/or an attorney reach an appropriate determination about a defendant's capacity to receive a fair trial, to be appropriately sentenced or incarcerated, to be competent to make certain life-sustaining decisions, or (in cases involving custody hearings) to address the "best interest of a child."

One of the more important factors distinguishing *forensic* work from *clinical* work (as also noted above) is that of the forthrightness with which clients report existing problems. Over the years, the clients I've assessed for *clinical* purposes have almost always been upfront reporting existing problems. Occasionally, this would not be true as there have been times when a client's psychiatric symptoms or cognitive/intellectual functioning limited their ability to communicate existing problems effectively. But for the most part, the clients I have worked with clinically usually wanted me to get an accurate picture of what was causing them problems so I might be able to help alleviate their distress.

Forensic clients, on the other hand, have oftentimes proved less forthright. Individuals, for example, who may have been involuntarily hospitalized out of a concern for their being a danger to self or others (a legal determination), were frequently prone toward underreporting existing symptoms in hopes that doing so would expedite their release from the hospital. On the other hand, many of the incarcerated defendants with whom I worked were given to exaggerating symptoms in hopes of either gaining release from jail and being transferred to a hospital setting or of influencing a jury or judge to render a lesser sentence for any crime they might have committed. Such dissimulation would require I become skilled in assessing not only an individual's actual symptoms but acts of under- or overreporting symptoms as well.

Another factor making forensic work difficult would be its requiring me to be ever vigilant about suspending any judgment I might have regarding the morality of the offense for which a defendant had been charged. Again, most of us, and especially psychologists, like to see ourselves as caring and nonjudgmental. But where an alleged offense is especially heinous (as in cases of rape, murder, child molestation, and the like), living up to this goal is not always easy—even though it is clearly necessary.

Providing forensic services would also require I remain neutral regarding any legal finding or sentence being considered by the court. And this would be particularly true for those cases wherein severe punishment and/or the death sentence were under consideration. Undertaking forensic work required I avoid advocating for either a defendant or society. Accordingly, my job would be to provide the court with accurate and reliable information as regards the substance-use, mental health, intellectual, and/or cognitive functioning of the defendant and how this data *might* pertain to any legal questions the court had raised. It would always be the judge's responsibility to make any *final* determination regarding the meaning of my findings relative to the offense alleged and in terms of existing law.

Lastly, forensic work would prove challenging because (as I'd quickly discover) both prosecuting attorneys and defense attorneys were frequently more concerned with my helping them win their cases than with my providing competent and ethical psychological data/evidence. Striving to maintain integrity and to do ethical work while completing these evaluations would be an ongoing and stressful task. And then there was the reality that a judge and/or the attorney for the opposing side were always scrutinizing my work. Mistakes or poorly done work could easily leave me looking unprofessional (like a fool). While this was probably as it should have been, given the importance of the work and the legal findings rendered, it still made the work difficult. On the other hand, while the work would be stressful (as well as time/labor-intensive), because of the expertise and attention to detail required, the work would also be lucrative.

Again, as for some of the specific cases I'd work on, they pretty much represented a cross section of those noted above, including court-ordered evaluations for divorcing couples involved in child custody disputes, completing evaluations for those seeking guardianship over another deemed of questionable competency, criminal assault cases wherein the accused's mental capacity was in question, etc. In one instance, I'd be asked to complete an evaluation of a juvenile in a capital murder case, wherein the defendant was accused of killing another in a drug deal gone awry. The juvenile was being tried as an adult, and the death penalty was being considered.

The neuropsychology work I'd do primarily focused upon completing assessments for patients of local neurologists and certain claimants of the Department for Disability Determination Services. Neurologists are those medical doctors who specialize in working with individuals recovering from neurocognitive disorders associated with strokes, head trauma, dementias, etc. And in many instances, neuropsychological assessments would assist these physicians with better meeting their patients' needs. As previously mentioned, the Department for Disability Determination Services is that governmental agency responsible for assisting individuals applying for benefits due to a disabling condition that limits employability. And from time to time, their applicants also claim disabilities attributable to neurocognitive disorders. Due to my internship training in neuropsychology, my more recent postdoctoral education in this area, as well as my long-standing interest in working with individuals having these sorts of problems, expanding the practice to allow for my providing neuropsychological assessments seemed a "no brainer."

Because of the rather complicated nature of neurocognitive disorders, assessment of such conditions would also tend to be both labor- and time-intensive—sometimes requiring anywhere from six to ten hours to complete. Like most evaluations, they'd usually begin with a review of any supporting records provided by the referral source. This provided background information on the individual's existing problems and the reason for the assessment. Next, a clinical interview would be completed to allow for the gathering of life history data regarding achievement of developmental milestones, any illnesses or injuries experienced during the person's lifetime that might be related to the person's premorbid functioning, and information pertaining to the nature and onset of the current problems. A mental status exam would then be completed to highlight current cognitive functioning and capacity for attending to other tasks of the assessment. Once adequate rapport had been established and the client was deemed sufficiently oriented/intact to continue the evaluation, neurocognitive testing would commence. Finally, after completing the testing, it would be scored and interpreted, and a report would be prepared.

For these types of evaluations, the domains of cognition tested would usually include attention, gross and fine motor skills, visual-spatial abilities, both expressive and receptive language functions, reasoning, judgment, other executive functions associated with problem-solving, and a wide range of memory functions. The goal of all the work would, of course, be to identify any prevailing cognitive or motor deficits, propose a diagnosis of the organic/brain condition responsible for these deficits, and suggest meaningful treatment recommendations.

Again, my taking on neuropsychological and forensic work would allow the practice to expand while also giving Pam a way out of the community mental health center. Accordingly, Pam would assume responsibility for many of the standard evaluations I'd previously been doing for social security claimants and those seeking services through the Department for Vocational Rehabilitation Services. The transition to our office also gave Pam the freedom inherent in being her own boss. Although, like most work, life as a private practitioner would still have its own kind of stress.

While being one's own boss might seem glamorous on the surface, anyone who has ever run their own business knows that along with all the freedom also comes all the responsibility. In our case, running our own business meant it was up to us to generate our paychecks. And if we didn't make money, we wouldn't get paid. We were also responsible for cleaning the restrooms, doing much of the building maintenance, and paying rent, utilities, and other office expenses. Then there was the fact that we also had to generate enough income to pay for our own health insurance (in addition to our salaries). And running our own practice meant never getting paid time off for holidays, vacations, or sick days because if we weren't working, we weren't bringing in revenue. Thus, taking time off always meant time without pay. Still, we were in charge. We could set our own schedules and choose for ourselves how much and what kinds of work we wanted to do. And overall, having Pam in the office would work out well for both of us.

Two thousand three was the year I decided to get into recording music. My work with Gary Baxter had been going pretty well, and I was pleased with the way my guitar skills were developing. But while I would have liked to have been playing music with others, my career limited this as an option. First, I loved working as a psychologist way too much to give it up, and I had invested way too much time and energy into my education and training to just walk away from the profession (and income). Additionally, my work as a psychologist was both time- and energy-consuming. Being in a band necessarily requires time for regular practice, rehearsal, performing, etc. And between the hours spent practicing psychology, managing the business, and trying to be a decent husband, it would simply be impossible to schedule regular time for playing music with others. Finally, there was also the problem of finding other healthy musicians with whom to play music. Believe it or not, this can be a challenging proposition as musicians (like individuals from all walks of life) can also struggle with substance abuse, mental illness, overgrown egos, and other demons that lead to group dissension and in-fighting. Because of this, locating caring, stable individuals serious about playing music while also being free of the problems that create so much drama and undermine the music is simply not as easy as one might think. For all these reasons, I knew that playing music with others was an unlikely option for me. Still, I wanted to utilize my guitar skills in such a way that others might actually hear me play. The solution would be to develop a small recording studio in my basement.

As noted above, I had already created a music room in the basement of our Reed Valley home. This eventually led to my purchasing a self-contained, eight-track recording machine with a built-in capacity for burning CDs. The machine was a modest unit by today's standards but one that met my needs. Each of the eight recording tracks had eight additional phantom tracks, so I could essentially record up to sixty-four tracks of music to be used later when mixing down a finished song.

For me, the actual recording itself would be a three-stage process. I'd start by choosing recordings performed by other artists that I was familiar with and then try to identify the various parts making up the song. As noted earlier, I'd always had a decent ear for music. So if I listened closely enough to the recordings, I could usually identify the different instruments and vocals that were blended together to compose the particular tune: one or two guitars, a bass, piano or organ, drums, lead vocal, harmony vocals, etc. Then after identifying the various components of the song (as best I could), I'd begin the task of learning to play the different parts. At first, I started with a few of the songs I had played as a youth. Later, I progressed to learning songs I knew from my past but that I had never learned to play. Finally, I'd start recording the individual tracks to make up the song.

Initially, I would record the rhythm guitar or percussion track. This would serve as the foundation for the remaining music. Then I'd use my headphones and listen to the initial track while simultaneously adding a second instrument or vocal track. Next, I'd add a vocal harmony track or another guitar track and so on. Upon realizing I needed a bass guitar to add low-end tones to the music, I headed back to Gibson's Music and purchased an inexpensive Epiphone bass. Later still, I realized some of the songs seemed to call out for organ or piano. Again, I tend to hear music fairly well, so after playing around with some electric keyboards at Gibson's, I decided I could probably play enough to justify purchasing one. With Pam's support, I bought a Yamaha piano/keyboard and began adding electric piano and/or organ to some of the recordings. Once all the tracks were recorded to my satisfaction, I'd combine them onto a master track. The final step would be to complete the "mastering" process so as to give the song a semi-polished sound.

Working this way, I had eventually recorded ten songs. And in a year's time, my first CD, *Heart's Work,* was finished. It didn't have much percussion, just a little tambourine and a few other handheld rhythmic instruments. But it sounded like real music. And this would be the start of what would eventually amount to sixteen years of musical recording fun. In the end, I'd produce seven such CDs. And beginning with my second CD (in 2011), I was sending the master recording to a company called Discmakers to have them mass-produced and professionally packaged (complete with photos, credits, and liner notes). Recording CDs wouldn't replace the joy I could get from playing music live or with other musicians. I've seldom been able to match that. But it would be a good second option, and it worked for me. In the liner notes of my first CD, I wrote, "Music helps keep me sane, in what can sometimes be a crazy world." This remains true today.

In 2005, my brother Dave developed advanced problems with heart disease. You may recall, my biological father had a long history of heart problems, so each of us kids were aware of this being an inheritable condition. Nonetheless, its emergence was an unwelcomed state of affairs. Ultimately, Dave required open-heart surgery and rehabilitation. And while his recovery would go reasonably well, for the next few months, the ordeal limited opportunities for our playing music together. Finally, once Dave regained his strength and stamina, we were able to resume playing. And this would lead to our recording music together for the first time. Some of the songs Dave and I recorded following his heart surgery would be included on the CD titled *Dave & Ken: The Starkey Boys*.

Also, 2005 was the year Pam and I adopted our boy Patch. We had been thinking about adopting a dog for about a year or so but couldn't decide on the breed. Pam was pretty astute at studying up on dogs so as to increase the likelihood of our choosing one that was a good match for our lifestyle. But before we could make a final choice, this sixty-pound, year-old, black-and-white long-haired herding dog started roaming around our neighborhood. He was a little timid at first but gentle. And once we began feeding him, he warmed up quickly. He had been sleeping under some bushes at a neighbor's house, and the little girl living there had taken to calling him Patch due to his having facial markings that made it appear as if he had a black patch over one eye. Unfortunately, the girl's mother said they couldn't adopt a dog. So as a result, after having him checked out by the local vet, we decided to give him a permanent home.

The vet eventually identified Patch as being part border collie and part Australian shepherd. And sometimes we'd refer to him as our "free born" dog because it appeared he had been living in the wild for a short while prior to our taking him in. Like most herding dogs, he was full of energy and loved to run. Because of this, on those few occasions when he'd escape his kennel or our yard, it would take us upward of an hour to track him down and get a leash back on him. It was not that he was looking to run away so much as he was just given to exploring. I also remember how, early on, Patch had the bad habit of chasing cars. As any dog owner knows, chasing cars seldom has a good outcome for the dog. So when he'd get away from us, we felt it important not to simply wait for him to come home on his own. All these issues aside, Patch would prove as good for our family as I believe we were for him. We used to quip that, with our family, Patch got steady meals, regular walks, plenty of toys, lots of love, and a good health-care plan to boot. He would be with us through our move to Mobile in 2007. And his story can be found on "Patch's Song," a tune Pam and I wrote for my CD titled *Dream Like Mine*.

By late 2005 and 2006, the London practice had become well established. Not only were Pam and I filling our office schedules, but we had each taken on part-time teaching positions for the department of psychology of Eastern Kentucky University as well. Then I'd be asked to provide supervision for the master's level psychology practitioners working at a nearby intermediate care facility. This program provided residential services for adults having significant intellectual disabilities and who, for a variety of reasons, couldn't be cared for at home. In Kentucky, as was true in Pennsylvania, psychology practitioners having only a master's degree could not legally practice without being supervised by a fully licensed and doctoral-trained psychologist. Consequently, I'd be hired to provide supervision for the facility's six master's level clinicians.

Because of the special needs of residents, and the difficulties involved with adequately meeting those needs, this too would be stressful work. Anyone who has ever worked with or known someone having such problems will understand what I'm talking about. But to further complicate matters, apart from the difficulties with meeting the resident's needs, the program had recently come under investigation by the Federal

Government's Department of Justice (DOJ) due to a series of allegations by family members claiming residents were being abused. Hiring me to provide supervision services for the master's level practitioners would be one step toward resolving some of the facility's legal problems and bringing it into compliance with state and federal regulations. Unfortunately, being under the watchful eye of the DOJ also meant the work of everyone, myself included, was forever being scrutinized by their investigators. And this made the job even more demanding. Again, the upside to the position was that it paid more than I might ever have imagined. I was making as much money in twenty hours of part-time work a week as I had previously made working forty hours through PPS. And I was still able to continue working the other twenty hours a week through our private office.

Then one Friday in 2006, after working several months at this site, I began feeling discomfort in my chest and experiencing extreme fatigue. I wasn't in any pain per se. But when I finished for the day and got into my car to travel back to London, I realized I didn't have the strength to drive home safely. After sitting in the car some twenty minutes, the discomfort passed, and my energy seemed to return. This allowed me to get on the road and make it back to London. But upon returning to the office and sharing my symptoms with Pam, she immediately called a cardiologist friend we knew to discuss the incident. He suggested I come straight to his office for an evaluation. After examining me and conducting an EKG test, Dr. Chatterjee told me I was having a heart attack. He then telephoned Pam to come over immediately and take me to the local hospital. I was admitted within the hour.

Eventually, I'd come to learn that heart attacks can present with many different symptoms. Some people have heart attacks so relatively mild they don't learn of their having had one until evidence shows up on an EKG screen at some later date (oftentimes during a routine physical). Other people have profound problems and die on the spot. One might think I would have known all these things, given that my brother had recently experienced heart problems and my father had suffered through so many heart attacks before he died. Still, at the time, much of this information would be news to me.

In retrospect, I'd realize that I'd been having warning signs for a while. A week or two prior to being hospitalized, while painting the ceiling of the workshop in our basement, I had gotten so out of breath that I truly couldn't continue. Again, I wasn't having any real chest pain or numbness in my left arm, as is sometimes symptomatic of heart problems, just a sensation of general discomfort accompanied by intense fatigue and shortness of breath. And when it occurred, I didn't know why I was feeling so tired or struggling to breathe. It just never dawned on me I might actually be having a heart attack. I remember hoping the problem was transitory and would go away on its own. Maybe I just didn't want to admit the problem because of the scariness of it all. Whatever the case, I knew I had to stop and take a break. So like many strong-willed (some might say, stubborn) males who struggle to talk about problems or admit their limitations, I didn't say anything to Pam until some fifteen minutes later. After finally mentioning the incident, we both agreed to monitor the situation. But when the second incident occurred a few weeks later, the symptoms could no longer be ignored. I'd have angioplasty surgery and stent placement the same day I was admitted.

The procedure seemed successful enough for me to be discharged within forty-eight hours. And I'd return to work (part-time) the following Monday. I was well trained as a youth not to complain about problems, and I also knew I had bills to pay. So staying home from work wouldn't be a viable option. Still, I didn't have as much energy as was previously the case. Then a few days later, Pam informed me that while I was in the recovery room following the first procedure, the cardiologist informed her of a second artery that might also need addressed at some future date. For whatever reason, they decided they didn't want to undertake the second procedure at that time. But all this left me wondering whether my current lack of energy was because of my being in recovery from the first procedure because of the medications they had me on following the procedure to protect my heart during recovery or because of the second artery blockage. I just didn't know. All I knew for certain was that I still didn't feel right.

Then as my lack of energy continued, I started worrying about whether or not I'd ever be able to return to working full-time and all the implications this might hold for my future. Inasmuch as I was self-employed, not being able to work full-time meant not having enough income to pay my health insurance premiums, let alone my monthly living expenses. If I couldn't pay for health insurance, I wouldn't be able to get the second procedure or additional medical care to ultimately restore me to health so I might be able to return to full-time work. And of course, if I couldn't effectively sustain full-time work, I also wouldn't be able to pay the office rent to keep it open, not to mention the mortgage on our home. Maybe you can see where all this was going. These were very real fears. And on top of all this stress was the understanding, based on my training as a psychologist, that anxiety and worry would only exacerbate my heart problems and/or further complicate my recovery. That was quite a conundrum.

Again I was faced with the reality that, when all is said and done, we are human beings first—with all the vulnerabilities and limitations associated therewith. Probably a week or two later, I was able to have the second artery blockage addressed and a stent placed. With the help of good doctors, Pam's support, and God's grace, this solved the problem. My strength and energy soon returned, and my anxiety subsided. By the following week, I'd fully returned to working through both PPS and the intermediate care facility with which I had contracted. I am also pleased to say that I would remain symptom-free for many years to come. But again, all this would serve as yet another reminder of my human frailties and the need for spirituality.

It's not unusual for health scares to make one question their priorities. This one encouraged Pam and me to start thinking about our situation in London and how little support we (especially Pam) actually had there. Other than a few friends, we were essentially alone. Had the heart issues resulted in my becoming permanently disabled, or in my having died, Pam would have been left alone to fend for herself until such time as she could sell our house, close the practice, settle our other affairs, and relocate to Mobile. And all this would have been a huge undertaking on her own. As a result, we began talking about moving closer to Pam's home and to where family might be more readily available.

Then as fate might have it, while we were discussing the move, I was offered a full-time position with the intermediate care facility where I'd previously been working part-time. Clearly, they were in need of someone with my skills and seemed to respect my work as a psychologist. And again, the money they were talking seemed unbelievable. Consequently, the invitation to join their staff full-time would be yet another of those difficult choice points wherein I had to decide the values by which I wanted to live and the priorities that would guide my life. What was I being called to do? Money truly can solve a host of practical problems. And everyone likes being wanted. On the other hand, given the stress the job would entail and the additional pressure it might create for my homelife and health, accepting the position would certainly come at a price. Then there was the fact of our still being stranded (so to speak) in Kentucky where little family support was available. After a few of weeks of Pam and me considering the offer, and more than a fair amount of prayer, I decided to pass up the job. God seemed to have other plans for me. I would never regret the decision.

Following the 2000 death of our stepfather, my brother Dave and his wife had assumed increased responsibility caring for our mom. Living only a few blocks from her house allowed them to be more available to provide support. And this seemed a workable solution to helping Mom meet her day-to-day needs. Given that Pam and I lived some distance away, we would contribute financially so as to help with hiring additional help when needed. And LouAnne pitched in as well. So having Mom's needs pretty well met (especially in light of my more recent health issues) reduced the need for Pam and me to stay in Kentucky and be as nearby. Again, on the heels of my heart surgeries and the emerging concerns for Pam's well-being in London, as well as in light of our earlier plans for one day living near Pam's family, we began exploring options for relocating to Alabama.

By early 2007, plans would be well underway for the move to Pam's hometown. We'd begun making arrangements to close the private office and located employment options near Mobile. We'd interviewed for jobs with the Biloxi (MS) VA Medical Center, located about an hour west of Mobile, and with a state psychiatric hospital located in northern Mobile County. And upon completing the application process for our Alabama psychology licenses, we accepted staff positions with the psychology department of Searcy State Hospital. Next, after sprucing up the house in London, we put it on the market and undertook the task of finding a new home near Mobile. By that fall, we'd sold our London house; closed Professional Psychology Services, PSC; and finalized the move down South.

PROFESSIONAL PSYCHOLOGY SERVICES—MOBILE

Our new house would be a three-thousand-square-foot, four-bedroom, three-bath, brick home located in the community of Semmes, Alabama, just west of Mobile. The lot was not as spacious as that of our home in Kentucky, but the house was of new construction, and it had a nicely fenced backyard in which Patch could freely run. It was also a bit of an upgrade from our previous house and much closer to Pam's family. Still, we would always hold fond memories of our Reed Valley home.

Searcy State Hospital was located in little Mount Vernon, Alabama, some forty miles north of Mobile. The facility was originally established around 1828 as a munitions arsenal for the US Army. It would then be appropriated by the Confederacy during the Civil War and, following the war, was used as US Army barracks (between 1887 and 1894). Dr. Walter Reid, conqueror of "yellow fever," served as post surgeon during that time. Later on, the facility served as a holding ground for Apache Indian prisoners (including Geronimo) being relocated to Florida. The facility was converted into Searcy Hospital proper around 1919 and served primarily black citizens until the late 1960s. By then, four new treatment buildings had been erected, and Searcy would begin serving citizens of all colors. At the time Pam and I took our positions with Searcy, a few of the buildings dating from the 1830s were still in use. Unfortunately, others were quite dilapidated, and even the newer buildings were in need of costly repairs. Aesthetically, it was a depressing setting, not only for those seeking recovery from the strain of mental illness but for the staff as well.

Like most state hospitals, Searcy mostly served those struggling with *chronic* mental health problems such as schizophrenia, schizoaffective disorder, bipolar I disorder, and the like. It also served those individuals from the region adjudicated as criminally insane. And for individuals with these kinds of issues, treatment would usually have a much narrower focus than for those having lesser or more transitory problems (such as single-episode depression, adjustment disorders, grief responses, anxiety, etc.). Here, the treatment would primarily consist of symptom reduction and management and the teaching of more basic social skills, communication skills, anger management skills, stress management skills, etc. In other words, the overall goal would be to help the client achieve an enhanced quality of life by establishing sufficient stability for him or her to successfully return to the community at large.

As noted earlier, many times individuals with chronic mental illness can live in the community provided their more pronounced symptoms are stable and adequate resources and support systems exist to sustain such placement. Unfortunately, this is not always the case. So when symptoms of a major psychiatric condition become florid or are exacerbated by coexisting problems like substance abuse, personality problems, unresolved legal charges, etc., treatment in a hospital setting often becomes necessary.

Previously, I discussed treatment for those having both mental health concerns and substance-use problems. Consequently, I'll not address that topic here. Personality problems, on the other hand, are those deeply ingrained, rigid patterns of coping that (in and of themselves) are capable of undermining one's interpersonal relationships and/or employability. Because they are deeply ingrained, these patterns also tend to be resistant to change. And because they are both capable of undermining relationships and employment and resistant to change, their impact on daily life can further exacerbate problems with chronic mental illness. Even when personality problems are not present, individuals with chronic mental illness may struggle to maintain close interpersonal relationships, stay employed, sustain reliable income, and keep a stable residence. But personality problems all too often compound this situation, in some cases contributing to struggles that leave the individual homeless, living on the streets or in a shelter, eating out of trash cans or dumpsters, etc. Then as these daily life stresses further aggravate an individual's psychiatric problem, symptoms become more pronounced and behavior increasingly erratic. Once a person becomes so troubled as to be an outright danger to themselves or others, they commonly end up in the legal system and are either incarcerated or involuntarily hospitalized. In these latter instances, state hospitals such as Searcy are the facilities most often used for treatment.

When feasible, the primary objective of hospitalization in a psychiatric facility is to quickly stabilize an individual's more troublesome symptoms such that they might be promptly discharged. In these cases, they may be returned to live with family or be placed in a less restrictive residential program providing appropriate care and monitoring. In those instances wherein a client has been convicted of a crime prior to hospitalization, once their symptoms are stabilized, they are typically returned to jail to serve out the remainder of their sentence. Finally, on those rarer occasions when an individual struggles to achieve the level of stability necessary to allow their return to the community/jail, or where they grow to feel safer or more comfortable living in the controlled environment of a state hospital, these individuals become longer-term hospital residents.

Despite all our misgivings about state-run psychiatric facilities, and all the dramatic horror stories portrayed on television or in the movies, many health-care professionals recognize that such hospitals usually represent a better alternative for the chronically mentally ill than do jails, prisons, or living on the street. And all too often, this is where persons with chronic mental health problems end up when state hospitals are not available. Unfortunately, providing care in a state facility is an expensive undertaking that many taxpayers usually prefer not to finance.

Thus, state hospitals are left to do the best they can with what little funding taxpayers are willing to provide. Generally speaking, I have found that state hospitals strive to provide humane care for those who otherwise can't fend for themselves and for whom society all too often chooses to neglect.

Pam and I had been fortunate enough to have sold our house in London after only a few months on the market, and for a handsome profit over the original purchase price. It was right at the end of the housing boom and right before the market collapse of 2007—perfect timing for us. Unfortunately, and unbeknownst to Pam and I, it was also near the time when the state of Alabama was looking to consolidate some of their state hospital facilities. As mentioned earlier, Searcy had become somewhat run-down over the years and was getting increasingly costly to operate. Thus, the state's plans for consolidation also included considerations for closing Searcy Hospital.

I'd work on the admissions unit at Searcy for a little over three years. Pam would end up working on a long-term unit for some five years or so. And I think both Pam and I would say we loved working with the patients at Searcy. Our education, training, and prior clinical experience had provided a good foundation for the work we were assigned to do. And our commitment toward working with those struggling with chronic mental health issues, as well as our being a part of a seasoned treatment team, allowed both of us to be comfortable enough to take on this new challenge. Again, on the admissions unit, my role was to work with a team designed to stabilize patients' acute symptoms (when possible) such that they might be quickly discharged to a community-based residential facility or halfway house or to a stable home environment. On the long-term unit, Pam worked with a team serving those whose symptoms could not be quickly stabilized or who had confounding coexisting problems such as severe personality disorders, histories of violence, sexual assault, etc. These coexisting problems would often render community placement less of an option. Patients on the long-term unit also included those who felt safer in the hospital setting (than in the community at large) and might have been considered "institutionalized."

Only a year or so after moving to Mobile and taking our jobs at Searcy, Pam would be diagnosed with adenoid-cystic cancer. She had noticed a small growth developing in her left ear and decided to have it checked out. That was when the cancer was discovered. For most of us, the very word *cancer* is scary enough as it evokes so many fears of the unknown. And cancer survivors know all too well how such a diagnosis disrupts one's life and how, with so little warning, raises questions requiring one to reorganize life's priorities. What is the prognosis? What might be the progression? Where do I go for treatment, and how will it be paid for? What impact will the disease have on my overall health, my future? Will cancer rob me of realizing long-held hopes and dreams? Will I face enduring pain? Will I suffer and die? And how will it affect my loved ones?

The word is scary for loved ones as well as cancer affects not only the identified patient but also all those who care about the cancer patient. In Pam's case, the extent of the tissue involvement could not be clearly established until the recommended surgery was completed. But shortly after the first procedure, it was determined the surgery had not successfully removed all the cancer cells and that a second procedure would be required. Thankfully, following the second surgery (and after several weeks of uncertainty), Pam would be determined "cancer-free," and there would be no need to undergo either chemotherapy or radiation therapy. Still, like many cancer survivors, Pam would need to have regular follow-up screenings for years to come. And while her particular kind of cancer might still recur at some future time, even migrate, as of this writing, we are happy to say that Pam remains cancer-free. Nonetheless, it was a scary ordeal and yet one more reminder of how life offers few, if any, guarantees.

As regards the work we did at Searcy, apart from the occasional concern over being assaulted by a troubled patient, or the more likely occurrence of getting injured breaking up an altercation between patients, both Pam and I generally liked our jobs. Unfortunately, much as had been true when working in other government-run institutional settings, I would gradually come to find all the administrative guidelines and red tape frustrating. It has just always seemed for me that systemic policies tended to be designed more for meeting the particular agendas of those politicians currently in power or for protecting the government from liability and lawsuits than for promoting quality patient care. I realize this might not be completely fair. And I don't mean to suggest that others, politicians and administrators alike, don't care about people. It's just that, for me, it sometimes feels like the proverbial tail-wagging-the-dog scenario. In any case, after the psychology department chair and the hospital director had a falling out over how the department should be run, the chair decided to move on. While I would be appointed "interim chair" of the department, my *interim* status and the ever-growing prospect of the hospital being closed on short notice left me questioning my own future at Searcy. So after a few months of prayerful contemplation, I decided to leave Searcy and again open a private psychology office. Professional Psychology Services (PPS) of Mobile would be opened in January 2010. Pam continued working at Searcy for another year or so. Then when the hospital finally closed, she too joined me in our new private practice.

> So, so you think you can tell,
> Heaven from hell, blue skies from pain.
> Can you tell a green field, from a cold steel rail?
> A smile from a veil?
> Do you think you can tell?
> —D. Gilmore/R. Waters

From "Wish You Were Here," words and music by D. Gilmore and R. Waters (1975), Copyright Columbia Records

THE PRACTICE OF CLINICAL PSYCHOLOGY

THE YEARS BETWEEN 2007 AND 2010 HAD been filled with the transition to Mobile, adjusting to work at Searcy, dealing with the scare of Pam's cancer, and ultimately setting up the Mobile private practice. Upon closing our London office, Pam and I had moved the furniture, file cabinets, testing kits, and related items into a Mobile storage facility. This would make setting up the new practice much easier than had previously been the case. And after a month or two of marketing, we were pretty well up and running in our new location.

Once again, I was providing neuropsychology and forensic services, as well as completing evaluations for applicants seeking benefits through both the Department for Disability Determination Services and the Department for Vocational Rehabilitation Services. But this time around, I also signed up on various panels for a wide array of private insurance companies. This allowed me to begin offering both assessment and therapy services of a more *clinical* nature for those policyholders seeking such help. When Pam joined the practice a couple of years later, she too would resume completing evaluations for the Disability Determination and Vocational Rehab agencies, while also providing clinical services to a limited number of privately insured individuals.

Earlier, I mentioned how psychologists usually gravitate toward practicing in certain areas of expertise. The same can be said for their overall domain of focus. Some prefer doing research or teaching. Others prefer doing forensic or industrial/organizational work. Still others emphasize *clinical* practice. Over the years, I've done a little teaching in a university setting. And I did research for my dissertation and am familiar with reading and interpreting research articles. Obviously, I've also done my fair share of forensic work. But my first love has always been *clinical* psychology and working with individuals directly to help them alleviate suffering and find meaning in life. So what does working as a clinical psychologist look like for me? How do I *approach* the practice of clinical psychology? As the reader might guess, my overall approach to practicing clinical psychology (like the other clinical work I've done over the years) has been deeply rooted in my own personal experiences and my training through Duquesne University.

Generally speaking, most doctoral-trained *clinical* psychologists have similar training. Still, it's not uncommon for individual psychologists to take somewhat differing approaches to their practice of clinical psychology. I mentioned a few of these approaches earlier when discussing my own experience with therapy, those being the analytic, humanistic, and behavioral approaches. I also noted how there are other approaches as well and how some psychologists adopt a more eclectic approach by utilizing elements from differing orientations.

Again, each approach to practicing clinical psychology can be beneficial (with no one approach being clearly superior to another). But some approaches do seem to work better when it comes to helping clients having certain problems. Personality disorders (e.g., dependent, antisocial, borderline, paranoid etc.) represent one such example. These syndromes are generally associated with highly dysfunctional parenting occurring during a child's early development. And while most of us probably encounter some parental shortcomings while growing up (as parents are never perfect), when parenting deficiencies are pronounced, they can result in a child developing attitudes and behaviors that are both rigid and unyielding. As the child grows into adulthood, these characteristics may then turn into pervasive and persisting *patterns* of coping that can undermine a person's daily functioning and create significant personal distress. The resulting dysfunction is what psychologists refer to as a personality *disorder*. And individuals with these types of problems seem to respond better to behavioral approaches. Clients with more compulsive behavior problems (e.g., substance abuse, compulsive gambling, compulsive sexual behavior, etc.) also tend to do better with behavioral or cognitive-behavioral approaches. And the same can be said for clients with intellectual deficiencies, who have more concrete thinking and problem-solving skills, or those with more chronic, severe psychiatric conditions.

On the other hand, clients having more sophisticated reasoning abilities, who are better adjusted socially and have more advanced problem-solving and stress-management skills, may respond better to a more cognitive or analytic approach, while clients given to social affiliation, to being empathic with others, and having more advanced verbal skills may do better with a more humanistic approach. And each of these latter approaches have also proven effective for persons having histories of more stable relationships, steady employment, and the like, and who are struggling with adjusting to shorter-term, more situationally based concerns. Uncomplicated depression and anxiety disorders may also respond more favorably to these latter approaches. *While none of these statements are absolutes, they tend to be more true than not.* And as always, one's approach typically works best when tailored to the individual client and prevailing goals for treatment.

In addition to the fact that certain syndromes tend to respond better to certain therapeutic approaches, a psychologist's approach to practicing psychology can also be influenced by factors that are not always under a therapist's control. Differences such as a therapist's gender, race, personal values, etc. (to name but a few) can all be important to any given client, thus impacting the therapeutic outcome. And anything affecting this outcome might influence a clinician's approach in certain situations (as clients who are not able to identify with or relate to their therapist, for whatever reason, usually don't get what they are seeking from the treatment and quit showing up).

Finally, one's specific approach to practicing psychology can also be influenced by factors such as the setting in which one works, the specific population being served, the existence of comorbid conditions, etc. How one approaches the practice of psychology in a prison setting can be very different from how one approaches their practice in a state psychiatric hospital or a private outpatient office. Working with children can be very different from working with grown adults or geriatric populations.

Now back to my approach for practicing *clinical* psychology. My own approach to clinical psychology tends to be more eclectic in nature. I probably lean a bit more toward the cognitive-behavioral/humanistic approaches, and I almost always try to apply my professional training in accordance with recovery guidelines found in the scientific literature. But in addition to my cognitive-behavioral and humanistic tendencies, my approach emphasizes working *collaboratively* with clients while incorporating a bit of an existential/spiritual component. Said another way, while I strive to meet my client's mental health concerns through conventional methods, I also try to stay open to the fact that many of the individuals with whom I work are seeking more than just a reduction of their presenting symptoms. Many of the people I see also want to make sense of their suffering within the greater scheme of things, to give their life experiences, including their troublesome ones, meaning. This is why, after years of clinical practice, I have found working collaboratively with a client to be useful. Collaborating with a client, working jointly to identify the problems leading them to seek my help, the goals for what constitutes successful therapy, and the steps to be taken for achieving these goals, has seemed to give me the best chance of assisting a client with *both* reducing their mental health symptoms and achieving greater meaning in his/her daily life.

Admittedly, there may be occasions when working collaboratively *only* means working to resolve presenting mental health symptoms (like anxiety, depression, alcoholism, trauma, etc.). And working to reduce troublesome symptoms can be important in its own right. So if this is all the client is interested in, I might utilize a solution-focused approach to try and satisfy this need or refer the client out to a psychiatrist for pharmacotherapy. But for those clients who are seeking more, for those clients who want to understand their life experience in terms of something greater than their individual ego or their day-to-day existence, for me, working collaboratively has proven essential.

By way of example, it's true that some addicts and alcoholics may only want to undergo detox so they can return to using drugs/alcohol without suffering quite so much as had become the case after years of use. But most of the individuals with whom I work are actually seeking a more stable and productive life experience as well. This is why most substance-use treatment programs distinguish between getting "sober or clean" and "recovering." For most programs, getting "sober or clean" constitutes only the initial phase of substance-use treatment. "Recovery" from substance dependence requires that one both get sober/clean *and* make real changes in how he or she is choosing to live his or her life. Only through sobriety *and* choosing lasting lifestyle changes can the alcoholic or addict both reduce the chances for relapse and get on with the task of living in a way that makes life meaningful.

Clinically, I've found the same to be true for those having other mental health concerns. Thus, when I have a client who is seeking more than just resolution of their presenting symptoms, working collaboratively allows me to address these additional concerns as well. Again, I don't mean to suggest that reducing troublesome symptoms isn't valuable. But reducing symptoms alone might be achieved by a physician or psychiatrist simply prescribing medication or by six to eight sessions of solution-focused counseling. As a psychologist, my role frequently goes beyond providing symptom relief to helping a client address the more existential question of what gives their particular life meaning.

Toward this end, collaborating with a client necessarily requires I attend to more than just the client's initial report of what he or she wants from life or the obstacles believed to be preventing the achievement of that which is wanted. Similarly, working collaboratively also means more than just accepting the particular steps a client might be considering for reaching that destination. Certainly, what the client views as his or her goals for therapy, the things keeping the person from realizing these goals, and the efforts made to date that may or may not have worked in helping him or her reach those goals are all important. These are all good starting points. But if the client knew exactly where he or she wanted to go or how to get there, then he or she probably wouldn't be coming to me for help. Usually, when one seeks the assistance of a psychologist, it is because the goals being sought or the steps being taken for reaching these goals have not been working. Hence, the client has decided to ask someone else for input.

Now please don't misunderstand: I am not saying I play God by trying to tell a clients what his or her problem is. And I don't try to tell the individual to where I think he/she should be going with their life or the choices he/she ought to make for getting there. Again, for me, the client (in conjunction with their Higher Power) is always the orchestrator of his or her life. I am only a facilitator who helps the client along the way. But what working collaboratively does mean is my *dialoguing* with individuals to help them clarify that which they do want from life and to identify those choices and decisions that might actually help them get that which they want. Said another way, working collaboratively means helping clients realize their own dream rather than that which others (myself included) might hold for them, helping clients clarify how their current actions are either leading them toward or steering them away from that dream and sometimes helping clients identify new or alternative *choices* for realizing their dream in light of the probable consequences of making those choices.

Through my own experience and professional training, I do have certain knowledge and understandings as regards what seems to work or doesn't work in people's daily lives. Some of the "choices" or "actions" may be self-evident. For example, most of us know that if you lie to and cheat people, you will likely create a reputation for being one who lies and cheats. And this may well alienate you from people or encourage others to lie to or cheat you in return. We also know that if you fight with and bully others, you will likely encounter others who are prone to fight with or bully you. We know that if you misuse or abuse alcohol and drugs, you are likely to develop related health, legal, relationship, and other life problems (at least over time). We know that if you deceive your partner and violate their trust, you run the risk of your partner treating you in a similar fashion or of your losing that relationship. And we know that if you abuse your children or reject any responsibility for raising those you help bring into the world, these children will likely grow up feeling abandoned, unloved, resentful, and angry (and you will likely feel guilty or ashamed as well). These are just a few of the things most of us realize to be cold hard truths of life. It doesn't require a psychology degree to understand them. Similarly, most of us also know that if you strive to be honest, caring, respectful, dependable, reliable, empathic, and the like, you increase the odds of being treated similarly in return. It isn't a *guarantee*, but if we treat others the way we want to be treated, it probably increases the odds of their reciprocating in a like fashion.

Unfortunately, as also mentioned earlier in my discussion of substance-abuse counseling, humans are prone to denial of the self-evident. They can be self-deceiving, rationalize deviant behavior, think irrationally, and even act impulsively or in self-defeating ways. And many times, *choosing* to behave in these ways keeps the person from getting that which is desired most from life while also contributing to his or her mental health problems. Again, this is not to say that these behaviors, these choices, necessarily *cause* one's mental health problems. As noted in my discussion of working with criminal justice clients, correlation is not the same as causation. And altering our choices and behavior alone cannot guarantee us a life free of tragedy or despair, fear or anxiety, depression or grief, trauma, etc. Invariably, a person who lives long enough *will* encounter hardships at some point in life. Still, *how* we live our lives, the *choices* we make from one day to the next, can reduce or help us to better manage those hardships we do face. The *choices* we make can perpetuate suffering or bring us more joy. And the *choices* we make can steer us further away from or lead us closer to our destination and a life of greater meaning and peace. In many respects, working collaboratively also means helping clients recognize this reality.

The actual practice of *clinical* psychology (much like substance-use counseling) is usually broken down into the domains of assessment and intervention or treatment. And most clinical psychologists are trained to view psychological assessment as that endeavor wherein a trained clinician utilizes history gathering, interviewing, and various psychological tests to identify mental health syndromes so as to more effectively guide the intervention/treatment process. Again, the purpose of assessment can vary when requested for forensic purposes, when requested by an employer to remedy job-related problems, or when used for military or interrogation purposes (which can be controversial in its own right). But in clinical psychology, assessment is usually taught as a tool used to guide the clinician in identifying and helping people address mental health concerns.

Domains of assessment in psychology can include such areas as intellect, mood, personality, anxiety, perception, trauma, cognition, violence potential, suicidal/homicidal tendencies, etc. Syndromes assessed can include intellectual disabilities, mood disorders (e.g., depression, bipolar disorder, etc.), personality disorders (such as antisocial, narcissistic, dependent, etc.), phobias and other anxiety disorders, and psychotic disorders (like schizophrenia, schizoaffective, and delusional disorders). Still, other conditions assessed might include post-traumatic stress or other trauma-related disorders, dissociative disorders, neurocognitive disorders (such as dementias, strokes, etc.), all in addition to yet other syndromes. Most clinicians are trained to identify clusters of symptoms making up disorders as described in the psychology literature and, in particular, the latest edition of the *Diagnostic and Statistical Manual for Mental Disorders* (published every so many years by the American Psychiatric Association). Again, the idea here is that accurately identifying the diagnostic syndrome can facilitate intervention or the treatment process and, thus, the amelioration of symptoms.

Hopefully, the reader recognizes that the approach to assessment outlined above is heavily weighted on the clinicians' training, expertise, and (ultimately) professional judgment. It typically places limited value on the clients' view of their concerns, except to the extent that a client may be asked what they see as the problem or if the treatment prescribed seems to be reducing their symptoms. Ultimately, if the client struggles to identify their presenting problem or the effectiveness of treatment (because of deficiencies in intellect, limited vocabulary, poor insight, lack of ego strength, severity of disturbance, etc.), or if the clinician and client disagree, the clinician usually makes the final call.

In my own work as a psychologist, there have been times when a client was either too limited or too impaired to be able or willing to report or describe their problems or to be able or willing to participate meaningfully in *any* assessment. On those occasions, I have identified a working diagnosis of my own. But my own *approach* to assessment, in keeping with an emphasis on valuing the person, has been to spend as much time and energy as possible enlisting the client's input such that any final diagnosis, as well as the goals for treatment, are *collaboratively* established. Yes, I may be the so-called expert on mental health problems. I do have specialized training and experience. I am the licensed psychologist. But once again, the client (in conjunction with their Higher Power) is the expert on their life. The client is usually in the best position to know what it is about their life that they would like to see improve. And it is the client who usually understands the resources they have at their disposal to draw upon for making change. A client may be coming to me for help, but in doing so, they are not giving up the right to make decisions about their own life. In many respects, the client is hiring me to provide a service for them. And yes, hopefully they trust that I will bring my education, training, and expertise to bear on the situation. But they are not asking me to take charge of their life.

So again, when assessing an individual seeking my assistance, I try to place as much emphasis on the client's experience of what is not working in their life as on my own perception of what might need to change. And I always strive to honor the client's right to decide what needs to be the focus of treatment. On those occasions when I believe a client seems in denial or lacking insight into a situation, as in the case of one who is behaving in impulsive or self-defeating ways (e.g., cases of substance use, criminal behavior, suicidality, etc.), I might try to increase his or her awareness of the possible negative or harmful consequences of the behavior or encourage recognition of alternate choices for dealing with a prevailing problem. Likewise, I might encourage a client to recognize the potential benefits of working toward goals otherwise not considered. But except in the rarest of instances (*imminent and serious* threat of harm to self or others, for example), I will not disrespect a client's right to make choices about the focus of treatment or to make choices about his or her own life. And I always strive to demonstrate my conviction that it's *the client*, not I, who is the real expert on what gives that life meaning. In many instances, demonstrating this conviction is what gives the despairing client hope that life is not unmanageable, that the life being lived does matter. On the other hand, it is my firm belief that where a psychologist fails to demonstrate conviction in the client's ability to make meaningful choices, then the psychologist has no hope of the client him or herself ever holding such conviction. Helping a client better manage mental health symptoms such as anxiety, depression, trauma, hallucinations, etc. is important, but so is respecting a client's right to make decisions about his or her own life, to maintain autonomy, to demonstrate self-determination, and to realize his or her own spiritual journey toward personal meaning.

My approach to treatment intervention (or therapy) is similar. The profession of psychology differs from that of psychiatry in that the latter "treats" mental health disturbances almost exclusively with medication. Occasionally, a psychiatrist might suggest a cognitive or behavioral strategy for managing certain problems or refer a client out for talk therapy, but in general, psychiatrists are not trained in formal psychotherapeutic approaches to treatment. Rather, psychiatrists use pharmacological techniques for managing symptoms. This is in keeping with their vision of mental health concerns being primarily genetically or biologically based.

Most mental health practitioners acknowledge that *some* mental health conditions do have a genetic or biological component (e.g., schizophrenia, schizoaffective disorder, bipolar I disorder, endogenous depression, etc.). And most recognize how pharmacological interventions can be essential to managing symptoms such as delusional beliefs, hallucinations, mania, and the like. But clinical psychologists also recognize that many mental health problems are not genetically based but, rather, a result of developmental factors and/or troubling life experiences and the toll these things take on one's ability to cope.

Again, by way of example, the available psychological research is pretty consistent in indicating that most forms of depression, anxiety, trauma, and personality problems are *not* a direct result of genetic or biologically based precursors. True, one may inherit a predisposition or vulnerability to depression or anxiety. But the scientific literature clearly indicates many types of depression, anxiety, and other problems of life to be more a function of one's developmental experiences and/or existential stressors than genetics.

Depression and anxiety, for example, related to relationship problems, separation, or divorce is something with which many of us are familiar. Both depression and anxiety accompanying the loss of employment, financial troubles, homelessness, chronic pain, death of a loved one, etc. are also commonplace. And the psychological research is also pretty clear about the relationship of anxiety disorders to behavioral conditioning. Associating an experience of anxiety (or fear) with a particular stimuli or trigger (an aggressive dog), and then generalizing this anxiety to other stimuli (dogs—regardless of their size or disposition), is a common scenario for developing a phobia of dogs. In like fashion, trauma arising with abuse, assault, natural disasters, or exposure to military combat is also well-documented. And while medication can certainly be helpful in reducing an individual's more acute symptoms, whether one is talking about depression, anxiety, or trauma-related symptoms, medication alone cannot resolve what are, many times, very real underlying life experiences. If your baby recently died in a house fire, all the medication in the world will not take away the reality of your loss. If you are traumatized following a sexual assault (or being robbed and shot or serving in a war zone, etc.), no amount of medication will take away the reality of your traumatizing experience or your difficulty readjusting to life after such trauma. Yes, medication may provide *some* relief of acute symptoms in these instances; it may facilitate sleep or slow down one's rapid breathing or racing thought processes such that a person feels less vulnerable to being overwhelmed. But true *healing* from these kinds of events usually requires some form of therapeutic (or pastoral) intervention designed to address the precipitating experience and to help the troubled individual adopt new strategies for *making sense* of it and its impact on his or her life.

Because of this, and much as is true with my approach to assessment, I strive to make therapy a *collaborative* process. This, I believe, is the most effective way of helping a client learn both to manage problematic symptoms and cope with the multitude of ups and downs that life brings so that he or she might one day discover a context within which the totality of their life experience has meaning. Maybe this sounds like I'm being redundant or have gotten a bit offtrack. But for me, this *is* what I consider the crucial goal for many seeking to experience truly successful therapy. Again, for many individuals, effective therapy cannot be limited to only alleviating symptoms or resolving a presenting problem. Rather, for many, effective therapy includes both reducing symptoms *and* helping the individual learn to place painful life experiences into a greater context so as to allow them to get on with living a more meaningful existence.

Like most clinical psychologists, I am trained in the techniques of systematic desensitization, cognitive restructuring, behavioral modification, etc. And all these techniques or disciplines (much like psychotropic medications) have their place in helping clients better manage mental health symptoms or otherwise alter dysfunctional responses to life stressors. When a given situation calls for it, I may utilize any of these tools. But for the person who is struggling with the bigger question of what a painful or distressing experience means in terms of life itself, such techniques or disciplines are of limited value. A soldier who has served a tour or two in direct combat and witnessed untold suffering, death, and trauma usually wants more than to just *manage* anxiety, anger, or sleep problems. They usually want to understand how their worldly experience and how all the suffering, death, and trauma they may have experienced make sense in the larger scheme of things. Accordingly, the real value of psychological techniques is similar to the value of spiritual disciplines such as prayer, yoga, fasting, meditation, etc. All these disciplines have value in promoting one's spirituality, in carrying one along their spiritual journey. But much as is true with religious disciplines, to help another find inner peace, to help another find real meaning in their life, requires the clinician help the client move beyond the psychological disciplines and beyond all the techniques and proceed to that destination the client is striving to reach.

Now if the process I've just described sounds a bit vague or even mystical, it is in this fashion, I believe, that therapy is as much an art as it is a science. Psychotherapy may rely on scientific inquiry, scientific research, and scientific understandings. But effective therapy also requires the therapist be much more than just a scientist. Effective therapy requires the therapist strive to be authentically human as well, for only by being authentically human can a therapist learn to recognize and suspend one's own values, one's own biases, one's own fears, one's own doubts, one's own hang-ups (if you will). And only when the therapist suspends these contaminating variables can he/she develop the patience, courage, love, and faith needed to facilitate therapeutic healing for a client whose life may have lost all meaning and who may well be on the verge of "throwing in the towel." Patience is what allows a therapist to listen to another without assuming he/she knows in advance that which the other is trying to say. Courage is what allows a therapist to help another experience and confront deep-seated or scary thoughts and feelings he/she might otherwise want to avoid. Love is what allows a therapist to suspend judgment of another's missteps or mistakes in order to help the other to believe in him/herself and move forward with his or her life. And faith is what allows a therapist to trust in another's capacity to make choices and (in conjunction with their Higher Power) to find solutions to problems otherwise viewed as unsolvable. All these are, in my opinion, essential components of effective therapy.

And I believe them to exist independently of one's scientific training.

As the private office in Mobile grew, I was able to be more selective about the kinds of work I was taking on. And this meant I could get more involved in couples therapy. In some respects, working with recovering alcoholics and addicts had always necessitated my doing a certain amount of couples and family counseling as promoting substance-use recovery usually meant helping the recovering individual repair some of the damage substance-use and related behavior had caused significant others. But as the years passed, as Pam and I learned more and more about nurturing our own marriage, passing this knowledge on to other couples in a more formal manner seemed increasingly appropriate. So while I'd continue doing substance-use counseling, individual therapy, neuropsychological assessments, and the occasional forensic assessment, at this point, my work would also expand to include more couples work.

Many people have asked about the secret to a successful or healthy relationship. My brother Kevin once suggested the most important factor for a successful relationship was to make the "right" choice up front. Others have probably suggested this as well. And there's probably some wisdom in this advice. Taking time to figure out one's own values and what gives one's own life meaning, as well as what one is looking for or needs in a relationship and how the other person matches up with these values and needs, can be crucial. Far too often, people jump into a relationship without either knowing what gives their own life meaning or who the other person truly is. Unfortunately, impulsivity will get you every time when it comes to relationships (and probably life, in general). Still, taking time to figure out your own life or who another person truly is can be difficult. Many times, we get caught up in the moment, the passion, the fantasy, the sex, the desire for love, the fear of being alone or getting left out, the desire to escape loneliness, or the illusion of who we think will make us happy. Once again, I am reminded of the words of young Siddhartha, "I can think, I can pray, and I can wait." It's easier said than done. And even when you do think, pray, and wait, even when you are careful, reflective, and mindful about your choice, there is no guarantee the choice you make will bring you what you seek.

In truth, there may be no one secret any more than there is one clear definition of what actually makes up a successful or healthy relationship. Some have defined a successful relationship as one of a lasting duration that helps give life meaning while alleviating such existential stressors as loneliness or the fear of death. But most of us have known couples who stayed together for long periods despite much discord, arguing, suffering, and even abuse. And then again, how long is lasting? And couldn't a dog, cat, or other pet alleviate loneliness and give one's life meaning? Many pet owners think so. So maybe a better answer to this question is that most of us know a successful relationship when we see it, or at least most of us seem to know what an unsuccessful or unhealthy relationship looks like when we come across it.

Relationships marked by *incessant* arguing, fighting, and battering are probably viewed by most as unsuccessful and unhealthy (even if the couple stays together for years). Relationships lacking in mutual respect for the other's mental, physical, and emotional well-being might also fall into this category. Likewise, relationships lacking in caring communication (i.e., wherein both parties feel free to express their thoughts and needs and where each feels listened to and understood by the other) might qualify as being unsuccessful or unhealthy. When relationships lack collaborative problem-solving (i.e., where both parties feel a solution to be fair or mutually acceptable) or successful conflict resolution (i.e., where both parties feel their concerns matter to the other), they too may be seen as unhealthy or unsuccessful. And finally, when relationships are lacking in mutual trust and intimacy, and in the nurturance of each other's hopes and dreams, these relationships may also come to be experienced as unsuccessful or unhealthy.

This is not to say that successful or healthy relationships necessarily embody such lofty ideals as *perfect* communication or problem-solving skills or conflict-resolution skills and the like. And I certainly don't mean to suggest that successful or healthy relationships *never* involve disagreements, arguing, disrespectful speech, etc. After all, as I have said many times, we *are* human beings, with all the imperfections and shortcomings this entails. We all get angry from time to time, we all get impatient, we all get controlling or demanding, and we all get selfish or caught in our own emotions and lacking in empathy. And any relationship between humans inevitably seems to include a certain number of problems arising from all these human flaws. But successful or healthy relationships seem to have more of those qualities that allow us to rise above these human shortcomings or flaws, thereby nurturing each party toward greater inner peace and a more meaningful existence.

In my own life, I've come to believe that living with another for an extended period has helped me understand more about patience, acceptance, empathy, and love. Apart from allowing Pam and I to identify each other's strengths and limitations, our relationship has also called each of us to learn more about ourselves, including our own deficiencies. All those self-serving and controlling attitudes and behaviors we might otherwise prefer to hide get exposed as a result of sharing our lives with each other over an extended period. And this exposure challenges us each to confront these undesirable attitudes and behaviors and to undertake the sometimes painful struggle of changing them so as to improve who we are as people. In some ways, facing these shortcomings and making these changes give our respective lives what some characterize as the resonance of a finely aged musical instrument. Or said more simply, facing these shortcomings and making these changes give both of our lives increased meaning. Sometimes, I even think nurturing our relationship and making these changes have brought us closer to our own mortality. As I've aged, as I've grown to face my own struggles with life, the thought of witnessing the death of someone I have loved for many years, of learning to give up that person who has been with me through all the good times and the bad, of one day helping her let go of human life or of allowing her to help me let go of life has even brought me closer to God. And these are just a few of the blessings I believe can be realized through a successful and enduring relationship. But having said all this, healthy relationships require more than *just* making the right choice, and they most certainly are *not* something that just seem to happen or something that one falls into or out of. Healthy relationships require a certain amount of work, especially during the tough times. Healthy relationships are something that we *choose to do.*

Now obviously, I believe in relationships. I believe in marriage. And I believe that, for most people, making a commitment to another person and working toward a relationship that spans a lifetime can enrich one's life above and beyond what might otherwise be achieved by living alone or in what some have called serial monogamy. Still, I also realize that sometimes relationships don't work out. So what is one to do upon finding him or herself in an unhealthy relationship? What about those times when two individuals who are struggling with unresolved personal issues or simply lacking in the necessary relationship skills for creating a healthy bond find one another? Unfortunately, such instances do arise. And on those occasions, when a relationship renders one or both parties stuck in a vicious cycle of trauma, suffering, and/or abuse, the well-being of one or both parties may necessitate the relationship to end. Sometimes, divorce may be the only solution to saving the individuals so involved. Nonetheless, while I understand this to sometimes be the case, I am not suggesting two people should simply throw in the towel at the first sight of problems. And I do not believe couples should ever take lightly the decision to divorce. The decision to end any long-standing intimate relationship, regardless how dysfunctional, is almost always an extremely painful process for those involved. Couples counseling can sometimes help people avoid this pain.

As for the decision to pursue counseling when times do get tough, the psychological research is pretty conclusive about couples counseling *not* being for everyone. For example, couples counseling is *not* appropriate for persons engaging in ongoing infidelity, persons struggling with active substance-use problems, persons actively engaging in battering behavior, or persons with currently untreated symptoms of a major psychiatric disorder (like schizophrenia, bipolar I disorder, etc.). Where these concerns exist, resolution of those problems needs to occur *prior* to partners pursuing couples counseling.

If you think about it, this only makes good sense. A person involved in an extramarital relationship which they do not intend to end will probably not make the necessary commitment to allow couples counseling to be successful. Likewise, one who is currently battering the other, troubled by delusions of paranoia, or drinking a fifth of liquor a night to deaden their feelings is probably not going to be able to create or establish the kind of trust needed to meaningfully engage in a constructive counseling process. Couples counseling works best when a mutual commitment is present and two otherwise healthy people run up against the limits of those communication, problem-solving, and conflict-resolution skills that are necessary for jointly resolving emerging life problems. Accordingly, when couples counseling is being requested, during a prescreening process, I'll try to identify any such concerns up front so as to assess the couple's appropriateness for the counseling. Where issues exist that contraindicate couples counseling, I advise the couple on a plan of action for remedying these problems. This can include referring one or both individuals to another professional to get the personal help needed to resolve the concerns.

In those instances where a couple is deemed appropriate for counseling, I frequently start the initial session by again reviewing the parameters of couples counseling, the limitations to this type of counseling, and the conditions under which it tends to be effective. This assures me of the clients' having a clear understanding of what couples counseling entails. Next, I usually challenge both participants to question whether couples counseling is truly right for them or not; do they truly want to work on their relationship and remain together? This encourages each to explore how committed they are to doing what's necessary for the relationship to survive and flourish. Sometimes, one or the other partner may already have decided (privately) to end the relationship but is struggling to be forthright about the decision or to take definitive action. Occasionally, the other party may also suspect the relationship to be over but be too afraid to press the issue. In any event, where either partner is determined to leave the relationship, couples counseling is seldom productive. And many times, helping a couple face the inevitable outcome of a truly broken relationship is more therapeutic than pretending otherwise or trying to force someone to continue doing something that he/she cannot do. In these cases, divorce mediation may even be a better alternative to couples counseling.

Where it is determined that two individuals are appropriate candidates for couples counseling and desire to undertake the necessary work, I will (once again) turn my focus to collaborating with the couple to identify what they want for the relationship and what problems they would like to see resolved. Therapy goals for a couple (much like those for an individual) may shift over time, but once a goal has been determined, I can then begin the process of helping the couple develop those skills needed to move them closer to that goal.

Some people think that couples therapy is only about such things as working through conflicts over sexual matters or settling parenting disputes or resolving money management issues, etc. But I tend to view such problems as simply symptoms of what are many times more fundamental issues. For me, while couples therapy may also address those specific kinds of problems, the real essence of couples therapy is that of helping of two individuals develop the necessary skills for building a more meaningful relationship. In this regard, I've found that when couples learn to communicate, problem-solve, resolve conflicts, and manage stress more effectively, the foundation is usually created for true intimacy, trust, and love to flourish. These skills, I believe, represent the necessary tools for overcoming those day-to-day struggles so many of us face and that all too often undermine lasting and healthy relationships.

In keeping with this vision, early on, I might introduce exercises that help participants reconnect with those qualities and interests originally attracting them to each other, the reasons they desired to be together in the first place. For example, I might have the individuals write down (in private) three qualities they *clearly* appreciate about the other. In the following session, I might then ask each to share these out loud with each other and to talk about the feelings associated with what is shared by the other. Encouraging individuals to reconnect with these things can help them recall times when their relationship wasn't so stressed or when their situation didn't seem so hopeless. Sharing and hearing such affirmations can also help the individuals to be more appreciative of the other and with regaining confidence in their ability to work together toward resolving existing problems. In all likelihood, both individuals initially found qualities they liked or were attracted to in the other when they first began dating. And probably neither partner expected the relationship to fail when first committing to it. Similarly, one doesn't usually enter into a relationship with the plan of becoming critical, controlling, judgmental, disrespectful, or abusive of the other. Rather, in most cases, individuals understand that relationships require a certain amount of mutual respect, support, compromise, sacrifice, and caringness. Reeducating individuals on the importance of expressing appreciation, gratitude, gentleness, and love, as well as on how to go about working together in a collaborative and supportive manner when addressing conflict or resolving day-to-day problems, can be crucial to reestablishing closeness and intimacy.

In another session, I might have the individuals write down three things they believe they need from the other in order to reestablish closeness, trust, and intimacy. Or I might have them identify three things they are willing to change about their own behavior in order to better meet the other's needs. These kinds of exercises can be an important starting point for helping the couple to again communicate feelings and needs openly, in the "here and now," and in a less threatening manner. They can also help individuals with reflecting on their own participation in the relationship and with assuming responsibility for its success or failure. And finally, these kinds of exercises can help the couple with choosing to create a new relationship that's more rewarding than the recent past.

At other times, I might utilize exercises that help the participants learn more effective strategies for problem-solving and resolving conflict. I may, for example, try to coach the couple on ways of looking for common ground amid differences in opinion or areas of conflict (i.e., shades of gray between black-and-white points of view). This can be more difficult than it sounds, especially where one or the other partner feels as if he or she alone has always been expected to make sacrifices in order to satisfy the other's needs or demands. In such cases, any compromise may initially feel like one is again "giving in" while receiving little in return. But helping a couple learn to find *mutually* acceptable solutions can help each to recognize the long-term benefits achieved by working together rather than selfishly or rigidly striving to get *all* of what one wants in any given situation. *There are countless exercises a therapist can utilize in couples counseling. But the exercises are not a solution to discord, only a means to an end.*

Couples counseling is not a place for couples to come and dwell upon or argue about the perceived shortcomings of the other person or that which one believes the other person needs to change. By the time two people come in for couples counseling, I can almost guarantee that each has shortcomings the other finds clearly irritating. I am also pretty sure that both parties do things the other finds difficult to tolerate. Occasionally, one party may have even done something the other party finds downright unforgivable. But the focus of couples counseling cannot be on changing the perceived shortcomings of the other, any more than it can be on seeking atonement for any "sins" the other may have committed. One of the simple truths about all therapy is that, for it to work, every client needs to keep the focus on one's self, and in the case of couples counseling, the focus needs to be on what each party wants out of the relationship and the personal changes each is willing to make to help bring about that which he/she seeks. Focusing on changing another's shortcomings or upon collecting a "pound of flesh" almost always dooms the counseling (and, in this case, the relationship) to failure.

There may, of course, be times when I allow for each to express frustrations regarding the state of the relationship or an existing problem. But similarly, effective couples counseling does not involve allowing one individual to judge or blame the other for the relationship problems. Yes, I have had times when one party sincerely believed the other to be solely responsible for the couples' problems. But one of the more destructive factors for any relationship is a tendency to think that one or the other person is totally at fault for existing conflicts. I have long found that when a relationship is working well, both parties are doing something right, and when a relationship is going badly, both parties are doing something wrong. Rarely, if ever, is one person solely at fault for a relationship's problems. And supporting this perception in any fashion at all is never fruitful. Accordingly, I work diligently not to let the counseling slip into complaining or blaming or accusing.

Finally, instead of focusing upon the negative or on trying to go back and fix past problems or hurts, I try to keep the focus upon what needs to change in the present moment in order to promote greater peace, harmony, and love. Placing undue emphasis upon the negative or the past, as opposed to what might be done in the present to improve the relationship, seldom yields positive results. Again, for couples counseling to be effective, the focus needs to be on what the couple wants from the relationship in the present and what each partner is willing to give up in order to help them get that which they want.

Many times, the early stages of couples counseling can be session-limited. In some cases, twelve to sixteen meetings can get a reasonably functioning couple well on their way to healing what ails them. For more complex cases, where prior parenting or past life traumas have resulted in significant trust issues, controlling behavior, fears of abandonment, passive/avoidant tendencies, anger management problems, etc., the counseling may take longer. And occasionally, with the passage of time, a therapist may come to realize that one or the other party needs to be referred out for individual counseling to resolve personal concerns while the couples counseling is ongoing. Finally, there have also been instances when I have needed to suspend the couples counseling until such time as these comorbid conditions were sufficiently resolved. But again, ideally, couples counseling is a *collaborative* undertaking wherein each party comes to realize that when the relationship is working well, *both* individuals deserve the credit, and when the relationship is not working well, *both* individuals share the blame. Couples counseling is where individuals go when each loves the other and each is willing to make some change in the hopes that a healthier relationship will give them both more of what they want from life. For me, it is also in this respect that couples counseling can be considered a spiritual endeavor because couples counseling is about helping individuals utilize their relationship as a vehicle for increasing their meaning in life.

In January 2012, shortly after her eighty-sixth birthday, my mother entered the hospital. She'd struggled with poorly controlled hypertension and congestive heart failure for a few years, but her condition seemed to worsen during this period. She'd be in and out of the hospital a few times over the course of January and February. Then her condition seemed to improve. Unfortunately, only a few weeks following her most recent discharge, she developed pneumonia. She died a few days later. My mother had lived a full life. She was the mother of four children, raised and adopted a grandson, and had multiple grandchildren. In her later life, following my stepfather's stroke, she gained increased independence and self-confidence, was active in her church, became an avid painter, and all but resolved her problems with depression. At the time of her death, I think she was at peace. And I was at peace with the many good times we'd shared over the last twenty-five years of her life.

As a clinical psychologist, I've had many opportunities to work with individuals and families struggling to manage the loss of a parent. Grief is probably the most common emotion people experience during such times. Sometimes the grief is accompanied by other feelings. Maybe one feels confused or scared or angry or lonely or abandoned. One may also be unsure how to respond. But even when life has resulted in a loved one growing distant from his or her parent, upon the parent's death, grief or some emotional response is common. And in some cases, the emotion can seem devastating. As I said earlier, for better or for worse, our parents are *always* our parents. Though we may have adoptive parents, stepparents, even other parental figures whom we grow to love dearly, our natural or biological parents are the only such parents we will ever have. So one way or another, with the death of a parent (as with the death of any loved one), we are each called to make peace with this loss.

Unfortunately, the second most common emotion I have encountered, especially with the death of a last surviving parent, is probably that of greed. I can't begin to tell you the number of times I've witnessed loved ones, particularly the adult children or heirs, turn on one another and engage in selfish, bitter, even hateful battles over the property or other material possessions left behind by the deceased. It is truly tragic and all too similar to the contentious child custody disputes that sometimes arise between divorcing parents caught in their hurt and self-righteous anger when a marriage becomes damaged beyond repair. In both cases, the people seem oblivious to the fact that whatever the outcome of their battle, the payoff they receive will never outweigh the cost. Thank goodness, with the death of our mother, my siblings and I were able to rally together with an understanding that no material possessions could be worth more than the experiences and relationships we shared as a family. Yes, Mom was gone, but we still had each other, and clinging to material possessions in hopes of hanging onto some semblance of Mom, especially at the risk of arguing and fighting with each other, would only destroy the love our mother had wished for each of us. Once again, I would be reminded of the spiritual lesson contained in the message that "while people die, love remains."

My brother Dave would be named executor of our mom's estate. And for the next year and a half, Dave worked to settle our mother's affairs and to sell the home in which my siblings and I had spent much of our lives growing up. Then about a year into this process, Dave again began experiencing increased struggles with his own heart disease. In the spring of 2014, Mom's house was sold, and the estate settled. On July 1, 2014, Dave died.

This was a tough time for me as Dave and I had grown particularly close over the years following his achieving sobriety. In his honor, I and a few of his closest friends would play music at his wake. The following year would see the release of my CD *Dave and Ken: The Starkey Boys*. It was intended as a tribute to the love Dave and I had shared making music together as most of the songs were those we'd recorded in my home studio and prior to Dave's death. Through the recordings, his children and grandchildren would have a lasting reminder of Dave's voice.

The following year, Pam and I would open satellite offices for Professional Psychology Services in Atmore, Alabama, and (after completing my Mississippi licensure requirements) in Hattiesburg, Mississippi. These locations allowed us to begin generating limited income from other sites in order to supplement the work we were doing in Mobile. As they say, "You never want to put all your eggs in one basket." These offices would also allow us to be even more selective about the kinds of work we agreed to take on while still making payroll. In particular, these offices allowed me to essentially eliminate the number of forensic cases I was doing and (with it) their related stress. It was a small change, but meaningful.

Then in the summer of 2015, my sister LouAnne, her husband (Mark), and Pam and I would begin a yearly tradition of attending the Abbey Road Beatles Festival held every Memorial Day weekend in Southern Indiana/Northern Kentucky. This festival consisted of five days of assorted tribute bands (from as far away as England, Finland, and Brazil, as well as those from across America) playing Beatles and '60s music from morning to night. It would be more music and fun than some might say should be allowed. But for LouAnne and me, it was an opportunity to renew a relationship that had not been close for years. As noted previously, I was four years older than LouAnne, so we had little in common growing up. Then as is often the case, when we were grown, we'd gone our separate ways. I moved away to school, and she married and began raising a family. For some forty years, we'd have limited contact. But with the deaths of our brother Kevin, our stepfather Marcus, our Mom, and then Dave, we'd become the only remaining relatives from our nuclear family. Even though my life was now in south Alabama, and we lived hundreds of miles apart, this would be our chance to start seeing each other again on a more regular basis. It also allowed us to share our mutual love for the Beatles and '60s music. I think we both needed to reconnect. The visits would continue for years to come.

This would also begin my most productive period for recording music. On a visit to her sister's house in Atlanta, Pam, her sister, and a nephew would pick up a snare drum for me at a yard sale. This encouraged me to purchase even more percussion items (drums, cymbals, congas, etc.) or my recording studio. As you may recall, earlier, I mentioned how Don Moore had once shared some of his drumming expertise with me when I was in junior high school. To this basic introduction on drumming, I was able to add some of what I had observed over the years playing with other musicians or by watching music videos and, in conjunction with my ability to play by ear, to further expand the music I would be recording. Between 2014 and 2019, I would record four additional CDs. And the more recent CDs would now have the full complement of band instruments: guitars, bass, keyboards, vocals, *and* drums.

You say you'll change the constitution, well you know,
We all want to change your head.
You tell me it's the institution, well you know,
You better free your mind instead.
—J. Lennon and P. McCartney

From "Revolution," words and music by
John Lennon and Paul McCartney.
Copyright 1968. Northern Songs Limited

MODERN TIMES

Two thousand sixteen was an election year for the US. It was also a time of social change and political upheaval the likes of which many of us had scarcely known since the 1960s. The candidates selected by the Democrat and Republican parties to represent their voters could not have been more different. They also could not have been more divisive. The Democrats chose the wife of a former president whom they hoped would be their flag bearer as the first woman president of the US. This candidate seemingly believed in an increasingly socialistic agenda that included extending the progressive policies of the recent past, further expanding the reach of the federal government, and sharing more of the nation's wealth through increased taxes on the wealthy and growing entitlement programs for the poor. She also advocated for open borders, more ethnic diversity, more cultural pluralism, and greater involvement in the global economy.

The Republicans, on the other hand, chose a populist candidate who sought to reduce taxes and restore America to a time when blue-collar jobs and employment opportunities, in general, were more abundant. This candidate also favored an American economy that was less dependent on the international market. Lastly, this candidate favored a nation where American freedom and values were not so vulnerable to the military might and cultural influences of other nations and where the federal government was smaller and capitalism clearly reigned supreme. The Republican candidate also ran on a platform of ridding Washington, DC, of those career politicians whom many believed were more committed to serving special-interest groups and maintaining their political positions than to serving the people who had elected them to office. He called it "draining the swamp." Again, the differences between the candidates could not have been greater, and the antagonism it created would reverberate throughout the nation in ways scarcely imaginable.

As suggested above, not since the 1960s could I remember a time when there existed more divisiveness, more civil unrest, more protests, and more hatred expressed by people all sharing the same nation. In truth, many viewed the Democratic candidate as deceitful, conniving, and manipulative, while others viewed the Republican candidate as abrasive, arrogant, and racist. The Democratic candidate and her election team would eventually be accused of fabricating a phony dossier of information intended to smear the Republican candidate so as to tilt the election in her favor. The Republican candidate and his election team would be accused of colluding with Russian authorities and engaging in sneaky, underhanded activities designed to sabotage his Democratic rival as well.

Most of the pollsters and political pundits predicted an easy victory for the Democratic candidate. So when election results revealed the Republican candidate as the victor, Democratic voters became incensed. Republicans cited the Electoral College count as proof positive they had won the election "fair and square." Democratic voters, on the other hand, contested the results by citing their having won the popular vote as proof the election had been stolen. Some Democrats quickly began calling for the Electoral College to be done away with so as to prevent such an "atrocity" from ever happening again. Even before the new president was sworn into office, Democrats in the House of Representatives (as well as the liberal press) were calling for an investigation into alleged election corruption and for the incoming president to be impeached.

While no such action would immediately ensue, the Democratic opposition never really settled down. Then once the new president was sworn in, an investigation would be launched by the newly appointed attorney general (a Republican appointee) to identify the source of the phony dossier and who was responsible for propagating the allegations of Russian collusion. Efforts to uncover those responsible for perpetuating the Russian "hoax" would drag on for years. And various administrators and agents in the FBI would be associated with having advanced the dossier and accused of abusing their power for political reasons. Some even resigned or were fired. But as of this writing, none were ever prosecuted. And few, if any, of the perpetrators were ever definitively identified.

I was as surprised with the election results as anyone. But what I remember most is being taken aback by all the resulting uproar and hostility. I have never been especially political. Not that I don't have strongly held values or am not socially minded. I have my opinions. I try to vote regularly in elections and share my views when asked by others. But I also try to remember that others may hold equally strong views of their own and that it's not my place to try and force them to believe as I do. Moreover, I've long been of the belief that people don't usually want to hear the opinion of others unless they ask for them, and even then, they may choose not to *listen*. I'm also of the mind that people having differing values or varying political perspectives usually get more of what they want in the long run by working together. As noted earlier, rigidly insisting or trying to bully others into agreeing with one's point of view or to get one's own way usually yields poorer results.

It was in a telephone conversation with Mike Sprague shortly after the election that I came to realize just how sharply defined his own liberal views had become. He too was beside himself with the election results and sought my input regarding what mental health diagnosis might be most appropriate for the incoming president. As a psychologist, my professional training had coached me well on never suggesting such a diagnosis (or opinion) for anyone without first completing a thorough evaluation. So in response to his clear disapproval of the election results, I could only express my hope that regardless whom the nation elected as its president, "hopefully the person would accomplish something meaningful without messing things up too badly."

Adding to all the initial uproar would be three contentious battles over Republican-sponsored Supreme Court nominees arising during the years immediately following the election. Each was marked by politically biased rhetoric and unsubstantiated personal accusations having little to do with the nominee's past judicial record or capacity to serve. And the upshot of all this would be to only further divide our country. The Democrats seemed intensely convinced the three newly appointed and more conservative judges would tilt the balance of power on the Supreme Court such as might result in undermining their progressive aspirations. They especially feared the new court would one day overturn the court's 1960's decision in *Roe v. Wade*, which supported a woman's unfettered right to abortion. Following confirmation of the third nominee, the Democratic leadership began threatening to "stack" the Supreme Court by adding two or more additional judges to the court's existing nine judges should the Democrats win control of the presidency and US Senate in the 2020 national election. While all these threats would be strongly condemned by Republicans, the resulting damage to our nation's psyche would remain.

As all the political conflicts raged on, racial tensions would again emerge in America. A so-called "Black Lives Matter" movement arose following a few isolated incidents of alleged police brutality perpetrated against blacks, with the group's mantra being that "systemic racism" was responsible for widespread abuse of power by police. The group also blamed racism for blacks not achieving economically or socially in a manner comparable to whites. The result would be protests (particularly in cities and states with supportive Democratic mayors and governors) that all too often turned into excuses for looting and rioting. Democrats would then blame the recently elected president and his policies for creating the new racial divide. The Republican administration, by contrast, touted an improved economy, increased household incomes, and drastically reduced unemployment rate among blacks, Hispanics, and other ethnic minorities as evidence of the administration's commitment toward promoting racial balance for all. Democrats were then accused of having stirred up the racial problems so as to advance their own political agenda. Regardless of who was at fault, all the destruction of property resulting from the protests only exacerbated the conflict. On the one side were those whose homes and businesses were being damaged or destroyed by the protesters and the police who had been hired to protect them, while on the other side were those seeking to correct what they perceived as racial and social injustices.

Out of concern for alienating a portion of their political base, few if any Democratic politicians would speak out against the protesters. And essentially all leaders of Democratically run cities refused the Republican president's offer to send in the National Guard to quell the riots. Instead, politicians in those cities proposed "defunding" police departments and increasing funding for social programs as the solution to reducing the crime and violence and ridding the nation of its cultural divide. Republican politicians, as might be expected, considered this idea as pandering to those who were breaking the law and railed against the Democrats' refusal to condemn such violence. They claimed that any instances of abuse of power and/or racism were isolated occurrences and not representative of the nation or police as a whole. They also insisted that defunding the police would only encourage more violence by career criminals. Finally, conservatives tried to remind progressive-minded advocates that America was founded as a nation of laws, wherein criminal behavior was to be prosecuted regardless of the race, creed, or nationality of the perpetrators. Some in law enforcement even pointed out that while blacks in America make up only about 20 percent of the nation's population, statistics showed blacks were responsible for more than 50 percent of all violent crime and gun offenses occurring throughout the country.

As the Black Lives Matter movement pushed on, protesters would soon be joined by disenchanted teenagers and young adults. They too struggled with problematic social adjustment, underemployment, and a lack of personal achievement and financial success and were intent upon getting their concerns heard and perceived injustices rectified. Throngs of young people started calling for the federal government to work more actively toward "balancing the playing field" through a redistribution of wealth and power. By contrast were those who proclaimed America to never have been about equality of success, wealth, or power but, rather, about equality of *opportunity under the law* for those willing to delay gratification, assume responsibility for their lives, pursue an education, and work diligently to achieve desired rewards. These voices blamed the discontent of so many young people on liberal-minded politicians whose socialistic ideology and "progressive" politics had imprisoned these youths and minorities in a world dependent on the charity of welfare programs and big government—thus leaving them with deep-seated feelings of entitlement and little hope for ever creating a meaningful life on their own.

Again, as a psychologist committed to questioning life and understanding people that I might better alleviate their pain and suffering, I'd be struck by both the irony and the tragedy of all this. It just seemed incomprehensible that so many seemingly bright and well-meaning individuals would get caught in their own perspective, their own point of view, their own opinion, and their own need to complain and point fingers at someone else when things weren't working out the way they planned. It was as if the people just couldn't see all the damage coming from their rigidity, damage that affected not only themselves but also everyone around them.

It's been suggested that disenchanted people need something or someone to blame for their frustrations, fear, anger, and discontent. As the old saying goes, "Haters hate. That's just what they do." But whatever the case, very few Democrats, very few Republicans, and certainly very few young adults or minorities seemed willing to speak of how existing concerns, real or imagined, might be symptomatic of some greater problem. Very few, for example, seemed willing to speak of how all these problems might be related to a breakdown of the nuclear family or the insidious decay of our nation's values. Very few seemed willing to speak of how all these problems might be attributed to a loss of national identity arising with the ever-expanding cultural diversity and pluralism we've come to experience as modern technology and international travel makes the world a smaller place in which to live. Very few seemed to speak of how all these problems might be associated with our nation's overall diminished interest in spirituality, prayer, and God. And very few, if any, seemed willing to look at themselves, at their own lives, and how their perceived problems and related dissatisfaction might be a result of their own attitudes and behaviors and how they were choosing to live their lives from one day to the next.

Psychologists understand how each of these factors *can* be associated with a nation's problems with poverty, violence, substance abuse, mental illness, and the multitude of other conditions associated with fear, anger, and social unrest. Undermine or destroy the foundation of a nation's family systems, social values, cultural ties, and sense of spiritual identity, and is it any wonder so many of its citizens would come to feel estranged from one another? Is it really any wonder so many people would come to feel confused about who they are or where they fit into this world or as if their lives have no real direction or purpose? And given all this, is it really any wonder that people would come to feel so angry and cheated by the very society of which they are a part that they blame their unhappiness and sense of despair on all those around them?

Again, psychologists know all too well the importance of family, of values, of cultural bonds, and of spirituality in forming both our personal and collective identities. These are things that invariably shape our perception of self, the rules and guidelines by which we choose to live, and our feeling of being connected with or estranged from those around us. These things help us to understand who we are within the bigger scheme of things. These things help us to realize where we fit in with the universe, with existence. And as importantly, these things teach us how to believe in something greater than our own individual egos or personal ideologies. These things give our lives meaning; they allow us to care, to love.

In many ways, all of us in this society seem to have become so caught up in the material world, in achieving our wants and desires, and in our well-intentioned efforts toward being more understanding, more accepting of differences, more tolerant, and more inclusive of others, that we seem to have lost sight of the things that matter most in helping us discover who or what we are, both as individuals and as a people. As a result, we act out of our fear, our anxiety, our anger, and our despair while self-righteously proclaiming ourselves to be justified in our actions. The Buddha might sit back, rub his belly, and laugh at all these angry people. Jesus might turn to prayer. But in a very practical sense, it is all truly tragic.

In 2019, Pam and I would finally be able to have our marriage blessed by the Catholic church. You may recall that when Pam and I initially married, the ceremony was performed by the chaplain of the hospital where I worked. Pam had agreed with this arrangement, although she had been raised in the Catholic church and always wanted her wedding to be a Catholic wedding. Unfortunately, this was not an option for us at the time as the Catholic church views marriage as a holy covenant between a man and a woman blessed by God and intended to be for life. Again, because I had previously been married, my marriage to Pam could only be blessed by the Catholic church once an official annulment of my previous marriage had been pursued and granted.

Anyone familiar with the Catholic church knows that obtaining an annulment tends to be a lengthy (some might say grueling) process. First, one needs to find a Catholic priest who believes enough in the intentions of the couple to sponsor the process of annulment and its presentation to the tribunal of the diocese. This is followed by the previously married individual (the petitioner) preparing a formal petition for consideration for annulment and completing the accompanying questionnaire. Then the petitioner prepares a detailed account of the circumstances leading up to the marriage, the events that occurred during the marriage that might have contributed to its dissolution, and the circumstances surrounding termination of the marriage. Once all this is done, the petitioner provides the church case instructor with the names of three individuals familiar with the circumstances surrounding the marriage and its termination who might serve as witnesses to provide additional evidence. The petitioner also needs to provide his/her birth certificate and evidence of his/her previously being baptized in a Christian-based church. In the event the petitioner was never baptized, he/she must pursue such baptism before the annulment proceedings can continue and a blessing of the current marriage be considered.

Once these steps have all been completed, the Catholic diocese sets up a series of interviews by representatives of the diocese who are assigned to review the materials provided and gain additional clarification regarding the circumstances of the marriage and its dissolution. I believe I was interviewed by three different such representatives. Next, if the interviewers find the materials to be complete and the case for annulment to have merit, the former spouse is notified of the request for annulment and provided an opportunity to object or otherwise respond to the petition. If no objection is lodged, the petition is scheduled to be examined by an ecclesiastical judge who places the request in line for consideration and ultimately renders a final decision. All these steps are the church's way of trying to assure that a mindful decision regarding the nature of the previous marriage has been reached and the requested grounds for annulment have been made in keeping with church doctrine.

In our case, the annulment process was begun in 2016 and spanned some two and one-half years. This explains why I hadn't pursued annulment proceedings some years earlier. But while it would end up being a lengthy and painful process, it'd also be a meaningful one. It was painful in that it required I examine all that which had transpired from the time Teresa and I first met and until well after our divorce was final. And this included getting honest with myself about all the mistakes I'd made contributing to the divorce. But once the annulment was granted, I realized that pursuing it had also encouraged me to reflect on myself and my investment in the meaning of marriage. And as a result, I would make a more conscious commitment to my marriage with Pam. I noted above that I have never joined the Catholic church. Nonetheless, I have found nothing in the teachings of the church with which I have a personal problem. And I have long believed that caring about those things which are of importance to my spouse is itself a spiritual endeavor. So as a result of obtaining an annulment of my previous marriage, Pam and I could have our marriage formally blessed by the Catholic church. This also meant she could again partake of the church sacraments, including the sacrament of the Holy Eucharist. Thus, completing the annulment process would greatly enrich both our marriage and our spiritual lives.

Two thousand nineteen would also be the year my Columbus High School graduating class would hold its fiftieth reunion. Since the death of my parents and my brothers, returning to Columbus had been reduced to the yearly excursions for seeing my sister and her husband, for visiting a few friends, and for attending the Abbey Road Music Festival. Nonetheless, I still considered Columbus my home. Admittedly, growing up there had not always been easy. And there were clearly times when I felt as if I didn't fit in. But though my life had called me away to destinations in Pennsylvania, Ohio, Kentucky, and (more recently) south Alabama, and while I'd not been able to return as often as I might have liked, I'd slowly grown to appreciate the stable environment Columbus offered me while growing up as a child. Columbus had been a safe place in which to be raised. It had protected me from some of the hardships of life. And as I'd gotten older, I had come to understand that being sheltered as a child might not necessarily have been such a bad thing. On a recent trip back, Pam commented on how seldom she heard emergency sirens while in Columbus. I guess when there is very little crime and very few true emergencies, police, fire truck, and EMT sirens are just less common. This has clearly not been my experience with any of the larger cities in which I have lived. But again, in Columbus, people don't usually settle differences with violence. Neighbors generally don't steal from or rob one another to get what they want. Kids don't take weapons to school, and people aren't generally given to shooting people when disagreements arise.

Sure, life happens. And no one ever truly escapes the evils of the world. Eventually, we all come to know such problems to be a real part of daily existence. But both as a person and as a mental health professional, I've become convinced that if we want children to develop into healthy adults, protecting them from growing up too fast and from being exposed to too much pain and suffering at an early age probably prepares them better for dealing with these concerns once they inevitably do arise. While I too needed to leave Columbus to experience the world, I'd be forever grateful for the solid foundation it had given me with which to undertake the journey. And while I would never have experienced the wonderful teachings of my professors at Duquesne University, never have become a clinical psychologist, and never have met Pam or so many of the lifelong friends who have forever changed my life had I not moved away, I will always cherish my roots. I am proud to call myself a Hoosier. I've experienced the "big city," so to speak. And though these experiences have taught me much, I am not sure bigger cities have a great deal more to offer than I could have gotten from staying closer to home. For every advantage I've found in larger, more diverse settings, I've also found a disadvantage. For every blessing I have encountered, I have also experienced suffering. Peace of mind may truly have more to do with *how* one lives his or her life than with *where* one lives it.

MODERN TIMES

Mike Sprague was on the planning committee for our fiftieth high school reunion and inquired about my attending. I agreed and, as an amateur musician, proposed we organize some former students to play live music as a form of entertainment. With a little effort, the "One & Done" band would come to pass and be scheduled to play. The music consisted of '60s tunes many of us had played as teenagers. And there we were, most of us near seventy years old, once again in the limelight. Sure, there'd still be some of the drama common to all bands: what songs could we agree on, who would play what parts, who would do the singing, what would we wear (believe it or not), etc. But eventually, we played two sets, some thirty-five songs, over the course of a two-and-a-half-hour period. The music wasn't terrific, but it wasn't bad either. And overall, the experience was great fun, both for the band members and guests alike. In many respects, for the first time in my life, it felt as though I was *truly* home. I was once again playing music in front of a live audience and probably felt more connected with my peers than I ever had as a youth.

Then upon returning to Mobile, life would throw Pam and me another curve. In 2017, Patch had begun experiencing lower back pain. The problem dragged on for months, and he'd gradually become less mobile. Various attempts to treat the problem with medication provided only limited relief. Then in late 2018, he developed problems with chronic pancreatitis. While a surgeon would later hypothesize the pancreatitis might have been caused by the medication he was placed on to alleviate his back pain, no one would ever know for sure. Repeatedly, our vet had reassured us that his pancreatitis was a treatable condition. But much of 2018 and 2019 were spent with his going in and out of the hospital as the condition worsened. And after some fourteen years with our family, Patch died in August 2019. I guess one might have to share life with a dog to fully understand the love Patch gave to us and the sense of loss we felt. He had touched our lives in so many ways, and his spirit will live on forever in our hearts. His story can be found on "Patch's Song," a tune written by Pam and me and recorded on the CD *Dream Like Mine*.

Pam and I both struggled with grief over the loss of our boy for the remainder of the year. Then in January 2020, Pam and I located another Australian shepherd in need of being rescued. He was a two and a half-year-old black-and-white male, also of some 60 pounds in size. His name was Tucker. The family with which Tucker lived had recently brought an aging parent into their home. Unfortunately, Tucker's active demeanor and the older woman's physical frailties were not compatible. As a result, the family decided Tucker needed to have a new home.

Tucker would turn out to be perfect for us. He resembled Patch enough physically to easily qualify as a brother. Still, his personality was sufficiently different to distinguish him as being his own dog. From the onset, it was clear that Patch was better adjusted socially than Tucker. Patch pretty much got along with all people and dogs alike. Only if another dog expressed aggressive tendencies would Patch respond in kind. Tucker, on the other hand, was a little slower to warm up to strangers and showed very little tolerance for other dogs. Both would be high-energy, but overall, Patch was a little more laid-back. Still, Tucker would be much more affectionate. He'd love snuggling up next to Pam and would be a real "kissy" dog. Before adopting Tucker, Pam had frequently voiced her desires for a "lapdog." I, on the other hand, always wanted a larger dog. In Tucker, we both got what we wanted.

Around this same time, in early 2020, I and others experienced what would become the defining world health crisis of our time. As if my never-ending quest to understand life hadn't already brought enough challenges, the COVID-19 pandemic would introduce a whole new array of questions. Near the end of January, I saw a news story about a viral outbreak in China that had resulted in the quarantining of the entire province of Wuhan. Everyone was being required to wear face masks, residents were being confined to their homes, and thousands of deaths were already being reported. While the virus had not yet spread to any other region of the world, reports of face mask and hand sanitizer shortages were already being cited, even beyond China.

Out of an abundance of caution, I was able to locate a pharmacy that still had face masks in stock and purchased a box of fifty "surgical" (single-use) masks. As reports trickled in of the virus spreading to Italy and producing even more deaths, I located a few more masks and some hand sanitizer. At this point, the virus had not yet arrived in the US. And most news stations were still reporting there to be little reason for Americans to be concerned. Still, the absence of *reliable* information was leading to conflicting accounts about the virus. Was it transmissible between people? Could it be transmitted by asymptomatic carriers? Were masks really useful in managing its spread? Could America really be spared? Then reports started circulating about previous US administrations not having stockpiled enough personal protection equipment (masks, gloves, gowns, hospital ventilators, etc.) to manage a nationwide outbreak, thus woefully underpreparing the country for any kind of pandemic.

In truth, probably nobody could have predicted the pandemic or just how widespread and deadly it would become, any more than one could have known how best to deal with it. Shortly after the virus was first identified, the president banned travel to and from China as a precautionary measure. He would endure a fair amount of criticism for this decision as some Democratic politicians accused him of overreacting while still others called him xenophobic. Again, given the hostile and divisive political atmosphere gripping America, none of this was much of a surprise. Nevertheless, and in spite of the criticism, the president stuck to his decision.

As the virus slowly spread across Europe, the president instituted additional bans of travel to and from Italy, Great Britain, France, and other nations reporting outbreaks. These measures were yet one more attempt to prevent the virus from reaching the US and potentially infecting millions of Americans. Ultimately, all these efforts failed. Within a matter of weeks, spokespersons at the Center for Disease Control (CDC) were reporting cases in America and predicting hundreds of thousands of deaths could occur. Major cities with frequent international air travel and larger Asian populations (e.g., Seattle, New York City, etc.) would catch the early brunt of the virus. But eventually, it spread across all sectors of the nation.

By early March, the NCAA had canceled the college basketball national championship tournament and suspended all other college sports (baseball, track and field, etc.) for the foreseeable future. The NBA followed suit by suspending its season. Then Major League Baseball suspended spring training and canceled the start of the baseball season "until further notice."

In hopes of further reducing the spread of the virus (or "flattening the curve" as they called it), the CDC then recommended closing down the country for a few weeks and quarantining all but the nation's most essential workers. After some consultation with advisers and the CDC, the president agreed and ordered all federal offices closed. He also encouraged nonessential private businesses to either lay off their employees or have them work from home. And this included businesses such as restaurants, bars, schools, churches, hair salons, etc. The lone exceptions to the recommendations would be for healthcare providers, first responders, grocery store workers, and the like. State governors would then issue "stay at home" orders for their constituents and limit travel for critical purposes only.

Ultimately, the actual shutdown of the national workforce and economy would last some four weeks. And predictably, the nation began to struggle.

In order to alleviate the financial strain associated with so many people being off work, the president and Congress promptly began working on emergency legislation to compensate businesses such that employees could remain on the payroll and continue being paid while out of work. This would help workers with meeting household expenses during the shutdown and while awaiting reopening of the economy. Unfortunately, because of continued political wrangling, the actual passing of the legislation through Congress would take weeks. And while many praised the act for its compassion, others complained both that it was undertaken at too great a cost to the national debt and was lacking (as might be expected with any large government payout plan) sufficient safeguards to prevent massive fraud.

Of course, with factories being closed, the production of goods would grind to a halt. Because small businesses were also shut down, the availability of services declined as well. And with hotels, theaters, and live music venues all being closed, the hospitality, movie, and entertainment industries all but collapsed. Finally, with school systems ending their terms prematurely, millions of students would be sent home and have their education suspended. Then as many had been predicting, the stock market took a dive.

As the pandemic dragged on, hospitals would be flooded with those sick and dying, and the nation's mental health concerns would explode. Problems with substance use, domestic violence, depression, anxiety, suicide, and other mental health issues all increased dramatically. Unfortunately, as the nation's need for mental health services grew, many health-care offices and practices had to reduce their hours due to worker shortages created by the spreading virus. This only further compounded existing problems.

Although the virus had clearly reached the US, the ongoing absence of reliable information continued undermining efforts toward managing it. Apart from the uncertainty regarding mode of transmission and usefulness of protective equipment, for the longest time, doctors were not even certain who was most at risk of getting infected. Eventually, it'd be discovered that the virus was particularly harmful to aging persons having comorbid health conditions, such as heart problems, respiratory problems, diabetes mellitus, obesity, and the like. But by that time, nursing homes and retirement centers were already reporting a dire picture. Residents had begun dying in large numbers and in isolation as family members were restricted from visiting loved ones in an attempt to further control the viral spread.

A few months into the pandemic, Pam and I would be fortunate enough to locate a small stash of N-95 masks. These were the masks the CDC believed to be most effective for protecting people against the virus. So after sharing a few with family and friends, we kept the remainder for use in our psychology practice. These masks, in conjunction with hand sanitizer and the single-use, surgical masks we'd provide to clients, would let us continue seeing our clients with a modicum of safety. A short time later, we'd implement even stricter guidelines (then being suggested by the CDC), limiting the number of persons in our offices, maintaining six feet of social distance between ourselves and others, sanitizing all furniture (including restrooms) after each client contact, wearing disposable gloves, and so on. But while all these efforts allowed us to continue helping some of our clients, because of the scariness of the pandemic, the reluctance of people to venture away from their homes, and the government shutdown, we still lost some 70 percent of our business between April and June of 2020.

Finally, by early August, efforts toward reopening the economy had gotten underway in most states. The president had implemented plans to fast-track creation of a vaccine, and effective treatment interventions were being pursued. The federal government had also disseminated guidelines to help governors and private businesses with reopening in as safe a manner as possible. Unfortunately, the guidelines would take months to instill as the recommendations were not consistently applied across all states. Some (particularly Republican-run states) seemed to reopen too soon or with inadequate precautions. Other states (particularly Democratic-run states) seemed to delay reopening far past the time many considered optimal for salvaging many of those businesses (especially restaurants, movie theaters, hair salons, etc.) damaged by the shutdown. Early on, some states mandated mask wearing in public places, while others did not. And while nearly all states would eventually pass such a mandate (at least for a time), some individuals complied while others refused. Thankfully, restarting the economy would help Pam and me with restoring our practice to about 80 percent of its previous business. And even though the office still wasn't generating as much income as it had prior to the pandemic, the improvement was much welcomed.

Given that we were in the midst of yet another election year, the candidates were intent on doing everything in their power to advance their political aspirations. Accordingly, they began climbing all over themselves to condemn one another's reactions to the pandemic. The party out of power complained how the president and current administration were mishandling their response, while those in power complained of how those not in power were sitting by and criticizing the efforts of others but offering no constructive solutions of their own.

By the end of summer, school systems would finally begin implementing plans for resuming the education of children.

By then, hundreds of millions of tax dollars had been spent upgrading school ventilation systems and implementing protective protocols nationwide. This would allow some schools to reopen with live instruction, particularly parochial schools and those from systems in more rural or Southern states. Other schools would offer varying combinations of in-class and virtual (computer-based) learning experiences. Unfortunately, teacher unions in many of the larger Northern cities (such as Chicago, San Francisco, Philadelphia, and New York) resisted any plan that involved returning to the classroom. Their expressed concerns would be of fears over contracting or spreading the virus and the need to protect teachers and students alike from health problems associated therewith. Still, all the emerging research seemed clear in suggesting teachers and students to be at *less* risk for contracting the virus in a school setting than in their home or community environments at large. Moreover, evidence was also mounting to suggest that depriving students of in-class instruction would yield long-standing academic problems for students, escalating dropout rates, growing social problems, and increased mental health concerns (especially problems with depression, anxiety, suicidality, and substance use). For months, the teachers unions refused to budge. And politicians in larger, again predominantly Democratically run cities refused to challenge the politically powerful unions. The result would be many of these schools offering only the virtual learning experience.

In late fall, Major League Baseball would commence playing games. This would be followed by the NBA resuming the previously postponed basketball season, the NFL starting up their season, and college football getting underway, all with precautions and/or modified formats and with limited fans in the stadiums and arenas. The NBA would actually quarantine (with remarkable success) all the players of playoff teams in the Disney World Complex of Orlando, Florida, until a champion was finally crowned. As might be expected, small outbreaks of the virus still occurred on teams in those sports where such quarantining wasn't feasible (despite the best efforts of all concerned), and some games had to be postponed or canceled because of this. But a World Series, College Football Championship, and Super Bowl would all be held in one fashion or another. I guess there was just too much public demand and too much money at stake not to hold these events. Still, none of these undertakings would be the same as usual.

As COVID "fatigue" kicked in, millions of Americans (as well as people worldwide) would become increasingly agitated by restrictions being placed on their personal freedoms. This was especially true for those living in states where mask wearing and social distancing were still being mandated. Over time, more and more people refused compliance with recommended/mandated safeguards, some even becoming argumentative (if not hostile) toward those politicians or neighbors intent on advancing such guidelines and minimizing risks.

Then as the nation struggled to persevere, a second wave of the virus hit Europe and the US. With Thanksgiving and Christmas fast approaching, the CDC recommended people refrain from attending any family gatherings of greater than eight to ten people. Again, some people followed the guidelines while many others defiantly refused. This resulted in America experiencing yet another surge of COVID cases by the end of 2020. This time around, the virus had mutated, thus producing a strain that appeared more contagious (although somewhat less deadly) than the original. All in all, before everything was said and done, over a million Americans would die from COVID-19. Some five million people would die worldwide. Many others would incur lasting physical health problems (e.g., respiratory problems, heart problems, anxiety, etc.) as the virus and its variants continued plaguing America and the world for years to come.

Amid all this craziness, the political antagonism emerging after the election of 2016 would intensify for the upcoming 2020 elections. Republicans began accusing the Democrats of wanting to use the COVID-19 crisis to keep state economies closed down and hamper the nation's recovery. This, they surmised, was the Democrats' attempt to further undermine Republican reelection hopes. Democrats, on the other hand, accused the Republicans of reopening the economy too quickly so as to advance their own political ambitions ahead of safeguarding American citizens.

As mentioned above, Republicans had already assumed the mantle of supporting law enforcement, maintaining lower taxes, limiting regulations on big business and industry, bolstering manufacturing jobs, and restricting legal abortion (all in addition to promoting more conservative values). Democrats, of course, had assumed an agenda of raising taxes on big business and the richest 1 percent of Americans so as to promote sharing the wealth and paying for expanded social, welfare, and other entitlement programs (including universal health care for all American residents, even those in the nation illegally). Now Democrats were also going all in on college student-loan forgiveness, downsizing police budgets and restricting policing powers, and placing stricter regulations on the energy industry. This latter effort was intended to advance plans for ending the nation's reliance on fossil fuels and to promote a "green new deal" designed to reduce greenhouse emissions and better preserve the environment. They'd also continue pushing the idea of eliminating restrictions on immigration and of opening the borders to any and all seeking entrance to the US (as well as promoting other progressive values).

Democrats also renewed their claim that Republicans had unjustly appointed three conservative Supreme Court judges in the preceding four years and, thus, upset the balance of power between conservative and liberal judges on the Court. In response to this perceived injustice, they resumed calling for an expansion of the Court from nine to eleven (or even thirteen) justices. This they hoped would allow them to appoint more liberal judges to the Court should they be successful in winning the presidency and control of the Senate. Democrats also began clamoring for statehood status to be awarded to Washington, DC and Puerto Rico (both Democratic strongholds) in hopes of increasing the number of Democratic representatives in Congress. And they'd renew earlier calls for doing away with the Electoral College out of a belief that the previous vote in favor of the Republican candidate had not truly represented the will of the people. They remained convinced that more than 50 percent of the American population supported their liberal agenda (even if more than half the nation's statehouses did not). Finally, leaving no stone unturned, the Democratic Party then encouraged Democratic governors and legislators to push for state laws allowing unrestricted mail-in voting for everyone listed on prior registration logs, with or without proof of their being dead or alive, legal resident or not, and/or having any verifiable signature. While the rationale for this move was that such action would encourage voter participation while protecting citizens from COVID-19 exposure, the hope was to increase turnout among registered Democratic voters who outnumbered registered Republican voters. These actions only further convinced Republicans that the Democrats were trying to steal the upcoming election by encouraging illegitimate votes to be counted.

As might be expected, all this insanity would have the end result of further reifying the political positions of each camp and of continuing to divide the nation along political lines. As election time rolled around, many merchants, particularly in larger Democratically run cities, had once again boarded up storefront windows, while governors were calling out the National Guard in anticipation of more social unrest and rioting should election results again be contested.

Some four days after the 2020 election, when the voting results were *finally* announced by the mainstream press outlets, the Democratic candidate was determined by most to have won the presidency. Still, there was no clear political mandate. And lawyers for the Republican president promptly filed suit in several key (primarily Democratically run) states, alleging voting irregularities ranging from voter fraud to failure to allow Republican observers adequate access to the vote-counting process. This led the attorney general to authorize the Department of Justice to open an official investigation into "significant" allegations of voting irregularities. No evidence of problems sufficient enough to overturn election results would ever be discovered.

In December of 2020, two of the COVID vaccines long promised by the Republican president, but touted as essentially impossible by opposing politicians, became available. A third vaccine would follow a few months later. The first two would be administered in two doses over a two-week period, while the third came in a single dose. Many scientists proclaimed their emergence in such a short time as nothing less than miraculous. But many Democratic politicians espoused concerns that insufficient research had been completed to assure their being safe. They also complained that an inadequate number of doses were being produced or made available quickly enough to effectively treat the population at large. Complaints also arose regarding plans for delivering the vaccine and how to prioritize who should receive the first doses.

While the sitting president had directed each of the governors to establish their own plans for dispensing the vaccines in their respective states, some governors struggled to devise plans in a timely manner. This created further delays in getting the vaccine to those in need. The fact is, expectations that companies could ever produce enough doses of the vaccine to supply the entire US population, or that politicians would figure out a way for making them available in any kind of timely manner, were probably unreasonable. Still, while the vaccination process would drag on for months, the vaccines would prove to be a godsend. Eventually, health-care workers, nursing home residents, and aging adults were designated the first to receive the shots in most states. And though some had complained of not being able to get their doses quickly enough, after the initial rush, it became apparent that many people didn't even want to get vaccinated—whether out of fears the vaccine might eventually prove dangerous, for religious reasons, or because of a belief they were safe enough without a vaccination.

By January 2021, election results from the previous election would be ratified by all fifty states. Unfortunately, this did not put an end to claims by some Republicans that (once again) the election had been stolen. Several members of the House of Representatives and Senate vowed to contest ratification of the Electoral College findings, which was an interesting turn of events given that Democrats had their own issues with the Electoral College. This, along with calls from the sitting president, further encouraged a vast throng of Republican supporters to descend on Washington, DC, January 6 (the day Congress was to meet and ratify the Electoral College results) in protest. Apparently, a few protestors even carried firearms. After the Republican president appeared in support of the "rally," the protestors became increasingly agitated. Eventually, a number of the participants stormed the Capitol building, creating havoc, damaging property, and sending representatives and senators scurrying for safety. Ultimately, some six people would die (from assaults and/or related medical emergencies), and everyone, Republicans and Democrats alike, condemned this situation. Many also questioned how the Capitol Police and Metropolitan Police of Washington, DC, could have been so poorly prepared as to have allowed the protestors to get out of control. Some even questioned how the president's actions might have provoked or exacerbated the situation. Later that day, the sitting vice president would oversee acceptance of the Electoral College findings as final.

Within twenty-four hours, Democratic politicians were again calling for the still-sitting president to be impeached, claiming his actions and words had incited the crowd to rebellion. Liberal-minded social media tech giants then promptly joined in the fray by suspending the accounts of the sitting president and voicing concern over how his communications may have provoked the hostility. The conservative platform Parler was also shut down by social media outlets, claiming content being disseminated thereon also propagated violence. This, of course, led to outcries of censorship and by pledges of some in Congress to pursue a formal investigation into social media's operating policies and authority.

Seven days before the Republican president was scheduled to transfer power to the Democratic president-elect and leave office, Articles of Impeachment would be prepared by the Democratic speaker of the House. A few days later, they would be passed, again, primarily along party lines and with no discussion or hearings. As might have been anticipated, however, the presiding Republican leader of the Senate refused to take up the Articles of Impeachment, citing lack of sufficient time for completing a fair and just hearing prior to the sitting president's leaving office.

The FBI then undertook an investigation into the riots and announced concerns that further protests might occur both in Washington, DC, and various state capitals across America on the day of the official swearing-in ceremony. To help protect Washington, DC, against such protests and more additional rioting, bridges allowing access to the area were closed off, fencing barriers topped with razor wire went up, and metal detectors were installed at all Congressional entrances. Next, the Washington Mall and assorted federal monuments were closed to visitors, and some twenty thousand plus National Guard troops (in addition to the local and federal law enforcement officers, and at a cost of five hundred million dollars) were brought in. Again, out of concern for possible looting, businesses boarded up their shops.

Not since the protests and riots of the 1960s, maybe not since WWII, was the nation's capital (or the nation itself, for that matter) on such high alert. While none of the anticipated chaos actually occurred in Washington, DC, or any of the state capitals, inexplicably, protests and looting by liberal-based groups again emerged in the Democratically run cities of Portland, Oregon, and Seattle, Washington. A "peaceful transition of power" would be completed with the Democratic candidate being sworn in as president, although the outgoing president was noticeably absent from the proceedings.

While the newly elected president would pledge to "work toward unifying the nation," from the start many remained doubtful of his intentions. Supporters of the former president remained concerned that the Democrats' unyielding plans for trying to impeach the now former president would only add more fuel to the political fires and further alienate the seventy-five million citizens who had voted to reelect him and who truly believed the election results to have been tainted. But even though Democratic leaders knew they lacked the two-thirds vote needed in the Senate for a conviction, they'd pushed ahead. Finally, the new leader of the Senate agreed to bring the Articles of Impeachment to trial. This hapless endeavor reminded me of the old story about how one day a person's feet and hands became aggravated at the stomach because they did all the work of gathering the food while the stomach just sat there digesting it. The feet and hands decided to go on strike, not realizing that refusing to gather any more food would ultimately mean they too would die along with the stomach. In the end, this attempt to pursue impeachment, in conjunction with fears regarding the overall progressive policies of the Democratic Party and how these policies might further denigrate conservative values, made any chance of reuniting the country seem unlikely at best.

Within a week, the newly elected president then began signing executive orders intended to undo the immigration control, energy, international trade, and national security policies of the former administration. This would be followed by his implementing a national policy intended to confront problems with "systemic racism" that he believed to be pervasive throughout the nation. He promptly began ordering all military personnel and other federal employees to undergo training designed to facilitate cultural sensitivity and raise awareness of "white privilege," and mandated all departments to undertake a hiring policy to promote diversity, equity, and inclusion (DEI) so government employees reflected the social and cultural makeup of the nation at large. Apart from the detrimental impact all these decisions would ultimately have on the nation's job market, household incomes, trade agreements, and national defense, the social implications of such actions only created further hostility and divisiveness. My own sentiments regarding all this were probably closer to those voiced by Coretta Scott King, wife of the late Martin Luther King Jr., who suggested that regardless of which party gains political power, elections come and go, only God remains.

**I believe it's a sin to try and make things last forever.
Everything that exists in time runs out of time someday.
Got to let go of the things that keep you tethered.
Take your place with grace, and be on your way.**
—B. Cockburn

From "Mighty Trucks of Midnight," words
and music by Bruce Cockburn, 1991,
published through True North Records, 23
Griffin Street, Watertown, Ontario.

ENDINGS

THESE DAYS, WHEN I RETURN TO COLUMBUS, I'm surprised by how, in so many ways, very little has changed. Sure, it's grown to some forty-eight thousand residents. And there's a good deal more ethnic diversity than when I was growing up. I also suspect there's more substance abuse and divorce than was true in the '50s and '60s. A few of the newer restaurant chains have moved in to set up shop. And as might be expected, Cummins continues building new plants every so often, whether to replace outdated ones or simply to keep the company relevant in today's ever-changing markets. But unlike so many small towns that have fallen on hard times with the decline of American industry, the emergence of new technologies, and our "progressive" way of life, Columbus seems to have remained the same small, family-oriented community it was when I was a kid. The streets are still clean, and city leaders work diligently to keep downtown flourishing and teeming with business. The parks and athletic fields remain well manicured, and city buses, albeit updated, still run on time (and with current fares ranging from a meager twenty-five cents per trip to ten cents for senior citizens). Crime continues to be low, and there is essentially no gun violence. Families still value staying intact; parents continue working responsibly at raising their children to be caring, respectful citizens; and neighbors, generally speaking, continue to treat one another with kindness.

This is not to say that Columbus has been totally immune to the happenings and occurrences of the outside world, just that the people there still seem to have a sense of their roots. As a result, the town has remained relatively free of the drama so many of us are accustomed to seeing on television or reading about on the internet of late; those troublesome realities sometimes attributed to a world caught up in attitudes of selfishness, materialism, entitlement, and so much displaced fear and anger.

Perhaps this sounds like I'm being overly cynical in speaking of today's world. Maybe I simply need to admit that the America wherein I and so many others were raised has long since passed. Undoubtedly, life is about change. Still, it troubles me to think that the values our nation once held dear and that were ever-present in my hometown seem to have become less important in this fast-moving modern world. Honesty, dependability, integrity, valuing one's reputation, keeping one's word, working hard to earn one's keep, and caring for family—all these things used to mean something special. Today, for so many Americans, these values just seem to hold less importance.

There truly was a time when marriage was viewed by many Americans as a spiritually based union between two individuals seeking to better understand their place in the world and their relationship with God. Unfortunately, in this day and age, marriage just seems to be one more social contract to be entered into or out of depending on the convenience or discomfort it provides. For generations, families really were considered the fundamental structure for helping children grow safely into healthy, caring, productive adults. Now families seem to be eroding under the onslaught of hedonistic individualism, wherein so many people repeatedly place their own impulses, interests, and desires over the needs of others, even those of the children they bring into the world. Religious institutions and spiritual values, once serving as the moral barometer for individuals and communities alike, seem continuously under fire by those who have lost sight of their value in the greater scheme of things. School systems that once served as vehicles for promoting knowledge, reasoning skills, and critical thinking currently seem inundated with the politics of social reform and with teachers spending more time promoting political correctness or managing the behavior of students (some might say parenting them) than actually educating them. Police officers, once seen as protectors of the peace, are now questioned at every turn and, all too often, expected to be more social workers than enforcers of the law. Factories and jobs that once provided people self-respect and a sense of self-worth (while also helping America become the most prosperous nation in the world) have been downsized or outsourced in the name of globalization, increasing profits, and/or protecting the environment. Finally, politicians who once seemed to understand that working together to find common ground probably benefits the nation more in the long run appear increasingly intent on self-righteously bullying those of opposing views into compliance with their own agenda. Certainly, "the times they are a changing."

On February 13, 2021, only five days after agreeing to advance the Democratically led House of Representatives' Articles of Impeachment for the former president, the US Senate voted to acquit. While most believed his actions may have contributed to or did little to quell the riotous behavior of early January, the impeachment process was again viewed by many as a largely partisan attempt by Democratic lawmakers to exercise their contempt for the former president and his policies, while also trying to assure he would never again be eligible to serve in public office. Whether it was a partisan power play or not, an insufficient number of senators believed either that impeachment of a *former president* was constitutional or that his actions reached those of the legal charge of "incitement to riot." Neither side had won. The political battles would continue.

Again, while the newly elected president had originally promised to work for all Americans and reunite the country, it seemed his actions were already suggesting other motives. The quick decision to reverse immigration guidelines and border protections put in place by his predecessor only succeeded in creating a new crisis at the nation's southern border with Mexico. Hundreds of thousands of people, many unescorted children being encouraged by adults or ferried by Mexican drug cartels, began pouring across the border into the United States. Some believed the migrants to be fleeing persecution in their Latin American homelands or seeking to escape drug violence. Others suggested drug cartels were using the children as a diversion so as to facilitate their smuggling of drugs into the US while immigration officials were busy rounding up those crossing the border illegally. Certainly, an explosion of fentanyl overdose deaths unlike anything ever seen in the US would accompany this change of immigration policy and influx of illegal migrants. Many Americans feared the migrants might be carrying the COVID-19 virus, were criminals affiliated with gangs or terrorist groups, or were simply individuals seeking the free health care and welfare benefits more readily available in the US. No one could be certain of their reasons for coming to the US. And there may have been many reasons. But whatever the case, by July of 2021 (only six months into the new president's term), it was estimated that more than five hundred thousand illegal migrants had crossed the southern border, more than at any time in the previous seven years combined. The number would swell to over a million by the end of 2021.

While those of us in Alabama were not immediately impacted by these events, the chaos accompanying this mass influx of illegal migrants could scarcely be denied. The secretary for the Department of Homeland Security was supposedly responsible for overseeing immigration and border patrol. But it soon became apparent that he was either not up to the task or unwilling to effectively manage the border crossings. Vast numbers of migrants were entering America undetected, while others were placed in detention camps to await processing of claims for asylum. Some would be deported, but most would eventually be released into the community with instructions to appear for a court hearing at some future date. While this may have seemed a workable solution for some, it was generally understood that most illegal migrants would disappear into the society at large and never return for their scheduled hearing.

Apart from the personal suffering experienced by those making the arduous journey to our borders from hundreds of miles away, the strain this arrival of illegal migrants placed on towns and cities across America would eventually prove unmanageable. The administration had seemingly assumed the numbers would be drastically lower and that the small communities across Texas, Arizona, and the greater Southwest would absorb the costs of providing housing, health care, education, and other services for the throng of newly established residents (many of whom did not speak English and lacked basic job skills). Unfortunately, the meager budgets of these little towns and cities would never prove adequate for meeting all the migrant's needs. Finally, the governor of Texas, in a desperate attempt to get the attention of the new president and encourage some understanding of the problems his state faced, began busing migrants to Washington, DC; Philadelphia; Chicago; New York City; Denver; and other major cities up North. This led the mayors of these Democratically run cities to condemn the action and begin asking the president for federal help. By the end of fiscal year 2022, over two million migrants had illegally crossed the American/Mexico border (with upward of six million illegals arriving by December 2023).

As already noted, the new president also altered the former administration's energy policies in an effort to move the nation away from its reliance on fossil fuels. This decision, it was proposed, was intended to reduce growing environmental problems attributed to "global warming" through promoting more efficient "green energy options." The changes would include the president ordering the closure of major oil pipelines and placing tighter restrictions on both the production of natural gas and the mining of coal. Again, this wouldn't immediately impact our family. But it would mean all those families and communities relying on incomes from jobs in the fossil fuel industry would promptly begin to suffer. As energy prices shot up some 35 percent and unemployed workers struggled to pay their bills, claims that all those losing their jobs would eventually be retrained for jobs in the new (and as yet undeveloped) environmentally friendly energy industry seemed to fall on deaf ears. More political backlash was soon to follow.

The Democrats in the House of Representatives then proposed a five-trillion-dollar "Build Back Better" infrastructure plan that would include money for everything from roads and bridges to the expansion of high-speed internet to full-time preschool for all those living in America to universal health care for anyone (legal resident or not) living in the US and a host of other projects deemed by some as having little, if anything, to do with infrastructure. Raising taxes on big business and the wealthiest of Americans was the proposed solution for financing the bill. Still, few really believed such tax increases could ever generate the income needed to offset its final costs, and most chose to ignore the obvious likelihood of big business and the wealthy simply moving their assets overseas so as to avoid the taxes. After much discussion, concerns for the impact the spending would have on inflation and the ballooning national debt resulted in the bill (as initially drafted) lacking the necessary support for becoming law. Consequently, it was split into separate "infrastructure" and "social infrastructure" bills. This succeeded in getting the infrastructure portion passed by both houses of Congress, with concerns regarding its impact on inflation and the national debt essentially being ignored. The social infrastructure bill would be tabled.

Frustrated by the Republicans' success at undermining the Build Back Better plan, Democrats in the Senate would then propose eliminating the filibuster rule. This was the long-standing rule that made it necessary for a sixty-vote majority to be present in the US Senate in order for major legislation to be passed by its members, thereby encouraging bipartisan negotiation on more controversial bills. Getting rid of the rule would effectively allow Democrats to pass *any* legislation they desired, including the remainder of their five-trillion Build Back Better plan, without the need for any compromise or a single Republican vote. Again, Republicans viewed this as yet another power play, and the proposal failed to garner even enough Democratic votes to pass.

Then while Democrats and Republicans in Congress were busy fighting with one another, the new president decided to establish a firm date for completing the total withdrawal of those US troops initially sent to Afghanistan to defeat the terrorist forces responsible for the 9-11 attacks. The previous president had originally proposed such a withdrawal of troops (after some twenty years of combat), but the manner by which this withdrawal would actually occur under the new president would be much different from that previously suggested. The result was a complete collapse of the Afghan government and a takeover by the Taliban (an Islamic extremist group) within eleven days of the US troop withdrawal. Thousands of Afghan nationals who had been supporters of the US occupation would be left behind, and some thirteen American soldiers would die in the chaos surrounding the final stages of the evacuation proper. Conservative politicians were once again incensed.

As the political struggles continued, the president then put together a commission to study "reform" of the Supreme Court. As previously indicated, the Democrats in the Senate wanted to expand the number of Supreme Court justices from nine to as many as thirteen so as to undo the perceived conservative bias of the existing court. Expanding the number of justices would allow the recently elected Democratic president and Senate to add up to four more liberal justices. Again, nearly all these measures had been hinted at (or proposed) by Democrats prior to the 2020 elections as a way of undoing changes brought about by the previous Republican administration to further their own progressive agenda. Now they were actually being advanced. The battles waged on.

In March of 2021, Pam and I received the first of our two doses of the COVID-19 vaccine. The second would be received two weeks later. The pandemic was still in full swing and proving to be distressing for all concerned. There were just so many unanswered questions, both arising with the virus itself and the medical establishment's recommendations for dealing with it. We'd waited on getting the vaccine for a few months after it first became available in order to alleviate concerns over its being new and having unforeseen side effects. But by March, we felt concerns over the consequences of going unvaccinated far outweighed any uncertainties associated with the vaccine. Accordingly, we'd decided on getting "the shot."

The CDC would continue advising Americans to wear masks in public, to social-distance, to wash their hands and/ or use hand sanitizer, etc. until some 70 percent of the population might be immunized and "herd immunity" could be established. But while the availability of the vaccine seemed to offer a light at the end of the COVID tunnel, as mentioned earlier, many Americans resisted getting it. Some continued to cite concerns over approval of the vaccine having been rushed and insufficiently tested to ensure its effectiveness and the absence of adverse side effects. Others cited reports spreading over social media regarding all kinds of unfounded problems with the vaccine (e.g., that it could leave women unable to bear children, etc.), none of which appeared to be based on any scientific evidence. Still, others continued rejecting the vaccine for religious reasons. But many people, whether out of stubbornness, outright defiance, or acts of self-denial seemed to minimize their chances of contracting the virus or the severity of the possible consequences associated therewith. Eventually, the resistance would wane as new strains of the virus emerged and people realized that, in the least, the vaccine might protect them against the more severe complications associated with infection. Still, some of the resistance would never die.

By early summer of 2021, Pam and I were clearly feeling the strain of the pandemic. We had been trying to keep the office open for a year and a half with no meaningful break, and I was beginning to feel the effects of age creeping up on me, especially the lack of energy and stamina. As a result, we decided to cut our office schedule from five to four days a week and to eliminate one of our two out-of-town clinics. This gave us some temporary relief from all the wear and tear of the previous year and a half, while also serving as a gradual movement toward retirement.

Then in June 2021, the planning committee for the Columbus High School graduation class of *1970* decided to plan anew its fiftieth reunion (some fifteen months late). The One and Done band would again be invited to play, and we aging rockers were all excited. After a couple of months of working up the forty-some-odd songs for the performance, pandemic or not, Pam and I scheduled our trip North. We could only hope that by the time the reunion rolled around in September that the pandemic would be on the way out. Unfortunately, a new Delta variant of the virus emerged from India that was supposedly even more transmissible than that coming over from Europe in late 2020. The positivity rate for COVID infections began climbing once again.

As of August, only 48 percent of Americans had been vaccinated, and the CDC was indicating the original vaccine *might* need to be updated in order for recipients to have ongoing protection. This would lead to Pam and me getting our first "booster" shots. Then sure enough, as the Delta variant hit America, a new "pandemic of the unvaccinated" broke out, and the positivity rate soared. In some instances, even those previously vaccinated for COVID (but not receiving the booster) were getting infected. By September, another one hundred thousand people per day would be hospitalized, more than at any time since the COVID-19 vaccine had first become available. While the Delta variant would prove even less deadly than the initial variant, hospital beds were filling up again as the suffering continued. Just when we thought things might finally be getting better, here we go again.

Given this new surge in COVID infections, and after much consideration, six days prior to the 1970 CHS reunion performance, the group made the difficult decision to cancel its performance. I was clearly bummed. At my age, I wasn't sure how many more chances I might get to play music in front of a live audience. My only real hope was that the band could get back together when our own fifty-fifth high school reunion rolled around (2024). Still, given the ongoing uncertainties of COVID, the social and political turmoil of the past few years, and emerging concerns over my advancing age, opportunities for again seeing family and friends seemed to be dwindling. As a result, Pam and I decided to take our chances and continue with our plans for traveling North.

Despite any risks, the trip would prove most rewarding. It allowed Pam and me to visit my dear friend Mike Sprague and for us to catch up on old times and all the political craziness. It also let Pam and me get up to Indianapolis and visit IUPUI. It was the first time I'd seen the campus in some forty years, and I could scarcely have imagined how the university would grow. At the time of this writing, I estimate it to have tens of thousands of students, quite a change from when I first attended.

Next, Pam and I traveled to the Dayton, Ohio, area and visited a colleague from my days at Wright State. Then Pam and I drove to northern Ohio to visit my brother Dave's widow (Joyce), their son (Shawn), and Shawn's wife (Katrina). We toured their small community, checked out Joyce's townhouse, and spent an afternoon visiting Amish country.

On our way back to Mobile, Pam and I stopped by Lexington, Kentucky, to visit friends we'd made while living in the area and playing music with the Firehouse Pickers. Of course, we had all aged and were struggling with our respective health issues, but it was a real treat to talk about old times, catch up on all the latest news, and discuss the "great" pandemic. Plans to see my sister LouAnne and her husband fell through as she and her husband were heading out of state. And hopes of attending the previously canceled Abbey Road on the River Festival (finally rescheduled from Memorial Day 2020 to September 2021) were doused as questions remained regarding how safe it was to be around the festival crowd.

Again, all in all, it was a wonderful trip, full of opportunities to see loved ones and to get away from the stress of work and daily life after eighteen months of the pandemic. Still, it was also good to get back to Mobile as by the time we returned,

ENDINGS

the CDC had become convinced the COVID vaccinations were losing their effectiveness as the virus evolved. Booster shots were now being recommended every six months to assure the best possible protection from the virus. While Pam and I had already gotten our first booster shots in August, now booster shots were part and parcel of the CDC's overall prevention plan.

In reaction to the CDC's new COVID guidelines, the president would decide to issue a mandate for all federal employees, as well as workers of businesses contracting with the government, to receive the vaccinations as a condition of employment or for conducting business with the federal government. The executive order would eventually be overturned by the Supreme Court. Unfortunately, while it was in place, it created intense anger and backlash from those viewing it as excessive government intrusion into people's daily lives, and many employees, including military personnel, would lose their jobs for refusing compliance.

By early December 2021, yet another COVID variant (Omicron) emerged, this time from Africa. Given that Pam and I were already "boosted," we again escaped contracting the bug. Unfortunately, much as some had predicted, many of those initially vaccinated but not boosted were getting infected anew. The positivity rate was again climbing, and increased hospitalizations were being reported. This led professional sporting leagues to cancel a number of games due to the lack of enough healthy players for fielding teams and to the College Football Playoff committee establishing emergency protocols for handling the forfeiture of playoff games should COVID outbreaks render teams unable to participate. Christmas gatherings were once again being threatened as well as airlines canceled holiday flights en masse due to COVID infections and related staffing shortages among its employees. Mayors and governors in some cities and states then renewed or expanded mandates for masks while also requiring proof of vaccination in order for individuals to enter public places (including restaurants, movie theaters, schools, etc.).

Thankfully, by this time, more effective treatment options had become available for those who contracted the virus. Thus, while the Omicron variant seemed even more transmissible than the Delta variant (if one can imagine), the number of hospitalizations and deaths proved less troublesome. Unfortunately, after all this time, the source of the virus remained a mystery, and no one could answer questions regarding its future course. Some even predicted the world would never return to pre-COVID status and that yearly vaccinations (much like flu shots) would be necessary well into any foreseeable future.

As if there wasn't enough turmoil in the world, given all the social, political, and health-related problems, in late February of 2022, the Russian president would launch a military invasion into neighboring Ukraine. While the Russian president claimed the assault was an attempt to free Russian citizens trapped in Ukraine since the demise of the Soviet Union some years earlier, the true reason for the incursion would never be made completely clear. Some believed the invasion was an effort to distract the Russian people from their government's failures at managing all the death and devastation of the COVID virus. Others believed it to have simply been the communist dictator's way of seeking to expand his territory during a time when the rest of the world was preoccupied with the pandemic. Still others felt it was the Russian president's way of fulfilling a long-standing dream of trying to restore the former USSR by taking advantage of what he perceived as a weak US president. In any event, the death and destruction created by the invasion would be all too real.

While some thought the conflict would be brief, perhaps lasting only a matter of weeks, the Ukrainian people had a different idea. As a result, the war would rage on well into 2024 (with over one hundred thousand-plus casualties). Eventually, the United States, Germany, England, and France would all begin providing assistance to Ukraine. Then viewing the conflict as one of communism versus democracy, the People's Republic of China, Iran, and North Korea started offering economic and military aid to Russia. Over time, it would become apparent that no one seemed to have any idea how or when the fighting might be brought to an end. Many Americans were comparing US involvement in Ukraine to the Vietnam quagmire of decades earlier. And some politicians expressed fears the conflict might escalate into a nuclear confrontation.

In March 2022, Pam and I would get our second COVID booster amid predictions of yet another variant being scheduled to strike by summer. This was our fourth shot overall, and again, it would let us safely travel to Indiana to visit family and friends. It also allowed us to resume attending the Abbey Road Festival over Memorial Day weekend (for the first time in two years). And once again, this would provide a much-needed break. Still, many Americans longed for the time when vaccines might not be needed and life could truly return to normal. Maybe by 2023? Regardless of what the future held, by now, I was certain people would be talking about the great COVID pandemic for decades to come.

As June of 2022 rolled around, the impact of all the money the government had spent for COVID relief and the president's infrastructure bill started making itself known. Too much money chasing too few goods, as they say, yielded inflation that would firmly grip the US economy. And this would make daily life even more difficult for the millions of Americans struggling to recover from the pandemic. Rising energy prices had increased manufacturing costs, the cost of transporting goods to market, even the cost of food production. Over-the-road truckers were now spending upward of two thousand dollars per tankful just to fill their rigs with diesel. And of course, all these cost increases were being passed along to the public. Not only did this mean consumers were spending more of their household budgets on food, clothing, and other necessities of life, but also now it was costing more just to get to and from work to earn money to pay the inflated prices.

Initially, the president blamed the inflation problem on Putin's invasion of Ukraine and the related disruption in the flow of Russian oil to nations throughout Europe. Clearly, this (along with the US president's own reduction in US oil production) had cut supplies and raised oil prices for much of the free world. But only a few weeks later, the president would blame the US oil industry, which he claimed was intentionally limiting oil production so as to carve out huge profits during a time of worldwide shortage. Later still, he'd blame rising gasoline prices on local station operators whom he believed to be gouging consumers. Republicans, on the other hand, blamed inflation directly on the president's spending increases and on his pledge to promote an environmentally friendly economy by ending America's reliance on fossil fuels. Certainly, closing oil pipelines and promising to do away with our nation's reliance on oil, natural gas, and coal (however unintentionally) would have the effect of undermining any desire of energy company stockholders for increasing production.

Climbing production costs and increasing prices would be further compounded by emerging supply-chain shortages. Suddenly, everything from household furniture to appliances to automobiles and even food was becoming increasingly scarce or difficult to buy. Some attributed the shortages to China's efforts at managing the spread of COVID by closing down entire provinces and suspending factory production. America, and in some ways the world at large, probably had become overreliant upon the cheap labor markets of China and on the products they produced. And with so many Chinese citizens being quarantined and factories being closed, China was generating fewer and fewer items for export to other nations. As a result, reducing the shipping of Chinese-made computer chips, for example, would end up affecting everything from home computers to cell phones and even autos. By 2022, new cars and trucks were increasingly unavailable or being sold at a 15 percent to 18 percent premium compared with those of the previous year and with no discounting by dealerships. Used cars, now in high demand because new vehicles were less available, were now costing some 30 percent more than the previous year.

Others attributed the food shortages to a lack of oversight by the FDA of American food producers during the early stages of the pandemic. This, it was believed, had led to a suspension of safe production standards and, ultimately, to the temporary closure of some food processing plants once their products were deemed no longer safe for consumption. Still, others attributed shortages of American-made products to the enhanced unemployment benefits offered to laid-off workers during the early stages of the pandemic. These benefits, it was argued, had left many individuals reluctant to return to work once the initial crisis had passed. And fewer workers meant reduced production.

By midsummer, inflation had reached a forty-year high of 9.1 percent, while the cost of living climbed some 20 percent over the pre-pandemic levels. Automobile gasoline prices had soared from 2.37 dollars a gallon in January 2021 to over 6.00 dollars per gallon in some places by summer 2022. And just as the stock market had begun recovering from its early 2020 drop, it once again began a downward spiral. Increasingly, politicians spoke of a national recession being imminent.

Then in the middle of all this craziness, a *draft* of a Supreme Court ruling designed to overturn the *Roe v. Wade* case was leaked to the press. As might be expected, this created an uproar among proabortion activists. In an apparent attempt to intimidate justices into changing a ruling that had not yet been rendered, protestors began picketing the homes of Supreme Court justices. Despite these protests being in violation of federal law, the existing Democratic administration and Department of Justice refused to condemn the actions or arrest any of the protestors. And Republicans were again beside themselves at the lack of any meaningful response and the perceived threat these acts posed to the stability of our nation as a whole. Eventually, an armed man was arrested near the home of one Supreme Court justice after traveling from California, with plans to kill the justice. Still, no action would be taken against any of the other protestors, resulting in one congressman threatening impeachment of the attorney general should Republicans regain control of the House of Representatives following the upcoming midterm elections.

Seemingly, in hopes of taking the focus off the struggling economy, in midsummer, the Democratic leader of the House of Representatives formed a committee to begin hearings on the former president's involvement in the January 6, 2020, riots. This led Republican members to become irate as the Democratic leader refused to allow the Republican leadership to either appoint members of their choosing to the committee or to balance the committee with a like number of conservative representatives. Accordingly, Republicans began calling the hearings a sham. Many Americans agreed. The hearings would drag on for months, with some sessions being broadcast on national television during prime-time evening slots. Again, this seemed an attempt to distract citizens from the nation's other problems while also encouraging prospective voters to vote for them in the upcoming midterms.

ENDINGS

In late June 2022, the Supreme Court issued its *official* ruling overturning *Roe v. Wade*. The new ruling stated the earlier court had grossly overreached its authority by granting federal protection for rights that were never explicitly guaranteed in the US Constitution. The court's decision wouldn't mean a woman had no legal right to an abortion, only that any decision regarding a woman's right to an abortion should be decided by state legislators in keeping with their own constituents' regional preferences. Many Republicans praised the decision as a long overdue victory for unborn children. But Democratic politicians immediately condemned the decision and called for voters to take to the polls in the fall to elect congressmen and women who might pass legislation codifying (once and for all) a woman's right to abortion. Some abortion rights groups went so far as to call for a "night of rage" throughout America, leading some protestors to call for the Supreme Court to be burned down. No one knew where all this might lead, but everyone expected further upheaval in the months to come.

By late summer of 2022, the attorney general and Department of Justice agreed to open an official investigation into the former president's participation in the January 6 riots. A month or so later, the attorney general would also order an FBI raid of the former president's private Mar-A-Lago home in Florida, in search of "top secret" documents that were believed to have wrongfully been retained upon his leaving office. This latter action would eventually result in the former president being indicted on some thirty-seven felony charges related to unauthorized possession of said documents and obstruction of justice. But for many Americans, these actions would only create additional upheaval and a widespread perception that the FBI and Department of Justice were being weaponized against the former president (in keeping with the apparent persecution first initiated by the phony Russian dossier of six years earlier).

The former president vowed to fight all the charges and filed his own suit against the Department of Justice and FBI for violation of his civil rights.

As inflation pressed into the fall, the Federal Reserve initiated a series of increases in the prime interest rate so as to stabilize the economic outlook. It would take several months for inflation to begin trending downward, and in the meantime, as the midterm elections approached, the political wrangling continued. In November, the midterm elections of 2022 would be held, with the Democratic Party gaining a 51–49 advantage in the Senate. But much to their chagrin, the Republican Party had gained a majority in the House of Representatives. Once again, we had a split Congress.

Then in early 2023, it came to light that "top secret/classified" government documents were also discovered at the current president's Delaware residence and in his private office on the campus of the University of Pennsylvania. Some of these documents dated from as far back as his time spent serving both as vice president and as a US senator. Much as had been true with the discovery of documents in the *former president's* Mar-A-Lago estate, this resulted in the DOJ opening an investigation of the current president for unlawful retention of classified documents.

With the midterm elections being settled, and with the Republicans' newfound power, the House of Representatives voted to establish a committee that would investigate the Democratic president's past dealings with foreign governments. In particular, it seems that while serving as vice president some years earlier, one of his sons had experienced a great increase in personal wealth when working for international companies located in nations with which his father (as vice president) had contacts. This increase of wealth was believed by some to be related to the current president having abused the power of his

ENDINGS

office while serving as vice president. It was further alleged that the now-sitting president had also been misusing his authority as president to obstruct DOJ investigations into related accusations against his son. The House investigation dragged on, eventually leading the DOJ to assign a special prosecutor to further examine the evidence. Then in late 2023, the state of Delaware filed charges related to the son's previously having falsified an application for the purchase of a firearm. This would be followed by the state of California filing charges against the son for providing false tax information. The House of Representatives would then undertake an impeachment *inquiry* into the current president, although at the time of this writing, no formal charges against the president had been made, and the son had not been convicted of any crime.

In the spring of 2023, the fed's efforts to reduce inflation through its series of rate hikes had begun yielding positive results. Inflation had moved down toward 3 1/2 percent. Unfortunately, it still outpaced the growth of household incomes and left millions of American families scrambling to keep up with the rising home-heating costs and mounting food and gasoline prices. The interest rate for thirty-year fixed mortgages had also jumped to nearly 8 percent, thus drastically limiting options of homeownership for millions of Americans. And as the national debt was growing larger and larger in response to the spending coming out of Washington, concerns for our nation's long-term economic outlook were again being raised. Some believed we had mortgaged our children's future. Others feared we were jeopardizing our national security by creating more debt than we could ever repay.

By the summer of 2023, progressive-minded Democratic politicians had clearly gained ground with efforts to defund the police in larger metropolitan areas such as New York, Chicago, San Francisco, Washington, DC, and others. Liberal-minded district attorneys had also joined the movement by refusing to pursue charges against criminals accused of committing anything other than the most violent of crimes. But much as some feared, all these actions led to an explosion of crime and gun violence throughout these communities. Emboldened by the absence of law enforcement, gangs conducted "smash and gab" robberies of major retail stores, sometimes taking as much as twenty thousand dollars worth of merchandise in a matter of minutes with little fear of being arrested or ever being held accountable for their actions. Drug users and homeless individuals would all but overrun San Francisco, pitching tents and setting up house on the sidewalks of major retail districts, defecating in the streets, and assaulting those who complained. In New York, Philadelphia, and Chicago alone, the homicide rate climbed by 30 percent in just three years. Many longtime residents and business owners of these cities eventually became so frustrated by the problems that they'd sell their properties and move to states where life was safer and where the values were more conducive to healthy living.

Republican politicians, seeking to improve their standing with voters before the upcoming 2024 presidential election, then began citing all these problems as evidence the existing Democratic administration's policies were failing. Many Democratic politicians, on the other hand, blamed the increase in violence and crime on inadequate gun control laws and an American system that favored white Americans while leaving minorities with few options for meeting their needs other than resorting to violence. The current president would tour the nation, proclaiming reduced inflation and the overall low unemployment rate as proof that his policies were succeeding. But polls reported him to have a national approval rating well below 40 percent.

ENDINGS

In August, just as the presidential primary season was ramping up, the former president would be indicted in various jurisdictions across America. Charges ranged from misrepresenting his financial worth when seeking real estate financing in New York to election interference (also in New York) to conspiracy to overturn the 2020 election results in Georgia. Within three days of having his mug shot taken for the first indictment, campaign contributions had surpassed seven million dollars. He was ahead of all other Republican presidential hopefuls by as much as 40 percent in most polls, and his prospects for again being nominated by his party to run for the presidency in the 2024 election had never seemed brighter. As the charges had all been filed by progressive-leaning prosecutors, many still believed the former president was being openly targeted and vowed to vote for no one else. The country still seemed hopelessly divided.

Then in late September of 2023, the prime minister of Israel and Saudi Arabia's crowned prince publicly announced their nearing completion of a joint accord that would bring both peace and economic prosperity to their nations for years to come. As the Middle East had long been a region of conflict between Israel and some of its Arab neighbors, the agreement was eagerly awaited by those seeking peace and stability. But within a week's time, Hamas, the militant arm of the Palestinian people, would launch an all-out attack on Jewish communities along Israel's southern border with Gaza. When all was said and done, over twelve hundred Israelis had been slaughtered, many women and children, some of whom had been raped or beheaded. Another hundred or so Israelis (and some twelve Americans) had been taken hostage and were being held by the militants in scattered locations throughout Gaza. Not since the Holocaust had so many Jewish people been killed in such a fashion.

The prime minister of Israel promptly announced plans to retaliate by eliminating Hamas once and for all and vowed the Jewish nation would never again have to exist with sworn enemies living on its border. As much of the world joined in on condemning the attack, the president of the United States announced our nation's full support for Israel and our willingness to supply its military with anything needed in order for the Jewish nation to defend itself. This included intelligence, military advisers, and even weaponry and ordnance. Accordingly, within weeks, two American aircraft carrier strike groups were moved into the area, one in the Eastern Mediterranean and one in the Persian Gulf. A nuclear-powered submarine would also be moved into the region, and over 1,200 US troops would be "made available." Then in reaction to all this, Hezbollah, a militant group based in southern Lebanon, threatened to attack Israel's northern border should either Israel decide to invade Gaza or the US get directly involved in the conflict.

In stark contrast to the presidents' expressed assurance of our nation's support for Israel, progressive-minded students and professors on more liberal college campuses began holding open protests condemning the president's position. These protestors refused to condemn the horrific attack by Hamas and instead accused Israel of causing the conflict. And as the demonstrations escalated, so too did the hate speech and anti-Semitic rhetoric. As a result, there'd be a dramatic increase in assaults on Jews nationwide.

Sure enough, as promised, upon Israel making final preparations for its assault on Hamas, Hezbollah then began firing missiles and rockets into northern Israeli communities. This would be followed by Palestinian militants of the West Bank joining in with rocket attacks of their own and by Houthi rebels (a terrorist group based in Yemen) undertaking a series of rocket attacks on US military bases located in Syria and Iraq.

ENDINGS

The initial attacks by the Houthi rebels wounded over fifty American troops.

Knowing Hamas, Hezbollah, and the Houthi were all "proxies" of Iran, who had long provided them with military training and support, the president of the US warned Iran that continued attacks on US soldiers could have "grave consequences." Still, no meaningful military response by the US would be immediately forthcoming, and Iran responded by making threats of their own.

Finally, near the end of October, Israel launched the early stages of its ground offensive. As the Israeli assault on Hamas progressed, Hezbollah stepped up its attacks, and Houthi rebels began attacking ships transporting goods through the Red Sea. This latter move was viewed by some as a direct assault on international trade and a possible threat to the world economy. So in response, US warships would sink three Houthi attack boats. As the attacks on shipping transports continued, the US and UK would launch a series of air strikes against Houthi targets in Yemen. Iran then responded by ordering one of its Navy ships into the region and making additional threats about escalating the war.

In late January, a rebel attack killed three American soldiers and wounded some fifty more. The US retaliated by launching multiple strikes of their own against the attackers. And while the international community repeatedly called for a ceasefire and a return to peace, the Israeli prime minister defiantly pledged to fight "till the end."

In early April 2024, Israel then destroyed a building adjacent to the Iranian consulate in Syria. The strike reportedly killed two top Iranian military officers alleged to have been responsible for the shipping of missiles to the Hezbollah. A few days later, Iran responded by launching some three hundred drones and missiles toward Israel. The US and Israel successfully intercepted practically all the projectiles prior to reaching their designated targets. Still, Iran's actions were viewed by most as a clear escalation of the war.

By late spring, the college protestors had succeeded in establishing tent cities on college campuses across twenty-seven US states. The hate speech and intimidation had evolved into protestors increasingly shouting, "Death to America!" and "Death to Israel!" Still, college presidents resisted calls to confront the problem. Even the US president, out of apparent fear for alienating a portion of his political base, refused to criticize the disruptions. Finally, as the protests turned to violence, many American citizens demanded action. Police would be called in to dismantle the encampments, and hundreds of students (as well as outside agitators) would be arrested (although few demonstrators would ever be officially charged with a crime). Still, graduation ceremonies for many universities would be canceled.

As Israel continued to press its assault into Gaza, the president's own position seemed to waver. On the one hand, he expressed support for the rights of protesting students. On the other, he acknowledged Israel's right to defend its borders. Months of trying to broker a ceasefire had proven fruitless, and any hope for a quick resolution to the conflict appeared to have all but vanished. Some even feared that it could become an all-out war as none of the warring parties seemed interested in resolving the matter peacefully.

By late May, juries in New York would convict the former president of "fraud" charges and "interfering with an election." Democrats praised the verdict as proof positive that "no one was above the law, even a former president." But Republicans viewed the rulings as yet another example of Democrats manipulating the legal system so as to prevent the former president from ever again holding public office. None of the verdicts were considered final as the former president would appeal the decisions and he had not yet been formally sentenced. Moreover, prior to any such sentencing, the Supreme Court would decide that a former president was constitutionally immune from prosecution for official acts committed while in office. So for the time being, this ruling effectively threw all the court cases regarding the former president into limbo. But immediately upon hearing of the New York court's decision, political contributions for the former president poured in again, this time to thirty-four million dollars in the first twenty-four hours. Clearly, his political base had not been shaken, and the upcoming national election was promising to be as contentious as ever.

Finally, in late June, a much-anticipated debate between the former president and sitting president would be held. It had long been suspected by some (perhaps many) that the sitting president was manifesting the early stages of cognitive decline. When appearing in public he oftentimes seemed unsteady on his feet, stumbled, and nearly fell on more than one occasion. Then there were those occasions whereupon he seemed to lose his train of thought when responding to questions raised by the press. Finally, he also seemed increasingly given to distorting, if not fabricating, anecdotal stories. Spokespersons for the White House and broadcasters for the more liberal media outlets generally made excuses for these problems. They repeatedly claimed the president to be in full control of his faculties and to have boundless energy when carrying out his day-to-day responsibilities. These same supporters attributed the latter incidents to his "misspeaking" or mere embellishment. But others accused the president of simply lying for political gain. And some clearly believed his problems to reflect more pronounced memory lapses and cognitive confusion. Most simply questioned whether he was getting "too old" and lacking in the cognitive capacity for effectively performing his presidential duties.

Then as the debate unfolded, it quickly became apparent that the president was becoming distracted and confused when trying to answer debate questions. He repeatedly stared blankly off into space and generally seemed lost while standing at the podium. At other times, his responses to questions appeared disjointed or only marginally related to the debate topic at hand. On yet other occasions, he appeared to making blatantly false statements. By practically all accounts, the president was considered to have had a "disastrous" debate. The upshot of this would be to confirm much of the prior speculation regarding his increasing age and declining health. Within a matter of hours the press, major financial donors, and even some of his most ardent political supporters began calling for him to consider withdrawing from the presidential campaign. As national polling conducted immediately following the debate began showing a marked drop in the president's chances for winning re-election in the fall, concerns increased over the possibility a landslide defeat would have a down-ballot effect, costing the Democrats not only the presidency but both houses of Congress as well. Still, in response to all the expressed concerns, the president adamantly declared that "only the Lord Almighty" would make him withdraw from the race.

The drama surrounding the current president's debate performance would drag on for the next two weeks. Then, on the second weekend of July at a campaign rally in western Pennsylvania, a lone gunman attempted to assassinate the former president. The attempt would prove unsuccessful, although the former president did sustain a gunshot wound to the right side of the head. Still, the image of the former president brazenly rising up after being shot, blood running down his face and with his fist raised in the air, appeared to all but guarantee his being unbeatable in the upcoming election. From that moment on, there were few options for the sitting president but to drop his bid for reelection and for the Democratic Party to nominate his running mate, the vice president, as the Democratic nominee.

Given the havoc created by the recent health pandemic, all the social and political turmoil in the world, and ever-growing military conflicts, I couldn't help but wonder where it all might lead. When would it all be over? Could the pandemic truly be coming to an end? Would the racial divisiveness ever end; would the sparring ethnic groups ever learn to set aside their differences and come to see themselves as Americans first? And would the Democratic faithful ever drop its fear and hatred of the former president and all that which he represented? And what of the former president? Might he actually be incarcerated or would the convictions ultimately be thrown out? Moreover, could the Republican base ever give up seeing this man as a messiah and move on to support a less contentious candidate? And what of the sitting president's son? Would his legal problems result in jail time, and if so, would such an outcome have repercussions for the current president? And could the new Democratic nominee actually surprise everyone by winning the upcoming election after only twelve weeks of campaigning? As importantly, was it possible the nation could be in for four, even eight, more years of all the recent chaos?

And what of all the military conflicts? What about the Russian invasion of Ukraine? How many people would have to die, how much destruction has to occur before it comes to an end? Would there be any hope for peace in the Mideast, or was the conflict between Israel and Hamas destined to become a regional war involving Iran, Lebanon, Syria, the US, and others? Much like the 1960s, the world had once again become a confusing, angry, and scary place.

As already noted, since the divorce of my parents and my world having become less certain, I've been given to questioning life. Questioning life is what helps me manage the existential ambiguity inherent to living in a world over which I have limited control. Questioning life is also what helps me cope with all the pain and suffering of the world, while finding answers allows me to help those in need through my career as a mental health practitioner. This, in turn, has brought me much inner peace and given my life meaning. Still, if I have learned anything over the years, it is that I have few answers for most of life's more perplexing questions. I understand that change is inevitable and, in many respects, even good. Many of the greatest advances throughout history have arisen during times of change, even times of chaos. And certainly one can argue that such advances have greatly reduced human struggles and improved the quality of our daily lives. But change always seems to come at a certain price. For everything gained, it appears something must be lost.

I also understand that where all the world's current struggles lead, where all the pain and suffering, the racial discord, the social violence, the cultural upheaval, the political unrest, and the wars take us, is something beyond my capacity to change. As I've said repeatedly, it is my belief that we get more of our needs met and achieve more of our goals in the long run by making mindful choices and working together collaboratively. I believe love makes a difference. I believe that caring about others and treating people respectfully matters. I still believe in the value of striving to live spiritually. Admittedly, I don't always measure up to these ideals as well as I'd like, but I still believe in them. And yet I'm not so naive as to ignore the reality that, for whatever reason, some people choose a different path.

Through the course of my lifetime, I've witnessed individuals so full of fear, anger, and hatred that they cling desperately to dysfunctional attitudes and behavior while creating needless suffering for themselves and others. I've seen young people become so confused with their own identities or where they fit in with the world and so alienated from themselves and others that they turn schools and shopping malls into shooting galleries, effectively extinguishing the lives of countless boys and girls their own age. I've witnessed intimate relationships become so filled with bitterness and enmity as to end in hostile acts or contested legal disputes that all but destroy the very souls/hearts of those who once loved one another deeply. I've observed individuals become so trapped in their own religious beliefs that they create bombs to destroy churches, planes, office buildings, etc., killing countless numbers of innocent bystanders all because they reach a point where they cannot coexist with those holding conflicting points of view. Of late, I've even encountered politicians so intent on forcing their own political ideology on others as to undermine any hope for dialogue or compromise. On the grandest of scales, the world has witnessed countries going to war and destroying entire cultures and nations when differences between those in positions of power became so great as to leave them unable to work together to resolve conflicts.

I'm not sure I know how to explain any of this. Maybe this is what has to happen from time to time for humans to go full circle and once again regain a sense of perspective. Maybe this is what has to happen for people to recognize the limits of their egos and again achieve some semblance of balance. Maybe humans have to suffer deeply to again be able to recognize the beauty of peace and love. Maybe humans have to destroy all that is right and good before they can, once again, humble themselves to accept a Power greater than oneself. I'd like to believe this isn't the case, that it doesn't have to be this way. But in truth, I just don't know.

During my training as a psychologist, I learned how humans don't respond well to sudden or drastic change. Sudden, unexpected change, as when one suffers a stroke or heart attack "out of the blue" or when one experiences the unforeseen death of a loved one, often leaves us feeling unsettled, scared, and out of control. Profound or drastic change, like that resulting from a paralyzing accident or injury, or when one is faced with rebuilding their life after a devastating assault or natural disaster, often leaves us feeling traumatized. In such times, people are known to experience a wide range of destructive emotions and to react with a host of disturbing behaviors. Some people shut down completely, some people choose to harm themselves, and some people strike out against others or the world. If we are to respond effectively to change, human beings, and I suspect societies and nations as well, need the change to be gradual and accompanied by periods of stability between the times of change. Gradual change is what allows people an opportunity to adjust. Periods of stability are what allow people to accommodate and assimilate the disruption that change causes to existing frames of reference. They allow us time to heal the damage change sometimes brings about. Unfortunately, over the past few decades, we as individuals, as a society, as a nation, and as a world seemed to have experienced so much change in such a relatively brief period that efforts toward adjusting to the change appear to have taxed our collective souls.

When I think along these lines, it gives me hope that maybe, just maybe, the problems we're all facing in these current times aren't so insurmountable—that maybe, just maybe, these problems are simply the natural consequence of what happens when a people, a society, a nation, or the world changes too quickly or when the change is too drastic. So maybe change is what accounts for so much of the anger, hostility, social unrest, and upheaval that we as a people, as a world, have experienced of late. Maybe too much change in too short a time has eroded our individual sense of self, our understanding of the importance of family, our shared sense of community, and the foundations of our social and cultural identity. Maybe we've just lost sight of the shared ideals, the shared values, and the shared sense of purpose otherwise needed for holding us together. As I suggested earlier, these are the things that seem to give our lives meaning. These are the things that help us to feel grounded, to be able to identify with one another, to care about one another. These are the things that help us to realize that we are all one, all part and parcel of the same human experiment. For without a stable sense of self, of family, of community, of social and cultural values, we as humans become vulnerable to feeling confused, scared, full of doubt, and lacking in faith. So maybe too much change over too short a time is what's undermining our ability to work together and find meaningful resolution to prevailing differences and challenges. Maybe too much change too quickly has left individual egos so threatened and so rigidly committed to their own belief systems that neighbors turn on one another in acts of violence. And maybe, just maybe, this is even what encourages those elected into positions of political power to self-righteously lead a country into civil war or nations into worldwide war.

Of course, maybe it's not about change. Maybe it's about overcrowding, about the stress created by too many people living on an ever-shrinking planet. Or maybe it's about too much cultural diversity, about social traditions and values becoming so diluted that people lose their foundation, their roots, and their sense of personal and collective identity. Maybe it's about something else. The truth is, we may never know for certain. But to the extent it is due to change or overcrowding or some other such cause, would it really be asking all that much if we as individuals, as a society, as a nation, as a world just decided to slow things down a bit, just decided to scale back on all the tail-chasing in hopes that by doing so it would help reduce some of the craziness we are now facing? I'm not advocating we try to stop change. I know this isn't possible, any more than we can stop progress or prevent population growth. But would it truly hurt so much if each of us just spent a little less time with our electronic devices and a little more time actually being present to one another? Would it really be so painful if we just set aside some of our daily tasks and spent a little more time communing with nature or meditating or praying? And would it really be all that difficult to just invest a little more energy reflecting on those things for which we might be grateful rather than dwelling on the things we want or don't have? Would it really take so much more effort to give back to the world and the people around us just a tad bit more than we take or to strive for making the mindful choice to treat one another more caringly, with more kindness, patience, and love? And is it just possible that if we did all these things, it would allow for a collective "catching of our breaths"? That maybe, just maybe, doing these things would allow us to rediscover our true selves, to once again feel connected with rather than isolated from one another, to recognize the many things we all share in common rather than those things that make us different and to help us again find God. I just don't know.

Because there remains so much I do not know or understand, I try limiting myself to speaking only of that which I do know, my life as I have experienced it. And on balance, I guess I've been pretty blessed. For a boy born and raised in relative poverty and from a small Indiana town, I've tried to develop the natural gifts I was given to the best of my ability. I have tried to be a good student, to pursue a formal education, and to listen to and absorb the knowledge and wisdom of those teachers and mentors with whom I have come into contact. I have tried to take reasonably good care of my health and to avoid those activities and substances that could prove harmful to my body and mind. I have tried to keep physically active, although more so in my early years than of late (arthritis, heart disease, diabetes,

ENDINGS

etc. all have a way of slowing you down). I have tried to be a good son, a good sibling, a good friend, and a good husband. I have tried to be honest, reliable, and responsible and to carry myself with some integrity, to say what I mean and to mean what I say. And throughout my life, I've tried to remain gainfully employed, to earn my keep, to pay my bills, and to not live beyond my means. I've made some really good friends along the way, played some music, and devoted much of my adult life to helping those around me manage their day-to-day struggles so they might discover greater peace and meaning in their own lives. As a clinical psychologist, I have tried to listen to my clients and to remain open to learning as much from them as they may have learned from me. I have learned to love. Maybe above all, I've tried to live my life in a mindful and caring fashion, to question life and to make conscious choices amid the situations and challenges in which I find myself, to strive toward creating a meaningful life experience rather than being a victim of circumstance, to try and find peace and at least some good in everything and everyone I encounter, and to live my life in harmony with my Higher Power. When my story is done, I hope I will have made a difference; I hope I will have left this world in a better place than where I found it.

And in the end, the love you take,
Is equal to the love you make.
—J. Lennon and P. McCartney

From "The End," words and music by John Lennon and Paul McCartney. Copyright 1969. Northern Songs Limited

ACKNOWLEDGMENTS

Special thanks to Dr. Robert and Ms. Penny Cook,
Dr. Anton Salinski, and Dr. Pamela Starkey
For their invaluable contributions to the
Editing of the manuscript for this book.

Last but not least, thanks to Samantha
Amaryl and all the good people at
Page Publishing for their work on turning my
Manuscript into a book. I sing your praises.

REFERENCES

Easwaren, E, tr. Bhagavad Gita, second edition, 2007, the Blue Mountain Center of Meditation.

Giorgi, Amedio. *Psychology as a Human Science: A Phenomenologically Based Approach*. New York, New York: Harper & Row, 1970.

Heidegger, Martin, translated by John Macquarrie and Edward Robinson. *Being and Time*. New York, New York: Harper & Row, 1962.

Hesse, Hermann. *Siddhartha*. New York, New York, 10014: New Directions Publishing Corporation, 333 Avenue of the Americas, 1971.

Hesse, Hermann. *Steppenwolf*. New York, New York: Modern Library, 1963.

Huxley, Aldous. *Doors of Perception*. New York, New York: Harper & Row, 1963.

Lao Tzu, translated by Gia-Fu-Feng and Jane English. *Tao Te Ching*. New York, New York: Vintage Books Edition, Random House, 1972.

Persig, Robert. *Zen and the Art of Motorcycle Maintenance*. New York, New York: A Bantam Book/published by arrangement with William Morrow and Company Inc., 1974.

Major, Charles. *The Bears of Blue River*. New York, New York: Macmillan, 1908.

Ram Dass. *Be Here Now, Remember*. New York, New York: Hanuman Foundation, 1978.

Watts, Alan. *The Book: On the Taboo Against Knowing Who You Are*. New York, New York: Random House Inc., 1972.

Watts, Alan. *This Is It: And Other Essays on Zen and Spiritual Experience*. New York, New York: Random House Inc., 1973.

Whittaker, James. *We Thought We Heard the Angels Sing*. New York, New York: E. P. Dutton and Co, 1943.

ABOUT THE AUTHOR

DR. STARKEY WAS BORN AND RAISED IN the small Midwestern town of Columbus, Indiana. He completed his bachelor's studies through Indiana University–Purdue University of Indianapolis (Indiana) and received his master's degree from Duquesne University in Pittsburgh (Pennsylvania). He completed his doctoral training through the School of Psychology at Wright State University in Dayton (Ohio). His predoctoral internship was completed through the Veteran's Administration Medical Center of Lexington (Kentucky) and his postdoctoral training through the Baptist Regional Medical Center of Corbin (Kentucky). Dr. Starkey has served as a mental health professional for over forty years and currently works as a licensed clinical psychologist alongside his wife, Dr. Pamela Starkey, through their private offices in Mobile (Alabama).